The Good Crisis

Edited by John Seager and Lee S. Polansky

Developed and Produced by Print Matters, Inc.

Printed in the United States

ISBN 978-0-979-6685-7-9

Contents

Introduction: Debunking the Birth Dearth

John Seager

What with global warming, terrorism, poverty, refugee crises, nuclear pro-liferation, endangered species, and the rest of the all-too-familiar litany, it hardly seems as if we need to add anything to our "worry" list.

Yet, there is a constant chorus of concern about the possibility of eventual population decline and a so-called "birth dearth" based on the notion that women are not having enough children.

Articles in mainstream publications such as the *Wall Street Journal*, the *New York Times*, *Foreign Affairs*, and the *Guardian*, as well as books like *What to Expect When No One's Expecting: America's Coming Demographic Disaster* and *The Other Population Crisis: What Governments Can Do about Falling Birth Rates* focus on this issue.[1] Many assert that we can't possibly thrive in a world of declining fertility—and perhaps someday declining population.[2]

Among the earliest voices calling for an end to lower fertility rates was Ben Wattenberg. Wattenberg first decried "depopulation" nearly three decades ago. In his 1987 book, *The Birth Dearth*, he claimed that countries with low fertility rates would be confronted by serious economic, social, and political problems. He went so far as to release a *second* book on the subject in 2004.[3]

The United Nations' 2015 population projections emphasized a decrease in birth rates in developed countries, noting, "It is now estimated that 46 per cent of the world's population lives in countries with low levels of fertility where women have fewer than 2.1 children, on average"—and these countries include the United States.[4]

Is this so-called "birth dearth," as Wattenberg first dubbed it, really a prob-lem? It is not. The world is beset with social, political, and environmental challenges and crises—many caused or exacerbated by rampant population growth. In light of this fact, lower fertility can represent a great potential opportunity. Indeed, voluntary population stabilization would help solve some of the worst problems we now face.

World Population – Still Growing

Before dealing with the implications of fertility decline, it's time to say, "Not so fast." Yes, the *rate* of population growth has declined over time. And, yes, fertility rates have declined substantially since the middle of the 20th century.

Yet, the world continues to add some 83 million people each year—mainly in developing countries. And the most recent UN figures show an alarming jump in projections for 2100. In 2002, the UN medium projection for world population was 9 billion. Now it's 11.2 billion. The increase in the 2100 projection is equivalent to the entire current population of the Western Hemisphere plus all of Europe.[5]

The Total Fertility Rate or TFR (i.e., the average number of children born to each woman) remains extraordinarily high in many places. There are 73 countries where women have more than three children on average. While this may not seem particularly high, consider Guatemala, where women currently have an average of 3.1 children. Should that birth rate continue, population will increase by more than 400 percent, from 16 million in 2015 to more than 81 million by 2100. Western Africa has a TFR of 5.4 TFR. And Niger has a TFR of 7.6. This is far above the replacement rate in healthy places, which can occur at a TFR of 2.1.[6]

These high fertility countries unequivocally illustrate that rapid population growth is very much a reality in today's world.

What about U.S.?

Some birth dearthers, who tend to lean politically to the right, argue that lower fertility rates are a symbol of "moral decay" and predict economic collapse as the consequence. For the most part, these alarms are being raised about fertility declines in affluent nations, including the United States.

Ross Douthat of *The New York Times* called for "More Babies, Please" in a 2012 op-ed, writing, "The retreat from child rearing is, at some level, a symptom of late-modern exhaustion—a decadence that first arose in the

West but now haunts rich societies around the globe. It's a spirit that privileges the present over the future, chooses stagnation over innovation, prefers what already exists over what might be."

Douthat further asserts that lower fertility rates will "knock the United States off its global perch."[7]

Another frequent commentator is Nicholas Eberstadt, who predicts that smaller and unconventional families will lead to a "collision course" for children and the elderly when there aren't enough people to care for them.[8]

David Brooks, a prominent columnist for the *New York Times*, has joined in with this group, asserting that the United States will be harmed by what he terms "an aging and less dynamic world."[9]

These writers sound an alarm that warns of catastrophe. But it's a false one. Throughout this book, authors show how lower fertility rates—if they continue and eventually lead to population stabilization and even reduction—pose no real threat. In fact, falling birthrates offer great promise.

In Europe and Japan, family size has dropped in the past few decades. Some observers contend that this is the canary in the coal mine for the U.S. *The Good Crisis* focuses on the positive impact that population stabilization might have on the U.S. economy. When it comes to our national well-being, the birth dearthers are sounding a false alarm. A smaller proportion of youth dependents can largely or even entirely offset the rise among those who may age out of the workforce. In 1960, Japan had 56 dependents for every 100 working age people. By 2010, it was virtually unchanged at 57 dependents. In Germany, it went up slightly during that half-century from 48 to 52. These are small shifts of no great consequence. Note also that the U.S. dependency ratio improved greatly during this same period from 67 to just 50.

Retirement Security Depends on Productivity

The "birth dearthers" seem most worried about funding for retirement schemes as national populations age. In *The Empty Cradle*, Philip Longman writes, "The financing and long-term viability of social security systems throughout the world depend on an assumption that each generation of taxpayers will be larger than the one that came before."[10]

Every social benefit system depends on the availability of funds sufficient to cover the level of benefits provided. Since Social Security was constructed during a period of substantial population growth, it logically took that growth into account. The two determinants of any social benefit system are the amount of wealth held by any society and how it is allocated. The future of Social Security depends on our national productivity. There is a wide variety of options available to address future potential shortfalls in Social Security.[11] The notion that there will be insufficient funds available to cover future retirement costs is not supported by the facts.

Whither Growth?

The anxiety expressed by birth dearthers transcends concern about retirement programs. Longman, for example, asserts that "capitalism has never flourished except when accompanied by population growth, and it is now languishing in those parts of the world (such as Japan, Europe, and the Great Plains of the United States) where population has become stagnant."[12]

It's more than a little stretch to say that economies are languishing in these places. Europe, for example, is hardly in the grips of a depression. It certainly has its challenges, many due to the huge differences between the economies of northern Europe and those in the south, with both areas having relatively low fertility. Per capita GDP, however, has generally continued to grow over time.[13]

It is fair to note that more people working can result in more total goods and services. But, while population growth can play a role in overall GDP growth, it is not essential for per capita economic growth, which is the common economic measure of individual well-being. One study found that, between 1985 and 1999 in the United States, "Economic resurgence reflected the impact of three critical components of growth: an expanding pool of labor, robust levels of capital investment and rapid productivity gains."[14] Clearly, there is more than one way to grow a healthy economy. There comes a point where, one hopes, and this book explores, societies can shift from the quantitative accumulation of consumables to more sustainable lifestyles.

Longman, in *The Empty Cradle*, caps his dismal economic argument with the astonishing assertion that "we are living in an age of declining inventiveness."[15] How so? Never in history has there been an age so replete with innovation on every level, even levels never before imaginable, from genetic decoding to nascent nanotechnology to the still-unfolding digital revolution. Consider this: a $350 IPhone 5 has nearly three times the processing power compared with the 1985 Cray-2 supercomputer. And, at $16,000,000 that Cray-2 was a bit more expensive than the IPhone.[16] Plus, it didn't fit in your pocket.

Beyond Zero Population Growth

Population aging and the promise of eventual population stabilization can provoke anxiety, as social change tends to do. Certainly, economists tasked with adapting pay-as-you-go benefit schemes will be kept busy. But, population growth isn't the answer. Maybe most people could survive in a world of ten billion or even 20 billion—the way people now struggle day-to-day in the poorest places on earth. Yet they would not thrive.

Lower fertility rates and the resulting stable or declining population levels would not, by themselves, halt environmental destruction, let alone reverse damage—much of it irreversible. In fact, the affluence that is both a cause and effect of lower fertility rates is closely linked to rampant consumerism and a "throwaway society." As Professor John Kenneth Galbraith pointed out, "Consumer sovereignty, once governed by the need for food and shelter, is now the highly contrived consumption of an infinite variety of goods and services."[17] It will take more than an end to population growth to create a sustainable society. But population stabilization is an essential step.

Wherever women and couples have full access to reproductive health information, education, and services, most choose to have smaller families. We don't know what the global average family size will be in the future. But eventually it may dip below replacement level as a result of women's empowerment and access to highly effective methods of modern contraception.

Population stabilization has been a great rallying cry for many years. But there's nothing magic about "zero population growth." Smaller could be—would be—even better for people and for the planet. We should embrace this opportunity for it offers nothing less than a world of hope. Hope for restoration of deserts back into forests. Hope for the return of species to streams once again allowed to flow freely. And hope for the three billion people on the planet who now struggle to survive on less than $3 a day.

Can the U.S. adapt successfully to a larger percentage of older people and fewer young people? Over the past century, we've witnessed an unprecedented rate of change with an extraordinary array of new technologies. Millions of people are employed in occupations that weren't even dreamed of 100 years ago. These developments have made things better in many ways, such as medical advances, and worse in some others, such as pollution. The "graying" of the U.S. and other developed nations in the 21st century, if it happens, will provide challenges as well as opportunities.

We can find the workers needed in tomorrow's world by opening up more jobs for women, people of color, people with disabilities, and others who have been marginalized. Workplace flexibility, just one suggested change, could take better advantage of their skills and talents.

Perhaps, when referring to the 16 million American children living in poverty, we should think of them as the next generation's potential doctors and engineers, teachers and entrepreneurs, if we can break the cycle of economic despair through quality education programs and delayed parenthood. As things now stand, the aggregate impact of this lost resource is a national disgrace.

As for the world at large, the three billion or so people at the very bottom of the global economic ladder want decent lives. A less-crowded nation—and world—would improve prospects for many. As Dr. Joel Cohen of Rockefeller University eloquently wrote, "The real crux of the population question is the quality of people's lives; the ability of people to participate in what it means to be really human; to work, play and die with dignity; to have some sense that one's life has meaning and is connected with other people's lives."[18]

That is the population challenge. Many economic, social, and political obstacles still block the path to this better world. The Good Crisis includes a thought-provoking array of scholarly perspectives—along with compelling stories—to dispel the notion that smaller families lead to economic or social decline.

The possibility of a less-crowded world is no cause for anxiety, let alone panic. Rather, it's an achievable dream worthy of our efforts. And it's an essential first step toward restoring a planet now straining to meet the wants and needs of seven—soon eight-billion people.

Editors' Note: The reader will see that this book contains both scholarly chapters and feature-type articles. We felt that it was important to show the human face of the complex issues addressed; the feature articles do just that.

NOTES

1. Jack A. Goldstone, "The New Population Bomb: The Four Megatrends That Will Change the World Fertility Rates," *Foreign Affairs*, January/February 2010. www.foreignaffairs.com/articles/2010-01-01/new-population-bomb, accessed September 16, 2015. "Europe needs many more babies to avert a population disaster," *Guardian*, August 22, 2015. www.theguardian.com/world/2015/aug/23/baby-crisis-europe-brink-depopulation-disaster, accessed September 16, 2015. Recent books on this topic include Jonathan Last, *What to Expect When No One's Expecting: America's Coming Demographic Disaster* (New York: Encounter Books, 2013) and Steven Philip Kramer, *The Other Population Crisis: What Governments Can Do About Falling Birth Rates* (Woodrow Wilson Center Press / Johns Hopkins University Press, 2013).

2. J. Kennedy, "Baby boom goes bust in Pennsylvania," *Morning Call* (Lehigh Valley, PA), April 18, 2015. www.mcall.com/news/nationworld/pennsylvania/mc-pennsylvania-low-birth-rate-20150418-story.html%23page=1#page=2, accessed May 13, 2015.

3. Wattenberg first made his argument in 1987 with *The Birth Dearth: What Happens When People in Free Countries Don't Have Enough Babies?* (Pharos Books, 1987). He followed up with *Fewer: How the New Demography of Depopulation Will Shape Our Future* (Ivan R. Dee, 2004).

4. United Nations Department of Economic and Social Affairs/Population Division, "World Population Prospects: The 2015 Revision, Key Findings and Advance Tables" (New York). http://esa.un.org/unpd/wpp/Publications/Files/Key_Findings_WPP_2015.pdf. Accessed September 15, 2015.

5. Ibid.

6. Population Reference Bureau, "2015 World Population Data Sheet, with an emphasis on Women's Empowerment." http://www.prb.org/pdf15/2015-world-population-data-sheet_eng.pdf. Accessed September 15, 2015.

7. Ross Douthat, "More Babies, Please," *New York Times*, December 1, 2012. www.nytimes.com/2012/12/02/opinion/sunday/douthat-the-birthrate-and-americas-future.html?_r=0 Accessed September 3, 2015.

8. Nicholas Eberstadt, "The Global Flight from the Family," *Wall Street Journal*, February 21, 2015. www.wsj.com/articles/nicholas-eberstadt-the-global-flight-from-the-family-1424476179. Accessed September 16, 2015.

9. David Brooks, "The Fertility Implosion," March 12, 2012. http://www.nytimes.com/2012/03/13/opinion/brooks-the-fertility-implosion.html. Accessed September 16, 2015.

10. Philip Longman, *The Empty Cradle: How Falling Birthrates Threaten World Prosperity and What to Do About It* (Basic Books, 2004): 4.

11. "Provisions Affecting Payroll Taxes," https://www.ssa.gov/oact/solvency/provisions/payrolltax.html. Accessed December 4, 2015.

12. Longman, *The Empty Cradle*, 4.

13. Per capita GDP in Europe grew by 12 percent from 2000 to 2013. www.ers.usda.gov/.../ProjectedRealPerCapita. (Basic Books, 2004).

14. Porter, M.E. & D. van Opstal (2001). *U.S. competitiveness 2001: Strengths, vulnerabilities, and long-term priorities* (3). Washington, D.C.: Council on Competitiveness. http://www.isc.hbs.edu/Competitiveness2001.pdf (accessed July 2004).

15. Longman, *The Empty Cradle*, 116.

16. http://pages.experts-exchange.com/processing-power-compared/ Accessed December 3, 2015.

17. Galbraith, J.K. (1998). "On the continuing influence of affluence," *Human Development Report* 1998: 42. http://www.nieman.harvard.edu/events/seminars/galbraith.html (accessed July 2004).

18. Cohen, J. (1998, October 8). "How many people can the earth support?" *New York Review of Books*, 29.

Demographic Influences on U.S. Economic Prospects[1]

David E. Bloom and Jay W. Lorsch

The United States has experienced dramatic demographic and economic changes in the post-World War Two era. The overall population doubled, from 158 million in 1950 to 319 million in 2014—with the United Nations Population Division projecting a further sizable increase to 363 million by 2030. The ratio of the working-age population (ages 15-64) to the non-working-age population (ages 14 and under or 65 and over) rose from a low of 1.5 in the early 1960s to a high of 2.05 in 2006, and then down slightly to just under 2.0 in 2014—with a projected further drop to below 1.6 in 2030.

These trends matter because they influence the level and growth rate of income per capita and the relative position of America in the world economy. The higher worker to non-worker ratio, which began when the baby boomer generation (i.e., the 1946-1964 birth cohort) entered the workforce, led to a surge in savings, investment, and the supply of labor, and was accompanied by unprecedented prosperity. Since 1960, GDP has nearly quintupled in real terms, while GDP per capita has almost tripled.

But what is ahead for America? New demographics are clearly in the offing, most notably a dramatic rise in the share of elderly people and major changes in racial and ethnic composition. The median age of the U.S. population increased from 30 to 38 between 1950 and today and is projected to reach 40 by 2030. And the year from April 2010-April 2011 was the first time that there were more non-white babies born than white babies. Further, non-Hispanic whites are expected to make up less than half of the U.S. population by 2043.

This chapter assesses how future demographic changes may shape economic prospects for the United States. We aim to dispel myths about the inevitability of negative economic consequences associated with key demographic changes such as declines in the ratio of the working-age to the non-working-age population, population aging, continued immigration, and changes in the U.S. population's racial and ethnic composition.

Evolving Views on Population Growth and Economic Growth

For over two centuries, it has been commonly believed that rapid population growth stood in the way of improvements in standards of living. During most of the 1980s and 1990s, new evidence led most economists to think that population growth per se has no effect on economic growth. In the past 15 years, however, studies have found that, at least in some countries, rapid population growth does tend to impede economic growth and poverty alleviation, largely by elevating the burden of youth dependency. By contrast, declining fertility makes this burden more manageable by increasing the ratio of the working-age to the non-working-age populations. This ratio invariably rises as populations make the transition from high to low rates of fertility and mortality (mainly because the changes are asynchronous, with death rates declining first) and in the period following a baby boom. When that happens, there is considerable potential for increasing economic output on a per capita basis. The potential is due to the swelling of the labor force and of levels of savings per capita. These accounting effects are typically magnified by the rise in women's participation in the workforce that naturally comes with a decline in fertility, the boost to savings that occurs because the incentive to save for longer periods of retirement increases as people live longer, and society's ability to comfortably reallocate resources from investments in children to investments in physical capital, job training, technological progress, and strengthening other institutions.

The combined effect, known as the "demographic dividend," is estimated to have accounted for one-third of the rapid economic growth in the East Asian "miracle" countries between 1965 and 1990 (i.e., about two of the six percentage points in the annual growth of income per capita). Similarly, the near-absence of this change in the age structure of Africa, where

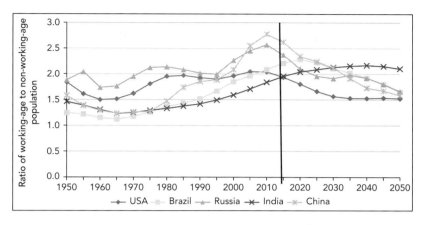

Figure 1. Ratio of working-age to non-working-age population in select countries, 1950-2050

high fertility remained the norm, is likely a decisive factor underlying that continent's slow economic growth. That being said, it is important to note that a demographic dividend does not take place automatically. It requires policies and practices that promote the efficient use of labor and capital, including policies related to education, governance, business, labor legislation, trade, macroeconomic management, and relations with neighboring countries.

Where do some of the world's biggest economies stand now in terms of this demographic trend? As Figure 1 shows, the United States is now descending from an all-time high in the ratio of its working-age to non-working-age population, and in the coming decades will see a large decline in this ratio, back to the level of the 1960s. Both Germany and Japan (not pictured) have already begun to experience a long projected decline in this indicator. China and Russia have also recently peaked with very high ratios, and will soon see rapid declines as well; Brazil is on a similar trend, although at a lower level. And India still has a way to go before it peaks.

Major U.S. Demographic Changes Under Way

With these facts in mind, we can look at the economic challenges and opportunities associated with demographic change in the United States now and over the coming decades. Several of them—population aging, and the changing racial and ethnic composition of the country—have set off alarms about the future of the U.S. economy. But are these alarms justified? Let's start with the trends themselves.

Immigration. The United States has long been a magnet for immigrants. The number of people obtaining legal permanent residence status first surpassed 1 million in 1905. At the onset of World War I, immigration plunged to about 300,000 per year, and it declined even further during the Great Depression. After World War II, immigration increased rapidly, reaching 640,000 in 1988 and then jumping to 1.1 million the next year and an all-time high of 1.8 million in 1991. The number fell again in the 1990s, but rose again and has exceeded 1 million in every year since 2005. Although the number of new legal immigrants was roughly equal in 1905 and 2012, the ratio of these new immigrants to the total population is much smaller today.

The distribution of immigration by country of origin has changed considerably over time. In the decade beginning 1900, Europeans made up more than 90 percent of all legal immigrants, but their share fell to 56 percent in the 1950s, with most of the rest from Canada, Mexico, Asia, and the Caribbean. However, in 2012, roughly 80 percent of legal permanent residents were from Asia or the Americas. Among this population, about 45 percent are between the ages of 20 and 39 (the corresponding figure for U.S. natives is 25 percent) and over half are female. Although immigrants distribute themselves very unevenly among U.S. states, the top destinations have been remarkably stable over time: California, New York, Texas, Florida, Illinois, and New Jersey.

As for the total number of immigrants living in the United States, this is unknown because of the difficulty accounting for undocumented immigrants. Estimates suggest that the total has reached approximately 40.7 million, which would represent a similar share of the total population compared with the beginning of the 20th century—although a much higher share than in the intervening years. For the undocumented immigrants, estimates range widely, from as low as 7 million to as high as 20 million. The Pew Research Center estimates that as of 2012, the number of unauthorized Mexican immigrants registered at 5.8 million (or 52% of the unauthorized immigrant population)—a share that has decreased slowly in recent years. Meanwhile, the numbers of undocumented individuals from other world regions including Asia, the Caribbean, the Middle East, and Africa are increasing gradually in the U.S.

Changing racial and ethnic composition. Non-Hispanic whites account for 63 percent of the U.S. population, a figure that has been, and is projected to continue, falling over time. The median age of this demographic group is 42, well above the median ages of 32 and 28 among the black population and the Hispanic population, respectively. Although Hispanics only make up one-sixth of the U.S. population, they will account for more than half of U.S. population growth from 2000-2015. An important contributor to the declining share of non-Hispanic whites is the relatively low share of individuals in their prime reproductive ages, and their relatively low rates of fertility during those years. Hispanic immigration is also a powerful contributor to the changing racial and ethnic makeup of the U.S. population.

As is well known, the average income of blacks and Hispanics in the United States is far below that of whites. The gaps in wealth tend to receive less attention, but they, too, are enormous. In 2011, the median net worth of white households was $110,500. The figures for Hispanic and black households were $7,683 and $6,314, respectively. These differences in economic circumstances reflect many underlying factors, among them education and training.

Population aging. The share of the elderly is rising worldwide, with the highest levels occurring in developed countries (especially in Japan and Europe). However, some of the sharpest increases will take place in countries in the developing world, most prominently Brazil and China. In the United States, those aged 65 and older have shot up from 13 million in 1950 (8 percent of the population) to 46 million (about 15 percent) in 2014—and this figure is projected to grow to 20 percent by 2030. Also notable is the growing share of the "oldest old"—those 85 and older—whose needs and capacities are substantially different from those aged 65-84. The 85+ crowd in the U.S. has also grown rapidly, from 1.2 percent of total population in 1990 to about 2.0 percent in 2014, with projections of 2.4 percent in 2030. Rising elder shares reflect the aging of large baby boom cohorts and increased longevity, as well as changes in fertility and net immigration.

Economic Salience of These Demographic Shifts

So what are the economic and political worries associated with these demographic trends?

First, U.S. productivity might fall. In general and for a variety of reasons, blacks and Hispanics have lower levels of education and skill than non-Hispanic whites. As a result, these populations are generally less prepared than non-Hispanic whites (whom they will increasingly be replacing in the labor force) to enter occupations with relatively high levels of compensation. In turn, a lack of appropriate action—such as increasing educational attainment and skills training of minority populations—could potentially translate into slower productivity and income growth for the United States.

Second, skill shortages may impede competitiveness. Some have argued that certain pockets of the U.S. workforce suffer from unemployment, which may be due, in part, to the perceived "skills gap" identified by many employers. Others, on the contrary, find no evidence at all that such a skills deficiency exists and argue that unemployment is due primarily to lack of aggregate demand.

Third, population aging might create numerous financial problems. Concerns center on the large portion of the population that will be, to varying extents, dependent on the working-age population for financial support, physical care, and companionship. For most of the elderly, financial support comes from a combination of sources, including personal savings, family members, Social Security, private pensions, and continued work. The long-term viability of some of these sources largely depends on the overall economy and (in some instances) the productive output of younger generations. The elderly may also legitimately worry about companionship, as smaller families, larger generation gaps, geographic mobility, and in some cases changing expectations lessen younger people's connections to their parents and grandparents.

Health care. Rising health care costs have the potential to hobble the U.S. economy. In 2012, the United States spent 18 percent of GDP on health care (the highest by far from both a historical and comparative perspective).

A rising share of the elderly in the population has led to fears that health care costs will inevitably continue to increase, as the elderly are more prone to experience one or more costly-to-treat chronic conditions such as cardio-vascular disease, diabetes, cancer, and chronic respiratory disease. Evidence on the "compression of morbidity" into a (relatively or absolutely) smaller part of a longer life cycle is thin and is doing little to silence alarms that have been sounding in various quarters about the fiscal implications of population aging.

Social Security. The rapid rise in the elderly share of the population has, appropriately, focused attention on the financial unsustainability of our pay-as-you-go Social Security system. This public finance challenge creates huge risks to the economic well-being of the elderly, especially those who traditionally rely more heavily on Social Security benefits for support: the less educated, less skilled, and less wealthy. Although politically contentious, there are a number of reforms to contribution and benefit schedules that could address this issue.

Fourth, social welfare dependency is poised to rise. Many Americans benefit from social welfare programs. Unemployment benefits, food stamps, Medicaid, and Social Security payments to the disabled and to survivors of Social Security recipients are prominent among these. Increasing shares of elderly and black and Hispanic populations suggest greater demands on these programs, which may crowd out investments in myriad forms of physical and human capital, and technological progress—all classic drivers of economic growth.

Countervailing Demographics

Some of the demographic trends discussed above imply potential economic difficulties for the United States in the years ahead. However, there are two countervailing trends involving fertility and immigration.

Fertility. Unlike in many other developed countries, the fertility rate in the United States has not fallen well below its long-run replacement level (roughly 2.1 children per woman). Indeed, as shown in Figure 2, fertility has actually increased since 1980 and is now just below replacement level. By contrast,

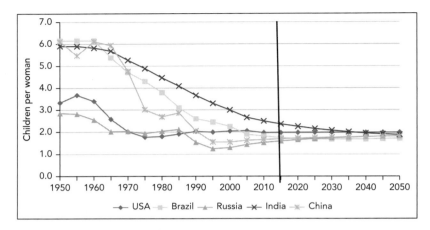

Figure 2. Fertility rates in select countries, 1950-2050

Source: UN World Population Prospects, the 2012 Revision

many other countries, including Germany and Japan (both at 1.5 children per woman) have fertility rates that are far below the long-run replacement level. As for Brazil, Russia, India, and China, the BRIC countries also in Figure 2, fertility has decreased dramatically over the last few decades, while India's fertility rate (at 2.5 children per woman) remains above the replacement rate.

Relatively high fertility in the United States means that there will be a correspondingly robust rate of new entrants to the labor force in the coming years, a trend that will likely be reinforced by continuing immigration. Income per capita in the U.S. could stand to benefit from having large numbers of potential workers and savers; the fiscal integrity of Social Security and health care financing stand to benefit as well.

Immigration. Immigrants are often self-selected for their work ethic, ambition, and willingness to take risks. Moreover, as noted earlier, a large portion of immigrants are of working age. The influx of working-age immigrants is a factor that pushes the working-age share of the population in the United States to decline more slowly than in many other developed countries that have more restrictive immigration policies. Liberalizing immigration policy, especially for skilled migrants, could provide a further boost to the size and quality of the U.S. workforce.

Countervailing Public Policies and Business Practices

Public and private policymakers in the United States can also adopt policies that will adapt to the demographic changes that lay ahead.

Human capital policy. Whether or not there is any skills gap right now, it is clear that the fortunes of the U.S. are tied closely to the education, training, and health of its future workforce. Investing in school and health can offset the projected decline in the share of the working-age in the population. Such investments have the potential to magnify the size of the effective labor force insofar as more and better education and better health results in more productive adults. Investments can also be disproportionately directed toward minority populations to promote their employment, productivity, and earnings and stem the tide of further increases in income inequality.

Retirement policy. Life expectancy in the U.S. has increased much faster than the normal age of eligibility for full Social Security benefits. This disparity suggests that raising the retirement age is a natural approach to addressing the tightening of the labor market that may be expected to accompany population aging. Indeed, expectations of greater longevity are plausibly associated with the desire to work to later ages, which may account for recent increases in the legal age of retirement in a number of wealthy industrial countries—including the scheduled increase in the U.S. from 65 (for people born prior to 1938) to 67 (for people born after 1959). On the other hand, life expectancy at age 65 for male Social Security-covered workers in the upper half of earners rose from 15.5 years for the cohort born in 1912 to 21.5 years for the cohort born in 1941, a gain of 6.0 years. By contrast, the corresponding gain for earners in the lower half of the distribution was less than 1.5 years. These data suggest that raising the retirement age beyond the two-year increase that has already occurred would impose a greater relative burden on low rather than high earners.

Human resource practices. Business has been slow to plan for population aging, but delay won't be an option for much longer. Unemployment is high now, but as the recovery proceeds, labor markets will tighten and companies will have little choice but to welcome older employees. Indeed, prompt action to harness—and enhance—the contributions of older workers will be seen as a key competitive advantage.

Older employees who wish to keep working may demand flexible roles and schedules. Allowing more part-time work and telecommuting will entice older workers to stay on, extending their careers by placing lighter burdens on them. Allocating demanding physical tasks to younger employees will produce a similar benefit.

Ongoing training, meanwhile, will help older workers master new skills as the economy changes. And employees' longer working lives give companies the benefit of greater productivity gains from their training investments.

Wellness programs produce healthier employees at all ages; on-site clinics save workers time and tend to lead to more prevention and early detection of illness and disease, which also lowers costs.

Last, moving from pay systems that are seniority-based to ones that give increased weight to performance will likely lead to a relaxation of corporate norms surrounding age at retirement.

Conclusion

The U.S. population will continue to grow at a robust pace in the decades ahead, ensuring a steady flow of new entrants to the workforce. But the combination of population aging and the fact that low-education and low-skill racial and ethnic minorities will make up an ever-larger portion of the workforce is raising worries about future worker and skill shortages and about the macroeconomic performance of the U.S. economy, especially when compared to the BRICs (Brazil, Russia, India, and China).

But demography need not be destiny. As ongoing political debates highlight, there are wide-ranging views of the public and private policy options that offer the most potent means of adapting to the new demographic contours of U.S. society. These include finding the means and will to control health costs for the aging population. They also must consist of educational policies at the federal and local levels that encourage learning that meets the needs of our changing workforce and the technological demands they will confront at work, whether in manufacturing or service jobs.

In this regard, now is the moment to confront the character of American education—to make elementary and secondary education appropriate to the development of skill and learning that the multicultural youth of America will require. It is also time to make a serious assessment of the state of American public and private higher education. Colleges and universities have been the pride of America since the creation of land grant colleges and the GI Bill after World War II. But now we need to reassess how these institutions might change to serve the country's needs in light of its changing population and the technological changes to come.

There is a need to rethink the role of older Americans in society. It is not only a matter of reinforcing the Social Security System to ensure its viability and providing quality health care at a sustainable cost. It is also rethinking how older Americans can contribute to society both through paid work and as volunteers for as long as they are willing and able.

Finally, this is the moment to consider immigration policies that both sustain the openness of the United States and ensure that newcomers can be assimilated as citizens who make needed social and economic contributions.

The predictability of demographic trends is a powerful tool in policymakers' arsenal. Being able to peer into the crystal ball improves our capacity to plan and devise both proactive and reactive strategies for heading off problems and taking advantage of potential opportunities. In that way, the demographic lens can help guide us to the economic future to which we aspire.

Notes

1. This chapter is an updated and revised version of an article published in the December 2012 issue of *Population Connection* magazine.
   The authors wish to thank Elizabeth Mitgang for her helpful assistance.

2

Their Best Assets: Why Companies Value Their Most Senior Employees

Hal Marcovitz

Donald Sommer shouts to make himself heard above the constant clashing sound of metal on metal. He holds up a tiny part—about an inch square. Just moments ago, the part displayed in Sommer's palm was one of several hundred stamped out of a huge sheet of metal. "It is used in seat motors,"[1] he says.

And by that, he explains, the part is a component of a bracket that sits under the seat of a Toyota. The bracket holds a motor that moves the seat. Tear apart any car and you will find tens of thousands of tiny parts, all with specific missions, all engineered with precision, all cut out of sheets of metal.

Sommer is a tool and die maker. It is his job to make the dies that are fixed to a press. The press operator then stamps out the parts from huge rolls of sheet metal. (That is what is making all the noise.) Ten million of these parts are produced each year at the factory where Sommer works, Tottster Tool & Manufacturing in Southampton, Pennsylvania. Tottster workers ship the parts to auto factories, many of them in Tennessee, where they are assembled into cars. "Some dies are simple but this [motor bracket] is a complicated one,"[2] Sommer explains, eyeing the part as he rolls it over in his palm.

Sommer is seventy years old. He has been cutting dies for fifty years. On his workbench before him he has spread out his tools—files, wrenches, clamps, hex wrenches, grinding wheels, and screwdrivers. Sommer cuts dies in the 21st century the same way he cut them when he started in the tool and die trade in 1964—using the simple hand tools of his craft.

He opens a wooden box to display his gauge blocks, which are also known as Jo blocks. They are tiny metal rectangles, each used to provide precision measurements. Not too long ago, a friend saw the collection and told Sommer he could sell the blocks for quite a tidy sum on eBay. That isn't likely to happen. Donald Sommer has no intentions of parting with his Jo blocks.

Not Ready to Retire

One of the dies Sommer has made during his career is used to stamp out a part so ubiquitous in the automotive trade that Tottster owner Linda Macht has named it "Donald's die." It is rare for people in the tool and die business to put such a personal stamp on their work, but Sommer has accomplished the feat. Indeed, there is no small measure of pride in Sommer's voice as he describes his work. The parts he shows a visitor may be buried deep inside the doors or dashboards of Toyotas or Nissans, but they are parts manufactured with the dies he has made.

If business at Tottster seems decidedly lo-tech, well, to some extent it is— but the tool and die business seems to be one segment of modern manufacturing that the high-tech geeks have yet to tackle. You won't find a computer screen or 3D technology on the Tottster factory floor. All of that is fine with Sommer. He doesn't seem like the type of fellow who would be comfortable designing dies with a keyboard.

He also doesn't seem like the type of fellow who is ready to retire. Sommer says he can't see himself sitting at home, watching TV all day, or finding some type of activity to fill his time. He likes being busy, likes making dies, and likes contributing to his company.

At Tottster, Sommer is not unique. He is the oldest employee among the few dozen Tottster workers, to be sure, but he only recently won that designation when Macht's secretary retired. "We just had a young lady—and I'll say young lady—retire here at eighty-six," says Macht. "She was my dad's secretary and as long as she was able to work, she worked here. She worked part time and she had to leave because of her eyesight. Eighty-six, not so bad."[3]

And so Sommer is now Tottser's oldest employee—but not by much. At sixty-nine, Tom Stewart is nipping at his heels. Stewart has been with Tottser for nearly forty years. He works as head of tool maintenance—a pretty significant job in a company where tools, both hand and power, are in constant use. Does Stewart plan to retire soon? "I'll check when I'm seventy and see how it looks," he says. "Donald checked when he was seventy and figured he'd keep on going. . . . A lot of doctors work into their eighties. They are making life and death decisions. They've got to keep up on what they are doing, too."[4]

Employees like Sommer and Stewart are an integral part of the culture at Tottster. Older employees—and their skills—are much valued. Certainly, there are younger workers laboring on the factory floor; Macht says some of their employees are barely into their twenties. But Macht, who took over the company after the retirement of her father—Bernard "Reds" Reichart—says there aren't a lot of young people who are learning how to make dies or run sheet metal presses. It is a trade that used to be taught in the vo-tech schools, Macht says, but now most younger employees join Tottster without skills, and so Tottster is forced to train them. Or, Tottster relies on employees like Sommer and Stewart who know what they are doing because they've been doing it for decades. "The skills I had when I started in the trade are almost obsolete, the way we are doing things now," says Stewart. "It's like a folk art."

Turning to Older Workers

Certainly, Tottster isn't the only American company that has adopted the attitude that older workers are among their best assets. At Vita Needle in Needham, Massachusetts, the average age of a company employee is sixty-five. That's right: People at Vita Needle are considered in mid-career at an age when most people their age are being feted by their coworkers at retirement parties.

Vita Needle is a lot like Tottster. The company operates a small factory providing a niche product—stainless steel needles and probes. The company's products are used to tranquilize animals, inject drugs into hospital patients, and test the temperature of food or the air pressure in automobile tires. The company employs forty-nine people, half of whom are seventy-five or older. Half the workforce is part time.

Vita turned to older workers in the mid-1980s when the company first experienced difficulty in recruiting employees. Located about eighteen miles west of Boston, Vita Needle placed an ad in a local newspaper offering part-time work to retirees. The first to answer the ad was Bill Ferson, who was then sixty-nine. In 2014, Ferson turned ninety-four and still shows up for work.

Ferson operates a swaging machine, which crimps the ends of the needles—creating the pointy part. Manufacturing was not new to Ferson—when he took the job at Vita he had recently retired from another manufacturer where he made precision measuring instruments. Still, he had never operated a swaging machine but was game for the challenge. "Bill was courageous enough to give it a try," says company president Frederick Hartman Sr. "He taught himself what to do."[5]

Like Tottster, Vita Needle seems stuck in the 1970s—there is a definite and noticeable lack of high-tech gear on the premises. Housed in an old theater in downtown Needham—the company doesn't want to move because most of its older workers are able to walk to work—the main workroom is filled with long tables where employees sit, sorting through needles, packing them in boxes for shipment. Elsewhere, employees operate lathes and drills.

And Vita Needle also has its share of employees like Sommer—set in their ways, hesitant to change, loath to part with their Jo blocks. According to Hartman, the company's office manager, Mary Bianchi, seventy-six, threatened to quit when he replaced her typewriter with a computer and keyboard. At first, the office staff wouldn't go near the fax machine and even today, many employees ignore the microwave oven out of suspicion. "I still think a third of our people won't go next to it,"[6] says Hartman.

At Vita Needle, the pace is slow, which enables workers to set their own hours. Indeed, in the hurry-up, need-it-yesterday world of manufacturing, that would seem like a handicap. After all, many manufacturers employ logistics managers—experts who are charged with getting the product assembled, packaged, out the door and on the trucks as soon as possible. A modern-day logistics manager may blanch at the notion of ninety-year-old hands, often afflicted with arthritis, moving products but at Vita Needle the company has found a way to make the system work. Everyone is scrupulously busy and scrupulous about the jobs they do.

Indeed, younger workers may be aloof toward the notion of placing damaged needles into the shipping cartons but not these workers: They take pride in their workmanship and know damaged inventory reflects badly on their company and the work they do. They feel a sense of accomplishment in their jobs that many younger workers have not yet learned. "You may not necessarily be reaching peak efficiency with this workforce in terms of output, but what we do get is very good quality,"[7] says Hartman's son, Frederick Hartman II, director of marketing and engineering for Vita Needle.

And the younger employees have taken notice of the work ethic of the older employees. At twenty-two, Rob Kurkjian is Vita Needle's youngest employee. He started at the company at the age of seventeen, intending to just stay there for the summer before beginning college. Five years later, he is still at Vita Needle—although he still sees himself enrolling in college one day. "They work harder than people my age," he says. "They aren't super speedy, but they put everything into the job. They make up for not being fast by making sure when something has to be done, they do it."[8]

More Than Just Money

For companies like Tottster and Vita Needle, there are benefits to both employer and employee. Tottster and Vita Needle get dedicated and reliable employees like Donald Sommer, Tom Stewart, and Bill Ferson. Certainly, particularly in the case of Vita Needle, the employers don't have to pay full-time salaries or benefits. Incomes of older employees are invariably supplemented by Social Security; moreover, their health care is covered by Medicare and not by a company-sponsored insurance plan. But at Vita Needle, Hartman Sr. argues that the employees are well-compensated and, in fact, the company provides generous bonuses each year—often equal to a few months' pay.

Moreover, at Tottster, Macht is quick to point out that in 2008—when the U.S. economy was on the verge of collapse and most automakers were in danger of going under—her business was hit hard. At the time, Tottster employed more than sixty workers but had to lay off all but eighteen. During the crisis, she asked Sommer to scale back his hours to part time. At first he agreed, but after a few weeks Sommer showed up and insisted on working full time, telling Macht that she didn't have to pay him a salary. "He said, 'You don't have to pay me, pay me in vacation, I'll do this for you.'"[9]

So the workers at Tottster and Vita Needle view their employers as something more than just a place to earn a paycheck. Says Bob O'Mara, a former chemical engineer who, at seventy-five, puts in several hours a week at Vita Needle. "If you are doing something that somebody values and is willing to pay you, then right away you feel affirmed."[10] Ferson says that if he couldn't work at Vita Needle he doesn't know what he'd do with his time. "You know, at my age, all my friends are gone," he says. "But I get up in the morning, I got some place to go, I got people to meet and I got something to do."[11]

For their part, employees like Sommer, Stewart, Ferson and O'Mara certainly do earn extra cash, but they also find ways to keep using their intelligence and skills, contribute to the economy and find meaning in life. "I wouldn't be alive if it wasn't for this job," says Ferson. "It lets me use the stuff upstairs in my brain. I see people, I socialize. They pay me."[12]

Good Places to Work

One of the reasons that older workers want to work at Tottster and Vita Needle is that employers like Hartman Sr. and Macht have made their companies into places that are attractive to older workers. At Vita Needle, for example, the part-time workers are free to set their own hours. Flex-time is the norm, meaning they can come and go as they please. Most of the employees have keys to the front door; they can come in as early as they desire and stay as late as they want—the last person to leave locks up. "People are letting themselves in at five in the morning," says Hartman Sr. "I'm not here telling them what to do."[13]

The employees can also take time off whenever they desire so if they want to spend a few weeks traveling they are able to do so without jeopardizing their jobs. Hartman Sr. acknowledges, though, that there can be a downside to such a liberal flex-time policy. If the company gets in a big order and it just happens to be summer, when many of the employees are enjoying Cape Cod with their grandchildren, well, the company just has to deal with it.

At Tottster, both Stewart and Sommer say they wouldn't be there if Macht didn't take pains to make the company into a friendly, family-oriented atmosphere. Says Sommer, "It's a nice place to work. Reds, Linda's father, was a nice guy to work for and Linda is similar. Some tool and die shops are full of nasty people. This has always been a pleasant place to work. I think when you go to work there's a certain satisfaction at the end of the day or the end of the week, certain accomplishments you have made. There's a die that's broken, you work on it. Boom, you are making parts, making stampings and making a profit for the company. It's a feeling of worth. It's better that watching CNBC all day and waiting for that Social Security check.... Why retire if you still have the skills to work?"[14]

At Tottster and Vita Needle, employing older workers does not represent a change with the past. These companies may find themselves on the cutting edge of social change, providing good products by utilizing the skills of people in their seventies, eighties and even nineties. But the fact is, that's the way they have always done business. At Tottster, Macht's father, Reds Reichart, worked until he was seventy-six. And Vita Needle's founder, Hartman Sr.'s great-grandfather, Oscar Nutter, founded the company at the age of sixty-nine in 1932 and worked until he was ninety-six, just days before his death.

Back at Tottster, a break-time has just ended. The presses fire up. Soon, the walls are reverberating with a thump, thump, thump as the massive machines stamp out tiny parts for Toyotas. Sommer leans over his workbench. There are dies to cut.

NOTES

1. Interview with the author, June 23, 2014.
2. Ibid.
3. Ibid.
4. Ibid.
5. Gretchen Ertl, "Older Workers: At This Company, Average Employee is 65," *Toronto Star*, June 17, 2013, www.thestar.com/business/personal_finance/retirement/2013/06/17/at_this_company_half_the_employees_are_75_or_older.html (Accessed July 14, 2014).
6. Julie Flaherty, "A Company Where Retirement is a Dirty Word," *New York Times*, Dec. 28, 1997, www.nytimes.com/1997/12/28/business/earning-it-a-company-where-retirement-is-a-dirty-word.html (Accessed July 15, 2014).
7. Katie Johnson, "Needham Firm Finds Success With Older Workers," *Boston Globe*, April 4, 2012, www.bostonglobe.com/business/2012/04/03/needham-firm-finds-success-with-older-workers/uy9yC2Br67TfwRCvljFilK/story.html?camp=pm (Accessed July 14, 2014).
8. Ertl, "Older Workers: At This Company, Average Employee is 65."
9. Interview with the author, June 23, 2014.
10. Johnson, "Needham Firm Finds Success With Older Workers."
11. Ari Daniel Shapiro, "In Their 90s, Working For More Than A Paycheck," NPR, Nov. 1, 2010, http://www.npr.org/2010/11/01/130566030/in-their–90s-working-for-more-than-just-a-paycheck (Accessed July 15, 2014).
12. Ertl, "Older Workers: At This Company, Average Employee is 65."
13. Flaherty, "A Company Where Retirement is a Dirty Word."
14. Interview with the author, June 23, 2014.

3 Economic Consequences of Population Aging in the United States

Ronald Lee

This article draws heavily on the recently released NRC report, "Aging and the Macroeconomy: Long-Term Implications of an Older Population," produced by a Committee of the National Research Council of which I was a Co-Chair. The views expressed here are my own, and not the Committee's.

The United States, like all rich industrial nations, will experience substantial aging of its population in the coming decades, even though its population is expected to continue to grow at a modest pace throughout the 21st century. If population growth were to cease, population aging would be more rapid. In this article, I will discuss the economic consequences of population aging in the U.S. drawing heavily on a report of the National Research Council on the long-term macroeconomic consequences of population aging, produced by a committee that I co-chaired.[1] However, the views expressed here are my own, not those of the committee or the NRC.

We naturally think of longer life as the root cause of population aging in the U.S. and elsewhere. Focusing on longevity leads naturally to the idea that we should adjust our individual life cycles, for example working longer or saving more. But population aging goes beyond changes in the individual life cycle and refers to the population as a whole. Population aging is certainly due in part to longer life, but it is also due to lower fertility and the slower population growth it causes. In the U.S., the timing of population aging is much affected by our massive Baby Boom which has just begun to turn 65, and which is beginning to raise rapidly the share of the older population. Low fertility and the aging of the Baby Boom mean that our economic adjustments will need to be much greater than those that would be sufficient to compensate for longer life.

Trends in life expectancy in the U.S. and in other industrial nations are shown in Chart 1. Around 1950 the U.S. was close to the leaders in longevity, but over the past sixty years our progress has been slow and we have moved to the bottom. Our life expectancy of 78 is five years less than Japan's at 83. Looking to the future, the heavy black line shows the projection of the Social Security Actuary that life expectancy will rise to 82.2. However, the NRC Committee concluded that life expectancy was likely to rise about

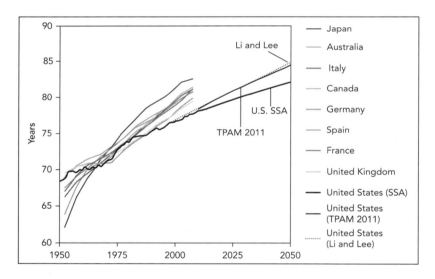

Chart 1. Life expectancy at birth in selected high income countries, and alternative projections to 2050 for the U.S. TPAM is the Technical Advisory Panel for the Social Security Trustees. SSA refers to the 2012 projection by the Social Security Trustees. Li and Lee refers to a projection by Nan Li and Ronald Lee.

Source: This is taken from Figure 3–1 of the prepublication version of the report of the Committee on the Long-Run Macroeconomic Effects of the Aging U.S. Population (2012). Based on United Nations (2011) data.

50% faster than that, to 84.5 years in 2050, as shown by the higher black line, and consequently that the population would age more rapidly.

Partly because of living longer, and partly because of retiring earlier, in the individual life cycle the ratio of years in retirement to working years also grew from 35 percent in 1962 to 41 percent in 2010, and is projected to reach 52 percent by 2050, which would mean that the average individual would work 2 years for each year spent in retirement.

The other major source of population aging is low fertility. Fertility in the U.S. has been at 2.0 or 2.1 births per woman for a long time, although the recession has brought it down to 1.9 more recently. In other rich industrial nations in Europe and East Asia, it is has long been far lower, averaging around 1.5 or 1.6. For this reason, population is younger in the U.S., and it will age less rapidly in the coming decades. Chart 2 shows the proportion of the population age 65 and over in the U.S. and other rich countries. We see that in 1950 France was the oldest of these countries while the U.S. was in the middle of the pack

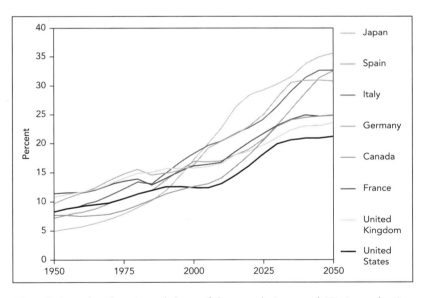

Chart 2. Actual and projected share of the population aged 65+ in a selection of high-income countries, 1950–2050.

Source: This is taken from Figure 3–17 of the prepublication version of the report of the Committee on the Long-Run Macroeconomic Effects of the Aging U.S. Population (2012), based on United Nations (2011) data.

21

and Japan was the youngest by far. Over the decades, though, the U.S. aged less rapidly and is now the youngest and is projected to remain the youngest through 2050. Japan, on the other hand, has aged very rapidly due to its rapid fertility decline and very long life. It is the oldest now and is expected to remain the oldest, with around 35% of its population 65 or older in 2050. The important point is that compared to other rich low mortality countries, the U.S. is not old now and is expected to age more slowly than the others in the future.

But what about immigration? Is that what is keeping the U.S. young? Immigration does contribute but it makes less difference than fertility. To get an idea of their relative roles, let's think about the so-called Old Age Dependency Ratio (OADR), the ratio of the population 65+ to the population 20–64. (The Committee concluded that treating 65 as the boundary of old age was a mistake, but in some contexts it is hard to avoid using it in this way.) The OADR in the U.S. is currently .22, with one "older person" for each five or so "working age" people. The Committee projected that this ratio would rise to .39 by 2050, or by 81%. The number of working age people per older person will drop by almost a half. Now to get back to immigration, how much would it have to increase in order to reduce the OADR in 2050 from .39 to .35, or by about 10%? The Committee calculated that this would require an average annual increase of 69 percent in the rate of net immigration, meaning there would be nearly 1 million more net immigrants every year than there are currently. By contrast, to achieve this reduction through fertility would require that women have an additional .5 births, a 25% increase in fertility. Neither of these changes seems very likely. Indeed the Committee concluded that it was almost certain (97.5% probability) that the OADR would rise by at least 60% by 2050. Population aging is not going to go away. We had better plan for it.

In addition to the aging population, it turns out that our consumption has also been aging in the sense that older people now consume much more relative to younger people than used to be the case. The dramatic changes can be seen in Chart 3, which shows the sum of private consumption by age plus publicly provided in-kind transfers such as health care, education, and long-term care (but not Social Security benefits which are income and need not be consumed). Compared to a 20 year old, an 80 year old consumed twice as much in 2007 as in 1960. Much of this change was due to the growing cost of publicly provided health care, and also growing private health care

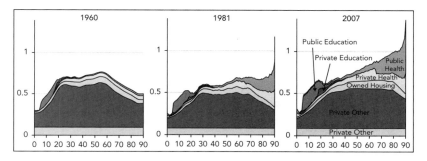

Chart 3. Consumption by age and by type in the U.S., 1960, 1981, and 2007, measured relative to average labor income for ages 30–49 in each year.

Source: This is taken from Figure 3–10 of the prepublication version of the report of the Committee on the Long-Run Macroeconomic Effects of the Aging U.S. Population (2012). Originally from Lee and Donehower, National Transfer Accounts.

spending. This increasingly costly consumption by the elderly compounds the economic cost of population aging.

Coming back to the OADR, it is based on an arbitrary age boundary at 65, and treats everyone above that boundary as a dependent, and everyone below it as a worker, while of course neither assumption is correct. Another approach is to estimate what the average person consumes at each age, as in Chart 3, and also estimate what the average person earns from work. These age profiles reflect the differences between people, some working in old age and some out of the labor force in their forties. We can use these age profiles to weight the age distribution of the population, calculating the "effective consumers" and "effective workers" in this way. The ratio of effective workers to effective consumers is the support ratio. As the population ages there are more people who consume more than they earn, and the support ratio drops.

The support ratio is projected to decline by 12% between now and 2050, or by about .3% per year. This means that other things equal (such as saving rates), consumption will grow .3% slower than it would otherwise between now and midcentury. If productivity were to grow at 1.5% per year, for example, consumption would grow at 1.2% per year. The decline in the support ratio in the U.S. will be much lower than in most rich countries where declines of .6% to .8% per year are common. The support ratio reflects both private and public consumption by age, and its projected decline will be fairly modest. But the costs of population aging are focused on the public sector programs for the elderly like Social Security, Medicare, and institutional Medicaid, which make up just a fraction of the national economy. The impact of aging on these programs will be proportionately much larger.

Whether the impact of aging is large or small, it must be borne in one way or another. Viewed broadly, there are four options: consume less during the working years and increase savings for old age; consume less during the working years and pay higher taxes to fund the government transfer programs; reduce public benefits for the elderly; increase the labor force by delaying retirement or raising the participation of women and other younger people. The task for policy is to choose an appropriate mix of these four options.

Later retirement would at most be one element among others in a larger policy response. Focusing on later retirement, it is important to consider the health status of the older population. For example, Chart 4 shows that the proportion of the population by age who report themselves to be in very good or excellent health declines strongly with age, and is substantially higher

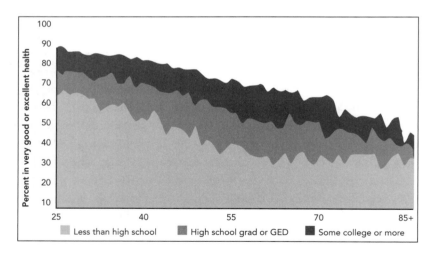

Chart 4. Age, education, and functional decline in the U.S., 2002–2004.

Source: Figure 4–1 of the prepublication version of the report of the Committee on the Long-Run Macroeconomic Effects of the Aging U.S. Population (2012). Originally from the MacArthur Foundation Research Network on an Aging Society (2009), based on data from the National Health Interview Survey.

for those with more education. Because enrollment rates increased decades ago, the current proportion of the older population with more than a high school education has risen steadily, and will more than double between 1985 and 2025, promoting improved health among the elderly. In fact, disability rates at older ages did decline steadily during the 1980s and 1990s, raising the ability of older people to enjoy life and to work. Unfortunately this trend appears to have flattened over the last decade, and some studies have found rising disability at ages 40 to 64, so the future outlook is uncertain.

However, health is not the main limitation on work at older ages. Half of men not working at age 70–74 have no health impairment, and more than half at ages 65–69. So far as health is concerned, labor force participation could be more than half again higher, even for men with no more than high school education. Looking ahead to 2050, a study commissioned by the Committee found very little change in the proportion of the population at ages 20 to 74 that could work, after taking account of all the expected changes with population aging, increasing educational attainment, increasing proportions of the Latino population, increasing obesity, and so on. Later retirement is definitely an option, although ill health, disability, and shorter lives are more prevalent among those in lower income groups, and their rights and welfare must be protected.

Throughout the 20th century, the age at retirement in the U.S. dropped steadily by more than ten years, until the 1980s when it stabilized. Around 1995, however, the age at retirement began to rise, and since then has risen by about 1.5 years for both men and women. Probably the main reason for this increase has been the change in employer-provided pensions from the traditional defined benefit kind to defined contribution, IRA and Keogh plans. Unlike most defined benefit plans, these others provide no incentives for early retirement, and in addition they shift investment risk and longevity risk to the individual.

Based on legislation in the 1980s, the Social Security full retirement age is already in the process of rising from 65 to 67. If policy makers wished to encourage longer work in other ways, a number of policies have been suggested. One is to introduce a new "paid-up" status for workers who have paid payroll tax for 35 or 40 years. They would not have to pay it on further earnings, which would effectively raise their real wages by 15%. Another suggestion is that Medicare be made the primary insurer for workers 65 and over, which would greatly reduce the health insurance costs to employers of older workers. Both these policies would raise the incentives for employers to hire older people, and for older people to continue to work. This would raise GDP, but it would have mixed effects on government costs and revenues with uncertain net fiscal outcomes.

One might wonder whether increased labor supply by older workers would take jobs from younger people. The Committee concluded it would not, any more than the enormous expansion of the female labor force since WWII has displaced male workers and raised their unemployment. Various international comparisons and analyses of country case studies support this conclusion, although during a recession the situation is likely different.

I will summarize more briefly some of the other conclusions of the Committee. One important question is whether an aging labor force will be less productive or less innovative than a younger one. Much uncertainty surrounds this question, but the Committee did not find convincing evidence that this was likely to be a problem. Another important question is how adequately older people have prepared for retirement. Studies have used different concepts of adequacy and different analytic methods to arrive at estimates that between one fifth and two thirds of older people have under-saved for retirement. Either way, a substantial number of people is inadequately prepared. These studies all assume that Social Security and Medicare benefits will be paid as scheduled in the future, and due to fiscal pressures this seems unlikely to be the case. They assume the same about private and public employer-provided pension plans, many of which are seriously underfunded. For these reasons, the estimates of the proportions with inadequate savings are probably too low.

There has been much concern that population aging would lead to a collapse of asset prices and rates of return as older people tried to sell off their assets, or tried to switch out of equities and into bonds. The Committee noted that asset markets are global, other than for housing, and that the global population is aging. They also noted that on the one hand, population aging would boost the accumulation of private wealth and assets, but that it would also tend to drive up government debt, with the net effect unclear. On balance, the Committee expected that there would be little effect of population aging on asset prices and returns.

Population aging will exert its greatest pressure on the public sector, tending to generate progressively larger deficits through the large public transfer programs for the elderly. The public sector is also important because it is through the public programs and taxes that policy can influence retirement age, or employers' demand for older labor, or change the relative consumption of the elderly compared to younger age groups, or influence which age groups or generations bear the costs of population aging. It is well known that the biggest fiscal problem is health care spending through Medicare and Medicaid. Population is one factor raising these expenditures, but increased costs per enrolled person are also very important. The future course of these costs per enrollee is uncertain, particularly in the wake of health care reform. Many other uncertainties also cloud projections of government deficits in coming decades. The Committee asked how large an adjustment would be needed to keep the ratio of federal debt to GDP constant at its 2011 level. According to an optimistic scenario, an immediate adjustment maintained every year through 2050 would require 1.1% of GDP in reduced benefits or increased taxes. But a pessimistic scenario would require a much larger 4.8% of GDP. In both cases, though, the needed adjustment would be much smaller if it were begun immediately rather than waiting another twenty years, at which point the adjustment would have to be larger by 1.3 to 2.9% of GDP.

Population aging will pose economic challenges, particularly for the public sector, but these challenges can be met by a range of policy options that might include increased labor supply by women and older people, in addition to adjustments to savings behavior, taxes, and benefits. We should act sooner rather than later to choose and implement some mix of these broad policy options both to control the costs of adjustment and to avoid passing most of these costs on to later generations.

Notes

1. Committee on the Long-Run Macro-Economic Effects of the Aging U.S. Population, National Research Council (2012) *Aging and the Macroeconomy: Long-Term Implications of an Older Population.* See http://www.nap.edu/read/13465/chapter/1.

4

Making Cities Green: Millennials Eschew Cars for Sidewalks and Bike Trails

Hal Marcovitz

We can thank the Millennials for selfies, Tweets, Justin Bieber, and enormously funny YouTube videos of people tripping into fountains while staring into their smartphones. But we can also thank them for saving the planet.

Yes, thanks to the Millennials, the post-World War II trend of plowing up farmland for suburban tract housing; of building miles and miles of highways so that oil-burning cars and trucks have places to go, and of giving auto companies and oil companies access to seemingly endless streams of consumers, may finally be over.

"The Millennials want to live in cities and towns," says Thomas Hylton, a Pennsylvania writer and founder of the advocacy group Save Our Land, Save Our Towns. "A perfect example is my nephew, who grew up in a rural township on a two-acre lot. He went to MIT and works for Google. He lives in Easton, Pennsylvania. It's a really nice neighborhood. He takes a bus three times a week to Manhattan from Easton. And the other two days he works at home because he is totally wired. He loves living in Easton. This is a guy who grew up on the typical two-acre lot where he couldn't do anything by himself. Mom and dad had to drive him to everything. He has a sister who went to Emerson College and still lives in Boston. She does not own a car. She takes public transportation or walks wherever she has to go. This is a generation that is attracted to cities."[1]

Hylton has lived in Pottstown, Pennsylvania, for more than forty years. Pottstown is a small, industrialized town on the fringes of the Philadelphia suburbs. In 1973 Hylton found a job as a reporter at the town's newspaper, the *Pottstown Mercury*, and eventually moved up to editor of the editorial page. In 1990, Hylton won a Pulitzer Prize for a series of editorials on the importance of preserving farmland. After winning the Pulitzer, he took a year off to write a book about preserving open space and maintaining livable cities and towns—the book is titled *Save Our Land, Save Our Towns*. After the book was published he returned to the *Mercury* for a short time before quitting to devote his energies full time to the advocacy group he founded, which he named after the book. Now, he travels the country giving speeches about the need to revitalize cities and towns and preserve farmlands and woodlands.

He thinks most school buses should be junked and children should walk or ride their bicycles to school. He thinks people should stop using cars and instead move into cities where they can walk or take public transportation to work—and also to theaters, restaurants, parks, and museums. He thinks governments should stop zoning the suburbs and rural districts for housing and commercial development and instead make it easier for developers to reclaim urban brownfields, where they can build townhouses and inner-city shopping plazas.[2] He also thinks all of that is, well, already starting to happen.

Statistics show Hylton's observations are more than just theory. A 2012 Case Western University study found that for the first time in generations, the population of the city of Cleveland has been growing while many of the city's suburbs have been losing population. According to the study, Cleveland's downtown population nearly doubled from 1990 to 2010, adding about 9,100 people—with young adults driving the growth. Between 2000 and 2010, more than 2,000 people younger than twenty-five moved into Cleveland's downtown. In contrast, nearby suburban communities experienced population declines. Among them were Cleveland Heights (down 8 percent), Parma (down 5 percent), Rocky River (down 3 percent), Shaker Heights (down 3 percent), and Eastlake (down 8 percent). And make no mistake, it is definitely the young people who are leaving the suburbs for city life. And many of these young people are college-educated, employed in the professions, and upwardly mobile. "There's a hidden brain gain going on," says Jim Russell, an economic geographer who specializes in the demographics of Rust Belt cities. "Not only is your inner city growing, but it's clearly because of an influx of young adults. You're trending in the right direction."[3]

Peak Car

Why the trend back to the cities? Hylton likes to believe the reality of climate change has finally resonated with a lot of people, causing them to question their lifestyles and whether burning carbon is the right thing to do. "What's happened is that everybody has recognized climate change," he insists. "Since we've had [hurricanes] Katrina and Sandy and the drought in California—enough things have happened that enough people are seriously paying attention to the fact that we have to start living in a different way. We are changing our lifestyles. The sizes of offices are shrinking and the sizes of dwelling units are shrinking after fifty or sixty years of steady expansion. I think people are beginning to get it, and will get it even more in the future."[4]

Certainly, climate change may be weighing on a lot of people's minds but when it comes to the twentysomethings, well, a short walk to the nearest Starbucks may be of at least equal importance. And they definitely do want to walk to their favorite coffee shops. In case anybody hasn't noticed, the U.S. reached what is known as "Peak Car" in 2004, meaning that was the year in which Americans drove the most miles in history—some 3 *trillion* miles, according to the national advocacy group Rails-to-Trails Conservancy. Since 2004, auto use has declined. Certainly, high gas prices have had something to do with that—although in 2014 gas prices took a dramatic dip. Still, there is no question Americans are driving less: In 2014, Americans drove about 2.5 trillion miles. That is still trillions of miles more than people like Hylton would prefer to see, but there is no question that times are changing.

And it is the Millennials who are making the change. According to the Rails-to-Trails Conservancy, people between the ages of 16 and 34 drove 23 percent less in 2009 than they did in 2011. Moreover, 85 percent of high school seniors were issued drivers' licenses in 1996; by 2014, that number had dropped to 73 percent. "Teenagers are driving less than their elders—when their elders were teenagers," says Hylton. "When we were growing up, we were dying to get our licenses; we could hardly wait. Now, the percentage of 19-year-olds with a driver's license over the past five years is actually declining. That is something I never could have imagined. It is like the fall of the Berlin Wall. It is shocking to say, 'Teenagers are doing less driving,' but the fact is they are.

"My niece doesn't have a car and doesn't want a car. I have a nephew who lives in New Jersey, and I know he hates driving. It's a chore, although he has to drive to work. He lives in a walkable area and he would much rather walk."[5]

The Venerable Sidewalk

It doesn't take much of an expert to know why young city dwellers are driving less. Parking fees alone in cities like New York, Philadelphia, Boston, and Chicago could run hundreds of dollars a month. Anybody who has found themselves driving in circles, vainly looking for a parking place, knows curbside parking is rarely available and, certainly, even if a parking place is found the meter has to be fed. Insurance companies charge their highest rates for city drivers. And there are, of course, costs for maintenance and fuel.

But the fact is, young people also live in places where they don't have to drive. Most of what they need—cafes, theaters, shopping, schools—is within walking distance of the nearest subway station. The venerable concrete sidewalk—the most basic form of infrastructure available in every American city—enables young people to walk to their gyms and yoga studios. And those sidewalks are the same sidewalks that have been underfoot since their great-grandparents walked wherever they needed to go. And, needless to say, subways, els, and buses have been a part of city life for generations. Therefore, most of the infrastructure the Millennials need to change our cities is already in place.

Most—but not all. Many young people like to ride their bicycles, and since they are gravitating toward city centers they want to be able to ride their bikes to work and other places. Some cities have recognized this trend and have made efforts to accommodate them.

Since 1986, the Rails-to-Trails Conservancy has been working with local governments and railroads to convert unused sections of railway track into walking and biking trails. There are now more than 21,000 so-called rail-trail miles in the U.S. But Rails-to-Trails sees itself with a new mission—creating bike trails through city neighborhoods. In other words, their new mission is to find ways for people to use bicycles in cities.

Of course, by employing no more than a can of white paint, a lot of cities have already dedicated portions of their streets to bicycle use: City streets frequently feature a "corridor" striped off from the rest of the street with "bicycle only" warnings stenciled into the pavement. Certainly, a lot of bicyclists use them—and even use city streets where there are no dedicated bicycle corridors, sharing the streets with cars and trucks. But there is no question that a lot of bicyclists would rather not take the risk. "For many people, painting a line is not enough," says Keith Laughlin, president of Rails-to-Trails Conservancy. "Too many cars actually impinge on that territory. I've taken so many pictures with my phone of delivery truck drivers parking in these lanes that are just supposed to be for bicycles."[6]

Some cities have gone beyond the paint can to accommodate bicyclists. Laughlin has seen city streets in which parking lanes have been created a few feet from the curbs, providing the bicyclists with a safe corridor between the curbs and the parked cars. Some cities have formed bollard lanes on streets, creating bicycle corridors. (Bollards are those squat rubber or plastic posts that emerge from the road surface, frequently appearing as though they have been run over by a truck or snowplow.) Some cities have even gone as far as erecting concrete barriers within the roadway, providing bicyclists with a secure corridor and strong measure of safety.

Laughlin would like to see cities do much more. As new neighborhoods are carved out of old brownfields or through similar urban redevelopment, he suggests, special bike-only trails can be laid throughout these new neighborhoods. Perhaps some streets can be completely dedicated to bicycle use—*no cars allowed!* "I call that a road-to-trails project," he says. "It's like a trail, except it's in an urban environment and it's not taking an old railroad corridor, but taking a road for the same purpose—to give people an opportunity for mobility without driving."[7]

Driverless Cars

Dedicated urban trails for bicyclists are the type of features that may be common in the cities of the future—and a lot of people see the future as basically devoid of the automobile, or at least the automobile as we have come to understand it. The basic problem with the automobile, Laughlin suggests, is that it is parked roughly 95 percent of the time. That isn't much of a problem in the suburbs because most people who live in single family homes don't have to worry about finding places to park their cars—invariably, they own garages and driveways and have plenty of room to park both of their cars, even if both cars are massive SUVs. And, as everybody knows, suburban malls have big parking lots. So do suburban schools, movie multiplexes, and parks. But in the cities where—as we know by now, more and more people want to live—finding a place to leave one's car 95 percent of the time can be a problem. And so, Laughlin says, in the future shared car services, such as Uber, will become more and more common.

When it comes to the city of the future, and the future of the American automobile, Laughlin says, "I think there are other forces in play, such as the notion of the self-driving car. Google is getting pretty close to having this ready to go. We're already seeing these changes in car-ownership trends. It is becoming a sharing economy, where there will be bike-sharing and car-sharing.

"Currently, cars are parked about 95 percent of the time and on the road 5 percent of the time. If you could flip that, the amount of road space and public right-of-way that is set aside just for cars could be reduced, and that could be reclaimed for walking and biking. Those are huge shifts in the way things have been done for the past sixty or seventy years; twenty-five years from now our cities may look very different."[8]

Regional Zoning

People like Laughlin and Hylton may have fashioned some optimistic images of the future, but both also acknowledge that none of this will happen without the assistance of the government. (And when talking about *government*, they mean all governments—state, local, and federal.) Some governments have been very helpful; some have not.

In Pennsylvania, for example, Hylton found state legislators and a governor (Tom Ridge, who served from 1995 to 2001) very open to his ideas. For starters, they passed legislation removing some of the environmental restrictions that were stalling brownfield redevelopment. "A lot of people would say that loosened up environmental restrictions but I would be one who would say it provided sensible environmental restrictions," says Hylton. "At the time, nobody was doing any brownfields, they were just sitting there—it was not financially possible to do it. That was a landmark bill."[9]

Legislators in Pennsylvania also adopted a bill that enabled communities to enact regional planning and zoning. Why was this significant? Pennsylvania has sixty-seven counties. Among those counties, there are big cities like Philadelphia and Pittsburgh, and small cities, like Allentown, Harrisburg, and Scranton. And there are also boroughs—small towns like Pottstown— as well as townships, which are often suburban but also often rural. In all, there are more than 2,500 cities, boroughs, and townships in Pennsylvania and, believe it or not, some of them maintain populations of a few hundred people or fewer.

But under law, each of those 2,500 cities, boroughs, and townships has the right to establish its own local government, which means it has the power to write its own zoning laws. Moreover, under Pennsylvania law zoning cannot be exclusionary—in other words, a township government can't say yes to residential development but no to commercial development. Therefore, if a developer approaches the most rural of Pennsylvania townships—say, Sweden Township in Potter County, population 872—and files plans to build a strip mall, under Pennsylvania law the Sweden Township Zoning Board has to find a place to put it. You can see the nightmare here. It means some 2,500 cities, boroughs, and townships in Pennsylvania have to be prepared to find places within their borders for strip malls. (Now, imagine this as a countrywide problem and the nightmare gets even worse.)

Hylton lobbied some influential state legislators and convinced them to adopt a law enabling Pennsylvania communities to band together for the purpose of performing regional planning and zoning. It means that, say, a half-dozen communities can get together and write a regional zoning code that says all strip malls will go *here*, all planned residential development will go *there*, and all heavy industry will go *way out there*.

It's all legal now, but sadly, the law is underutilized. A problem, Hylton says, is that many local government officials don't want outsiders—in other words, a zoning board member in a neighboring township—telling them how to zone their townships. "I think it's much more a cultural issue than an actual legal issue," says Hylton. "In a county, you may have fifty-seven municipalities. So there are fifty-seven zones for a Walmart, and fifty-seven zones for an office park. If you want to try and do open space preservation, it's hard because you have all these different municipalities. . . . The fact is you have township supervisors, you have township commissioners, you have constant turnover. They are looking for development, they are looking at the tax base. In practice, it doesn't work very well."[10]

Better Lifestyles

One answer, Hylton says, may be to take the problem out of the government's hands. Essentially, if a developer never approaches the supervisors of Sweden Township with plans to build a hundred single-family homes, the Sweden Township Zoning Board will never have to find a place to put all those homes.

So the answer is to convince a developer *not* to build those homes in Sweden Township but, instead, build housing in places like Pittsburgh and Philadelphia—or even Allentown or Scranton. The infrastructure for those homes (those venerable sidewalks) is already there; the desire for those homes is there, and—above all—the zoning is already there. But to make that happen, government has to do its part to make those places more livable. Governments would do well to make it easier for developers to reclaim brownfields. They must find ways to give support to bike paths for their Millennial residents—and, certainly, aging Baby Boomers who may have grown weary of subdivision life and see the benefits of returning to the cities as well. And governments have to clear the way for transportation that doesn't involve cars or, at least, provide access for cars that can be shared by the individuals who live in the cities—be they driverless or not.

"You have to get back to the culture," says Hylton. "When people don't want to live out in the middle of nowhere, when the developer finds it is not cost-effective to do it—that people want to live in places where there is the possibility for them to walk to places they want to go—that is the real solution.

"The converging elements of people who want to live in walkable places, the necessity of starting to live more environmentally sustainable lifestyles, the fiscal issues, are all coming together to encourage people to live more sensible lifestyles. Which is why I am optimistic."[11]

NOTES

1. Interview with the author, Jan. 7, 2015.
2. Urban brownfields: Abandoned or underused industrial or commercial property, often environmentally contaminated, that is considered a potential site for redevelopment.
3. Quoted in Robert L. Smith, "Cleveland's Inner City Is Growing Faster Than Its Suburbs As Young Adults Flock Downtown," *Cleveland Plain Dealer*, April 28, 2012, www.cleveland.com/business/index.ssf/2012/04/clevelands_inner_city_is_gorn.html Accessed Jan. 15, 2015.
4. Interview with the author, Jan. 7, 2015.
5. Ibid.
6. Interview with the author, Jan. 8, 2015.
7. Ibid.
8. Ibid.
9. Interview with the author, Jan. 7, 2015.
10. Ibid.
11. Ibid.

5 Ecological Economics Comes of Age*

Brian Czech

The ideas which are here expressed so laboriously are extremely simple and should be obvious. The difficulty lies, not in the new ideas, but in escaping from the old ones, which ramify, for those brought up as most of us have been, into every corner of our minds.

John Maynard Keynes

Of all the critiques of mainstream economics—Third World, feminist, Austrian, radical, Georgist, Marxist, and others—the one our grandkids would have us heed most is the ecological critique. The ecological critique says that mainstream economics has ignored some extremely important scientific principles that are especially relevant to economic growth in the 21st century. These principles, taken together, make it abundantly clear that there are limits to population growth and to the production and consumption of goods and services, no matter how efficiently we try to produce and consume. In other words, these principles make it clear that there is a limit to economic growth. Therefore, a full world in pursuit of economic growth finds itself in violation of the laws of nature and is penalized accordingly. As they say, "Nature bats last." Unfortunately, the penalties will be most severe for the grandkids, and this will be supremely unfair because the grandkids will have had no say in the formulation of our economic goals.

---

* This chapter is an excerpt from Brian Czech, *Supply Shock: Economic Growth at the Crossroads and the Steady State Solution* (Gabriola Island, B.C.: New Society Publishers, 2013: pp. 137–169). Chapters referred to in this section can be read in that book.

The ecological critique of mainstream economics is so strong and compelling that a large and growing academic movement has formed around it. This movement is called "ecological economics," no less, and is more or less embodied in the International Society for Ecological Economics, or ISEE.[1] There are ISEE chapters representing the United States, Canada, Europe, Russia, Australia and New Zealand, Brazil, Argentina, and India.

As with most movements, there are various views on how ecological economics originated. However, at least three couplings of people and their thought-provoking writings would be prominent in any discussion of ecological economics history. One is the controversial book by Donella Meadows, Dennis Meadows, and Jorgen Randers called *Limits to Growth*, published in 1972. Another is the highly theoretical work of the Romanian professor Nicolas Georgescu-Roegen, summarized in his book *The Entropy Law and the Economic Process* (1971). The third would be the profound but down-to-earth work of Herman Daly on the steady state economy, featured in books such as *Valuing the Earth* (1993), *For the Common Good* (1994), and *Beyond Growth* (1997).

Limits to Growth was a cornerstone of the American environmental movement and was eventually translated into 30 languages. The authors, based at the Massachusetts Institute of Technology (MIT) and commissioned by the Club of Rome, developed a computer model demonstrating how economic growth was leading to natural resource depletion and environmental degradation. Two of the computer scenarios, including a "business as usual" scenario and a dramatic technological progress scenario, predicted a disastrous collapse of the economy during the 21st century. The third scenario was essentially the steady state economy and assumed concerted efforts to stabilize the system. The book and its authors suffered a politically debilitating attack in the decades following its publication. At first, economists in academia chipped away at details, but soon pro-growth, free-market organizations such as the Competitive Enterprise Institute and Cato Institute piled on with an overarching accusation of "pessimism." Such criticism was similar to the 19th-century criticism of Malthus's *Essay on Population* and is hard to read without countering: "Don't throw the baby out with the bathwater." Perhaps Meadows and her colleagues weren't spot-on with every detail, but the principles they laid out were undeniable and the scenarios were rigorously constructed. Decades later analysts are documenting how prescient the authors of *Limits to Growth* were, especially with the business as usual scenario.[2]

In contrast to *Limits to Growth*, Georgescu-Roegen's masterpiece went mostly unnoticed in academia and was entirely ignored in public dialog. Its effect has been like the hands of time, tick-tocking perpetual growth notions into the dustbin of yesteryear's fantasies. The slow but sure ticking is apropos, given that *The Entropy Law and the Economic Process* is all about "time's arrow," or the entropy law.

The entropy law is a foundational concept in physics: the second law of thermodynamics no less. Perhaps the quickest, easiest way to describe it is that energy inevitably, invariably dissipates. Things that are hotter than their environment cool off. Of the billions of cups of coffee poured in the broad sweep of history, not one has warmed up of its own accord, not for an instant. The entropy process is as consistent and irreversible as Father Time; you can tell whether it's earlier or later based on the warmth of your coffee. Einstein said of the entropy law, "It is the only physical theory of universal content, which I am convinced ... will never be overthrown." Einstein was also impressed by the entropy law's "range of applicability."[3]

And apply it Georgescu-Roegen did, unto 457 pages! The main application, in a nutshell, is that absolute efficiency in the economic production process cannot be achieved. Nor can recycling be 100 percent efficient. Pollution is inevitable, and all else equal, more economic production means more pollution. These findings may seem like no-brainers to many, yet neoclassical growth theory has led to wild-eyed optimism regarding "green growth" and "closing the loop" by turning all waste into capital. Such fantasia cannot be soundly refuted without invoking the entropy law.

The Entropy Law and the Economic Process moves across a huge swath of philosophical and scientific terrain. As with most wide-ranging and intellectually adventurous books, *The Entropy Law* can and has been challenged. Most of its arguments and the counter-arguments are philosophical and not amenable to scientific proof or disproof. But the tremendous value of *The Entropy Law* is that it unequivocally established the profound relevance of thermodynamics to economic affairs. Unlike neoclassical economics, ecological economics embraces this relevance, putting ecological economics into a better position for enlightening real world affairs.

With regard to real world affairs, though, *The Entropy Law* as a book was not as useful as the entropy law itself. It was abstruse enough to appear esoteric, and Georgescu-Roegen's interests in economic affairs tended to be exceedingly long-term. While neoclassical economists pushed a perpetually growing economy, Georgescu-Roegen emphasized a perpetually eroding economy and indeed a perpetually eroding universe, all the way out to the "heat death" necessitated by infinity. This emphasis had the ironic effect of retarding the application of *The Entropy Law and the Economic Process* to the economic process itself.

Fortunately for ecological economics, one of Georgescu Roegen's students at Vanderbilt University was Herman Daly. A devout Christian, Daly too had an eye toward the longest of long terms, but he also had one eye focused on the wellbeing of present and upcoming generations. This tapestry of long- and short-term interests can be sensed throughout Daly's writings. Daly took the entropy law, emphasized its short-term relevance while acknowledging its long-term implications, and used it as part of a well-grounded macro-economic framework. He called this framework "steady state economics," which served as the catalyst for the ecological economics movement. Much of the remainder of this book is a natural progression from Daly's steady state economics.

With the passing of Georgescu-Roegen (1906–1994) and Donella Meadows (1941–2001), of the three only Daly, a professor emeritus with the University of Maryland, remains a major figure in ecological economics.[4] *For the Common Good* (coauthored with the theologian John Cobb) received the prestigious Grawemeyer Award for Ideas Improving World Order. Daly was also the recipient of the Honorary Right Livelihood Award (Sweden's alternative to the Nobel Prize) and the Heineken Prize for Environmental Science from the Royal Netherlands Academy of Arts and Sciences. Daly is no ivory-tower academic, either, having spent six years as a senior economist at the World Bank. The National Council for Science and the Environment presented Daly with its Lifetime Achievement Award in 2010. The tremendous respect for Daly is displayed in a festschrift authored by colleagues, students, and admirers.[5]

Of course, it is somewhat arbitrary to classify these relatively recent efforts as the "roots" of ecological economics. We saw in Chapter 3 that the classical economists, most notably Malthus, recognized limits to economic growth. John Stuart Mill went further and elaborated on the "stationary state." Daly's steady state economy is essentially the resurrection of Mill's stationary state, supplemented with a rigor gleaned from the natural

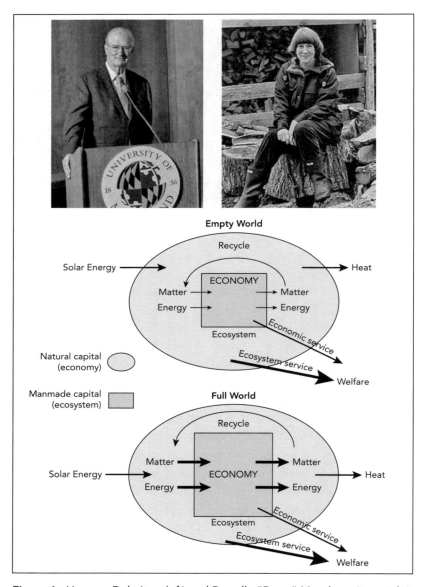

Figure 1. Herman Daly (*top left*) and Donella "Dana" Meadows (*top right*), founders of ecological economics. Daly and colleagues clarified the relationship between the economy and earth with a diagram (*above*) that was simple but powerful for illustrating limits to growth.

Credits: (top left) Herman Daly; (top right) Donella Meadows Institute; (above) From Ecological Economics, Herman E. Daly and Joshua Farley, ©2004 Herman E. Daly and Joshua Farley. Reproduced by permission of Island Press

sciences, an economic mastery honed in academia and first-hand experience with economic growth policy as implemented by the World Bank. After six years at the Bank, Daly left in disgust, noting the blind faith in neoclassical economics among the Bank's highest-ranking economists.[6] He offered the hopeful observation, however, that the Bank was becoming "more environmentally sensitive and literate."[7]

Daly was modest, for the newfound environmental sensitivity wasn't foisted onto the Bank by Wall Street or the Competitive Enterprise Institute. In fact, we have the likes of Daly himself and a noteworthy colleague at the bank, Robert Goodland, to thank.

With that brief historical account as background, the remainder of this chapter will comprise an overview of ecological economics, with an emphasis on how ecological economics treats the subject of economic growth. As with conventional economics, ecological economics can be broken down into micro and macroeconomics. Ecological economics is founded upon different principles, micro and macro, which lead to distinct conclusions and policy implications. These principles stem from the natural sciences (physical and biological) that are largely ignored in conventional or neoclassical economics.

While we keep the micro-macro distinction in mind, it will also be useful to think of three themes: allocation, distribution and scale. "Allocation" refers to the way the factors of production are devoted to different producers for different purposes. For example, land may be allocated among farming, forestry, recreational and other uses. Labor and capital may be allocated likewise. At a finer level, timber from a forest may be allocated among furniture-making, construction, boat-building, etc. Labor at the construction site may be allocated among carpentry, masonry and plumbing. Capital at an automobile plant may be allocated among the chassis, drivetrain, and circuitry floors. The efficiency of an economy depends to a great extent upon a well-balanced allocation among and within the factors of production.

"Distribution" refers to the distribution of income, wealth, or general welfare. This is the economic subject most often discussed by non-economists. Indeed, politics is mostly about distribution, which explains the classic definition of politics: "Who gets what, when, and how."[8] Bill Clinton could have elaborated, "It's the political economy, stupid!"

"Scale" refers to the size of the human economy relative to the ecosystem. This, of course, is our focus here, and it provides the primary distinction between neoclassical and ecological economics. Neoclassical economics deals almost exclusively with allocation and, to a much lesser extent, distribution. Why? Because neoclassical economics doesn't recognize environmental limits to economic growth. With no limit to growth, the concept of scale is superfluous, there is no conflict between growth and the environment, and the cure for social ills—including maldistribution of wealth—is always more growth. "A rising tide lifts all boats," as they say.

Ecological economics deals with allocation and distribution, but its emphasis is on scale, especially among the scholars and policy activists we might call "Dalyists." Scale deals with whole economies, usually national or global, so ecological economics is geared especially to replace conventional *macroeconomics* while accepting and incorporating some of the fundamentals of conventional (neoclassical) microeconomics. Before we delve into scale, however, let us briefly consider allocation and distribution from the perspective of ecological economics.

Ecological economists acknowledge that the market—that ubiquitous place where goods and services are exchanged—is reasonably efficient at allocating resources. The market is especially efficient when property rights are easily established and readily enforced. This is *not* the same as saying prices are a good indicator of absolute or long-run scarcity. For example, even if the market price of petroleum is far too low for the sake of the grandkids, allowing us to pull the carpet from under their future, the market will do a reasonably good job of allocating petroleum among today's power plants, airlines and trucking companies. For example, there won't be a huge surplus of petroleum at the power plant if the trucker down the road is desperate for gas. The fact that the invisible hand can handle this allocation problem is good indeed. Today's consumers will not only have electricity from the power plant, but goods hauled in by the trucker.

Adam Smith described this process in detail but also noted several problems, including monopolies and misinformed consumers. Such problems prevent the market from performing properly. Few have argued that point, and economists of all stripes talk about "market failure" and how to correct it. Nevertheless, neoclassical economists place a notorious amount of faith in the market. The invisible hand, they say, ensures that microeconomic behavior produces a desirable macroeconomic outcome. Supply and demand establish prices that send appropriate signals to producers and consumers, leading to economic activity that serves society's interests. For example, as a natural resource becomes scarcer, the price of it rises, resulting in more vigorous efforts to supply the resource. Theoretically, this will take care of the grandkids as well as today's consumers.

Richard Norgaard, a professor at the University of California-Berkeley and past president of the ISEE, points out the fallacy inherent to the neoclassical theory of prices.[9] The theory implies that she who sells the resource knows whether the resource is scarce or not. Otherwise, how would she know where to set the price? Yet how was she supposed to know how scarce the resource was, if price was supposed to tell her? It's a catch-22.

This is an important critique, because economists often argue that natural resources are actually becoming more plentiful just because prices are declining. (Not that many prices are declining today.) The late Julian Simon (1932–1998) famously peddled such pap, spawning disciples who found Simon's argument conducive to increasing their own money supplies. After all, their "theory" feeds straight into the hands of corporations that benefit from the resulting, pro-growth mindset of consumers and policy makers. The corporate community loves these disciples of Simon, and the new darling is the Danish statistician Bjorn Lomborg. Praise has been heaped upon Lomborg by the likes of the Competitive Enterprise Institute for his book, *The Skeptical Environmentalist* (see Chapter 4).

Yet for ecologists, ecological economists, and sustainability thinkers, *The Skeptical Environmentalist* is riddled with fallacies, straw men, and shoddy scholarship. I agree with them, having carefully reviewed the book for the journal *Conservation Biology,*[10] and websites have been devoted to exposing Lomborg's misinformation. Yet we saw in Chapter 4 how such books can be paraded by Big Money. In the process, their popularity may eclipse their notoriety, especially among the uninitiated, the gullible or those desperately wanting to believe that all is well, after all, in the environment. George Will comes to mind.[11]

But back to Norgaard, whose observation on the fallacy of pricing theory helps explain the confusion of economics students when they encounter the subject of supply and demand in introductory "micro." First they learn that prices are determined by supply and demand. Then they learn that the quantities supplied and demanded are determined by … prices.

There happens to be no lurking inconsistency here. But there's no magic trick to dazzle us either. It's just a matter of semantics. Supply is not the same as "quantities supplied" and demand is not the same as "quantities demanded." But these semantics do open the door for shenanigans.

The supply (per se) of raw diamonds, for example, is determined primarily by how many diamonds are in the ground and the technology available for mining them. Supply clearly does influence price; diamonds are expensive partly because they are so hard to find and extract. On the other hand, the "quantity supplied" is what is brought to the market by diamond sellers. Price clearly does influence the quantity supplied; the higher the price, the higher the quantity supplied, all else equal.

So the relationships among supply, price, and quantity supplied are really not so mysterious, at least not until a linguistically reckless or unscrupulous growthman wades in to muddy up the waters. The late Julian Simon has plenty of living counterparts. Robert Bradley, president of the Institute for Energy Research, believes that "natural resources originate from the mind, not from the ground, and therefore are not depletable. Thus, energy can be best understood as a bottomless pyramid of increasing substitutability and supply."[12] In other words, innovators supply the world with natural resources, including energy, from their minds. Therefore, the supply of such resources is no problem.

Clearly such a theory inculcates a healthy supply of manipulative political rhetoric, in which the word "supply" is quickly corrupted. It's a game anyone can play, so let's take a turn. Consider the supply of clean air at a party in an apartment. Smokers suck in the clean air and gradually replace it with second-hand smoke. Their lungs are like pumps in an oilfield, systematically extracting the resource, replacing it with airborne sludge. As more smokers arrive, the supply of clean air noticeably dwindles, and nonsmokers start to leave. Eventually even the smokers start leaving, beginning with the lighter smokers who don't like heavy smoke. So at first, more smokers means a lower supply of clean air, yet eventually—after enough smokers have polluted the place and many have left—the supply of clean air stabilizes. In fact the supply of clean air starts to increase a bit as the secondhand smoke is absorbed in the curtains and carpeting, and fresh air wafts in through fissures in the walls (assuming smokers weren't crowding the hallways outside). Next, we conveniently overlook the fact that it took a major reduction of clean air to make all this happen; too complicated to consider all that. So in a squirrelly sort of way we can now say that more smoking (that is, extraction of clean air) led to *increasing* supplies of clean air, and indoor air pollution due to smoking is a self-correcting problem. If we generalize a bit, moving out of the confines of this particular party, we can say that the key to less smoking in society is more smoking!

This ludicrous example mirrors the claim that the invisible hand of the market will "fix" any resource shortages that might arise. It's smoke-and-mirrors.

We've all been downwind of cigarette smoke. Certainly we have the right to poke a little fun, especially at the "Seven Dwarves," the CEOs of America's largest tobacco companies, who perjured themselves before a U.S. House of Representatives Subcommittee: "I believe that nicotine is not addictive."[13] The resulting news broadcast was unforgettable to many Americans, who learned a lot about Big Money that day. We fully expected the Seven Dwarves to announce, as an encore, the Tooth Fairy's engagement to Santa Claus. So Americans know quite well how Big Money pollutes the truth. Can we expect the mother of all money-making theories, neoclassical growth theory—along with all its crazy correlates—to come to us on wings of truth? Sure, sure, higher prices stemming from lowered supplies actually "increase" supplies because they provide an incentive to "supply" even more. And more smoke makes the air "cleaner" by providing an incentive for smokers to increase the supply of clean air. More traffic increases the supply of open road. More noise actually leads to a greater supply of quietness. Less of a good thing leads to more of it! More of a bad thing leads to less of it! Or, if you prefer, less of a good thing leads to less of a bad thing, and more of a bad thing leads to more of a good thing!

So if the Competitive Enterprise Institute, neoclassical economists, and growthmen at large want to claim that oil supplies, for example, are actually *increasing*, not decreasing, as evidenced by the occasional downturn in price, let them play with the word "supply" like the Seven Dwarves play with "addictive." Let them use "supply" to mean more, less, a harmless mess, anybody's guess … whatever. But may the rest of us not be dolts. Supply is how much there is, and as you use more, less remains.

Meanwhile, expecting the market to maintain our supplies is like expecting the political arena to maintain our ethics, the library to maintain our ideas or the sewage plant to maintain our intestinal tracts. Each of these pairings represents a relationship between two variables, but in no case is the relationship straightforward or dependable, much less positively reinforcing. Thus it is with market prices and supplies. The bottom line is that markets are all about the consumption of resources. No matter how efficiently they allocate resources today, *bigger* markets mean *more* consumption and *less* resources tomorrow.

Now we turn to the distribution of wealth. Many neoclassical economists view the distribution of wealth as a final stage or special case of allocation and therefore "covered" by the market. Others think of distribution as a matter for politics, ethics or religion and not even within the purview of economics. Ecological economists, on the other hand, emphasize that an equitable distribution of wealth is necessary for the long-term economic security of rich and poor alike, and is therefore a central issue for economic study and policy. In fact, distribution of wealth generally takes a higher priority than allocation in ecological economics.

Ecological economists also emphasize the distinction between allocation and distribution. Just because a consumer purchases something when he thinks the transaction will benefit him doesn't make the market equitable at distributing wealth. In fact, the market has little to do with the distribution of wealth. Wealth (in the economic sense) is the *means* to purchase and affects the *amount* that may be purchased. Wealth may be legitimately worked for and even invested in, so that labor markets and stock markets are conduits for wealth, but large portions of wealth are distributed via charity, inheritance, marriage, luck and shades of crime ranging from shoplifting to Enron. A whole subfield of ecological economics has sprung up around the distribution of wealth as distinct from the allocation of resources.

In considering the distribution of wealth, a good starting point is human behavior. Remember from Chapter 2 the neoclassical notion of self-interested, utility-maximizing *Homo economicus*, whereby utility is expressed in terms of consumption? This materialistic model of mankind is roundly condemned by assorted critics, often with Marxist or Georgist leanings, and more often with common sense. Ecological economics offers an additional, unique and original critique in which humans are viewed as having evolved in a variety of ecosystems, each of which posed unique constraints on economic behavior and resulted in unique cultural norms. As such, humans are subject to diverse, complicated, and even mysterious motives not satisfied by simply maximizing their consumption of goods and services. This way of thinking is called "evolutionary economics" in some circles.

Don't worry, this book is not about to turn into a Luddite manifesto for turning back the clock to caveman days. But it's worth thinking about human nature—the deeply rooted, promising aspects of human nature with economic growth at the crossroads. We know that people the world over have cultural, tribal roots and urges, exposed most obviously in outdoor activities such as hunting, fishing, and camping. Is there something deeper? Surely there is, especially traits, behaviors, and attitudes that would have contributed to individual and tribal survival. We should at least attempt to identify some of the ways human evolution has affected our economic behavior today, rather than settling for a model that makes us look like pigs at a trough.

Early human societies, or tribes, involved kinship, a common language, a common faith, some property in common, equity among members (especially within gender), and an economy adapted to and dependent upon a particular ecosystem. Long-lasting tribal societies consisted of individuals who valued their tribal identities, including their ancestors and descendents. In other words, they were concerned with the distribution of wealth not only among the living but unto future generations. Far from maximizing consumption, they monitored their use of resources and consciously conserved these resources for future generations. Of course, not all tribes can be characterized this way, but in many parts of the world tribal institutions evolved to ensure conservation.[14] Such institutions included totems that identified clan members with nonhuman species, dances that reinforced appreciation of natural resources, land-resting practices and, in almost all tribal cultures, redistributions of wealth ranging in scope and duration from the Chinook potlatch to the Mosaic Year of Jubilee. Tribal cultures that failed to develop the appropriate traits and institutions were not sustainable; they simply didn't survive.

The point is that both conservation of resources and redistribution of wealth are essential for sustainability—ecologically, economically, and ethically. As with the wealthy, there are needy people in all societies as a matter of luck, skill, age, health, inheritance, and other factors often beyond their control. The needy perish without some help from society, or else turn to *anti*-social means of acquiring necessities. In a tribal hunting culture, the needy would have resorted to indiscriminate harvesting practices that endangered future generations of wildlife and plants, such as the killing of pregnant does. In feudal times, the needy often hid along forest paths, begging, poaching, sometimes robbing. Today's needy tend to congregate, nameless, in big cities where food and shelter are more readily obtained. If there is no assistance, whether it be some form of workfare or pure charity, eventually violence ensues. That's just common sense, and only an intelligent and fair approach to distributing wealth is stable and sustainable.

So in the long evolution of tribal cultures, institutions for maintaining equity and ceremonies for redistributing wealth were selected for because they were sustainable. That doesn't mean tribal leaders said, "Let's select these institutions because they are sustainable." It means that tribes which developed those institutions lasted the test of time, while others didn't. It was natural selection operating at the cultural level.

It should be comforting and encouraging to know that sustainable economies are not an unprecedented condition for *Homo sapiens*, especially when we consider that we all have tribal ancestry if we search deeply enough into the past. Perhaps it is in us yet to limit consumption for the sake of society, present and future, instead of attempting (in abject futility) to satiate unlimited wants. Perhaps posterity, the "seventh generation" in more tribal terms, will yet recapture our attention long enough to put the likes of gas-hogging Escalades and McMansions in a new light, a light not nearly so positive as it apparently is today.

Meanwhile, we face a troubling question: "If we were all tribal, and natural selection was for sustainable tribal institutions, whatever happened!?" The answer seems straightforward enough. During the Neolithic Period, or the New Stone Age, beginning in the Middle East around 7,500 BC, tribes learned to grow their own food. Agriculture spread shortly thereafter to parts of Africa, India, China, and Europe, while Native American tribes developed their own agricultural techniques. Agriculture and the domestication of animals allowed a degree of separation from nature and independence from the wild animals and plants so important to tribal identity. It wasn't long before agricultural surplus freed the hands for the division of labor and the development of numerous technologies, occupations and cultural activities such as politics and religion. A sedentary lifestyle supported by agriculture was also conducive to larger families and higher population densities.

Friction among neighboring peoples, often for resources, resulted in the development of organized warfare. Some tribes became oriented more toward raiding than hunting, gathering, or farming. Post-tribal societies similarly produced a warrior class and, eventually, national armies and navies. So the world went through its stages of empires, feudalism, and monarchies; a dark age here, a renaissance there, periodically punctuated by religious crusades and revolutions. By sword or plowshare, tribal societies were replaced, one by one, often unto several post-tribal stages. For example, Polans, Silesians, and other Polish tribes were subjected to Viking invasions from the north and Mongolian invasions from the east long before there was a state of Poland, which then was invaded by Turks from the south, Germans from the west, and Russians from the east.[15] Yet the Poles retained their homeland, helped early on by sustainable tribal cultures, rooted to the land, with lasting traditions of loyalty and cooperation gradually melding with Roman Catholic ceremony.

Hebrew tribes had an even longer, more intense history of persecution. They retained their faith but lost their homelands and then their right to own land. Eventually, with no lands to coevolve with, or to farm, hunt on, or gather from, Jewish society naturally became oriented toward commerce. Lending, especially, required almost no land. Christians were not allowed to do it, so Jews occupied, expanded and at times perfected this unique niche in the financial history of the world.[16] Money-lending (a forced occupation) may not jump out as an icon of sustainability, but other tribal traditions do, such as the labor-and-land-resting Sabbath day, the land-and-labor-resting *shmita* (the Sabbath year), and the leveling of wealth known as Jubilee. These traditions were so sustainable—protecting land and spirit as one—that they lasted centuries after the lands themselves were out of reach.

All five of the world's major religions—Hinduism, Buddhism, Islam, Judaism, Christianity—have sustainable traditions, at least ideally. Hindus revere nature and eschew a materialistic lifestyle. Buddhists follow the middle path, a perfect metaphor for the balance of nature, with humans taking their share while leaving the rest for the other species of the world. Moslems establish "hima," or nature reserves, to balance their needs with the needs of plants and animals. Jews rest the land and participate in Jubilee. Christians are stewards of nature in the mold of St. Francis of Assisi. An argument could be made that protecting the environment, out of respect for nature and concern for future generations, is the most unifying theme of the major religions. Who among the bona fide faithful would deny its importance?

I'll never forget the day I was asked to give a talk on steady state economics to religious leaders in the Washington, DC, area. During the discussion that followed, a distinguished and pensive Unitarian minister finally revealed his thoughts by saying, "You know, the steady state economy—that's the kingdom of God." He elaborated to some extent on the theological basis for this statement, yet it is easy to sense how perpetual economic growth doesn't mesh with the ideals of *any* major religion. Neither does perpetual recession. That leaves the steady state economy as the theologically enlightened alternative.

Perhaps the environmentally ideal aspects of mainstream religion stem primarily from the earthy spiritualism, common sense and dignity of sustainable tribal traditions. But ideals are rarely achieved, and not all tribal traditions lasted beyond the tribes themselves. Many Native American (North and South), Australian, and African tribes were obliterated by imperialist European nations, who turned out not to represent ideal versions of Christianity, Islam, or other religions. Some of the tribes remain in name, at least, within and among modern nation-states, but only the deepest Amazonian rainforest or the driest Australian outback still have tribal economies rooted intimately in their ecosystems.

Meanwhile an explosive convergence of science and technology, all in the midst of an intellectual "Enlightenment," led to the Industrial Revolution of 18th-century Europe. In the evolutionary perspective of ecological economics, the very phrase "Industrial Revolution" is telling. A *revolution* is something that, by definition, has become unhitched from *evolution*. In a revolution, the pace and magnitude of change are pronounced. Industrialization happened in a flash compared to the long sweep of prehistory, and suddenly most of the world participates in globalizing, mass-marketing, manufacturing, and even "service" economies. Many of us have lost our connection to the natural world and wouldn't know a grouse from a grebe. We have lost the tribal institutions that kept us in touch with the natural resources the grandkids will depend upon. The challenge now is to develop counterparts to tribal totems, ceremonies, land-resting rules, and even distributional schemes that will work in today's political economies.

Some such counterparts limp along in disguise already. In the United States, for example, the bald eagle has been our nation's symbol since 1782. The identification of our populace with this majestic bird helps to explain the strong protections afforded to the eagle, dating back to the Bald Eagle Protection Act of 1940. It's a solid perch in the mostly unsustainable tree of American policy.

Certain seasonal events evoke a touch of tribal awareness, too. Thanksgiving is probably the closest thing in American culture to a tribally rooted celebration in which we ponder and appreciate the plenitude of the land. It is no coincidence that, of all the federal holidays, this one brings us closest to our Native American hosts. We are thankful to the Native Americans for helping those early, vulnerable colonists. Alongside the Native Americans, we are also thankful to God or Mother Nature for the fruits of the land. It's true that Thanksgiving has become a lot like an American Christmas—more about celebration than appreciation. The malls are open till midnight and a lot of Americans spend the day shopping for Christmas gifts. The sheer mass of this operation has become unsustainable, but at least an element of wealth redistribution lives on in the act of gift giving.

So now in the 21st century we must stand before the mirror and ask: Which of the following ladies or gentlemen will materialize? A long-evolved, tribally rooted, *Homo ecologicus*, or the self-interested, utility-maximizing, globe-trotting *Homo economicus*? Which, we might ask, would also deserve the title of *Homo sapiens*? Clearly we need *sapience* in a full-world economy.

Based on the above—our mix of tribal origins and industrial economies— I'd like to think we are *Homo ecologicus*, variety *economicus*. We are predisposed, while remaining efficient and adequately self-interested, to distribute wealth in a more sustainable fashion than the raw-boned, sociopathic *Homo economicus*. We've got just enough sapience to be vigilant, to maintain or restore our ecological and ethical fitness, to keep in mind that the unfit go extinct, with or without piles of money.

For purposes of ethical fitness, the distribution of wealth is our primary concern. For purposes of ecological fitness, the bigger issue is scale. The market may do a reasonably good job at allocating resources among competing ends, and is involved to some extent in distributing wealth, but it does nothing whatsoever to prevent the over-allocation of the entire collection of resources or even of a particular resource. Neither does neoclassical economics. In neoclassical economics, it's unclear if land is even a factor of production

(Chapter 4), technological progress perpetually increases economic capacity (Chapter 8), and population growth is required not only for long-term GDP growth, but for long term per capita GDP growth (Chapter 5)!

As with the distribution of wealth, there are tribal antecedents that enlighten our understanding of the scale issue. An oft-cited example is the Rapa Nui of Easter Island, who developed a culture obsessed with the conspicuous display of stone figures called *moai*. Moai often weighed more than 20 tons, and the desire to move them about the island resulted in a technology of transportation in which copious quantities of coconut palms were used as rollers.[17] Competition among islanders to display more and bigger moai took precedence over developing institutions for monitoring and conserving the palm, which also happened to be a crucial source of food and fiber. The Rapa Nui neglected other natural resources too, but the coconut palm was the cornerstone of their economic life. Once their island was denuded of coconut palm, disaster ensued. The economy had become far too big for the remaining resources to support. Cultural decay set in quickly, to the point of cannibalism, until the economy was adjusted to an ecologically supportable level by a not-so-invisible hand of nature.

Anthropology is not an exact science, but it appears that prior to the Industrial Revolution many economies on continents outside Europe had achieved relatively steady states (as in steady state economies), even while others were heading down paths toward Easter Island-like outcomes. For example, several tribes in North America had developed hunting economies in balance with the bison herds roaming the Great Plains, especially before the Spaniards introduced horses.[18] Among these noteworthy tribes were the Arapaho, Cheyenne, and Comanche. (The famous Sioux tribes came later to the plains in response to European colonization, moving in from the east and adapting quickly.)

Meanwhile, a more sedentary, Anasazi culture was waxing and waning in the Southwest. In Chaco Canyon (New Mexico), then at Mesa Verde (Colorado), Anasazi economies boomed and then collapsed in the 13th and 14th centuries. Scholars think the demise of these economies was largely a result of overpopulation and resulting resource shortages, especially of water. Not long afterward a similar fate befell the primary tribal occupants of what is now Arizona, although their wholesale disappearance from the archaeological record is a bit more mysterious. Indeed, the Pima Indians called them the "Hohokam," or "vanished ones." In the case of the Anasazi, pockets survived here and there, evolving culturally into the more sustainable Pueblo tribes of today.

Clearly, there was a natural selection for sustainable tribal cultures in North America, and a similar process was under way for millennia over large swathes of the planet that had avoided the Neolithic transformation and its discontents (the proverbial Vandals, Visigoths, and Vikings). Rather suddenly and very tragically, in an early episode of "globalization," the whole process was interrupted by a lethal combination of European "guns, germs, and steel."[19] Many tribes disappeared, and those that survived lost a great deal of cultural integrity, including in many cases the institutions that had made them sustainable.

We should avoid, of course, a pollyannaish perspective on prehistoric life. Even among the tribes that appear sustainable in hindsight, survival wasn't fun and games, especially for women saddled with heavy domestic workloads. Nor was peace a long-lasting condition, evidently, in regions of tribal interaction. Natural hazards were ever-present and, as many economists have emphasized, the average lifespan was much shorter than today's.

But we should also avoid the presumptions of economists who are pollyannaish in their perspective of *current* affairs. Yes, of course life spans are longer today, but there is ample evidence that many a tribal life was lived in magnificent, vigorous health, especially in the hunting cultures of North America and Africa.[20] We cannot know how much vigor was lost to humankind when tribal blood stopped coursing through its veins, or how much "disutility" we experience as a result of pollution, noise and the myriad other stresses of a full-world economy. It would be ludicrous for us to claim the slightest knowledge of comparative health, happiness, or general welfare. It is every bit as ludicrous for economists, à la the late Julian Simon, to conjure up such supposed knowledge.

This brings us back to neoclassical economics, which envisions the economy as a circular flow of money. Money flows from households to firms and back again in circular fashion. The circular flow of money is taught in introductory business courses but is roundly ridiculed by ecologists for its failure to reflect more than a measly amount of reality. It certainly makes tribal life look sophisticated.

The ecological critique of neoclassical growth theory begins by noting that the circular flow diagram omits a little detail called the ecosystem. The economy, as Daly pointed out, is but one subsystem functioning within the ecosystem at large. The problem with the circular flow model in neoclassical textbooks is that it fails to even mention the larger system—the ecosystem—within which the money flows. We could even argue that it is the ecosystem *from* which the money flows (and we will, in the next chapter).

It is true that many economics texts build upon the simplistic circular flow with additional factors and agents. For example, one common diagram incorporates the government as a major money handler, taking taxes from firms and households and doling out salaries to bureaucrats, among other expenditures. Another diagram will show not only the flow of money but also the broad categories of how the money is spent. For example, the diagram will show how firms procure the factors of production from households, while households procure finished goods and services from firms. The factors of production are sometimes referred to as capital, labor, and "raw materials." The phrase "raw materials"—natural resources coming from the land—is about as close as the neoclassical model comes to identifying the ecosystem as relevant to the economy. In a full-world economy, this is not nearly close enough. It's akin to identifying the engine as merely "relevant" to the automobile.

The neoclassical economist might say, "Of course the economy exists within the ecosystem; it goes without saying." The problem with this excuse is that, as we saw in the last two chapters, neoclassical economics does indeed overlook and minimize the relevance of land in the production function. The landless production function amounts to the same as overlooking the ecosystem's role in the circular flow of money. This oversight would not have been so harmful during the classical era when the human economy was like a drop in the ecological bucket, but with bottled water, global warming, and a burgeoning list of endangered species, isn't the oversight radically and recklessly unacceptable? In a full world, it behooves our economists, students, and citizens to *emphasize* rather than trivialize the ecosystem as the foundation, matrix and backdrop for all economies.

Just as a very basic neoclassical textbook may include the simplest circular flow diagram consisting entirely of firms and households and the money circulating among them, a very basic ecological economics textbook may include a diagram with the human economy embedded in a very simple ecosystem. Picture, for example, a brown sphere labeled "human economy" within a green sphere labeled "global ecosystem." As the brown sphere grows, green space shrinks.

However, even the most basic ecological economics textbook will include one more extremely important component: the sun.

The sun is the primary source of the energy required to fuel all economies, including the "economy of nature" and its human counterpart. Millions of years ago it provided the energy for the photosynthesis of plants that eventually decayed their way into becoming today's fossil fuels. Photosynthesis continues today, providing us with biomass fuels such as firewood. The sun warms the Earth, too, creating thermal currents and generating wind energy. In the process of evaporation, the sun "picks up" the water from the seas and drops it upstream of dams, thus producing hydroelectric energy. The sun also meets our energy needs more directly via solar panels, and sometimes even more directly, as with greenhouses.

The only other significant sources of constantly flowing energy are the moon and the Earth. The moon generates tidal energy with its gravitational pull, while radioactive decay (primarily) continues to generate heat energy at the Earth's core. In a sense, we have the sun, moon, and Earth feeding us energy. As the sustainability thinker David Holmgren pointed out, this is a curious fact when considered in the context of our tribal roots. It turns out that "Mother Earth, Father Sky, Sister Moon," are apt metaphors for the nurturing support we receive from the natural world. Yet there is no need to get "New Agey" about it. The religious call of "caring for creation" is probably a more relevant development in the spiritual world for saving posterity from an environmental and economic train wreck.[21]

On the other hand, there *is* something well worth noting about the relationship of New Age philosophy to neoclassical economic growth theory. While classical philosophers and classical economists recognized limits to economic growth, the current theory of perpetual growth touted by neoclassical economists, corporations, and politicians finds its spiritual counterpart in the New Age movement. The irony seems outlandish, given the tag "conservative" attached to the most adamant pro-growthers today, but judge for yourself: New Age spiritualism is a unique combination of technological optimism and a concept we might summarize as "mind over matter," whereby "natural resources originate from the mind, not from the ground." New Agers advocate extensive genetic engineering, "astral

Figure 2. Mountaintop removal for coal encroaches on one of the few remaining homes in what was the town of Mud, in Lincoln County, West Virginia.

Credits: Vivian Stockman and Ohio Valley Environmental Coalition (ohvec.org)

traveling" and wispy notions of energy transformation that are unabashedly referred to as "magic" or even "alchemy." The New Age movement constitutes a fantasizing, expansionist philosophy of human destiny in which the limits imposed by nature are transcended through a change in consciousness.

Beautiful dreams are still dreams, no matter how beautiful. Unfortunately, there is no more scientific basis for the New Age vision than there is for the neoclassical theory of perpetual growth. We get a certain amount of energy from the sun's rays, the moon's pull, and the Earth's core. Various useful forms of energy are derived from each of these sources. In addition to the aforementioned wind, wave, and hydroelectric energy noted above, we have geothermal energy derived from the ventilation of the Earth's core. Ecological economists refer to these as "renewable" energy because they will flow from the sun, moon, and Earth for a very long time.

There are still other, nonrenewable sources, and two are significant: fossil fuels and uranium. We will consider these, but first note that they are moot for economic purposes in the absence of sunlight, photosynthesis, and the resulting plants required for the existence of all animal and human economies. Fossil fuels and uranium may be used to supplement our energy needs, especially in the manufacturing and services sectors, but they cannot substitute for the solar energy that literally, through photosynthesis, powers the agricultural sector at the foundation of our economy. Energy income from the sun establishes an absolute upper limit to sustainable economic production, an upper limit to gross world product.

Some will argue that we can eventually replace photosynthesis with another process of food production, a process not requiring sunlight but, perhaps, only heat, so that nuclear power may be used instead. Such hog-wild fantasia makes even an ultra-liberal New-Age charlatan look like Charleton Heston (the late, ultra-conservative president of the National Rifle Association.) There will be technological developments that increase agricultural efficiency, and probably significant ones yet, but we should not allow our society to be seduced into complacency by the lunatic fringe of technological optimism.

In addition to the sources of energy, we need to understand something of the nature of energy. For this purpose we turn to the branch of physics known as thermodynamics. We encountered the second law of thermodynamics (entropy law) earlier in the chapter; we need only consider the basics a little further to grasp what the laws of thermodynamics mean to economic growth.

Thermodynamics is a branch of physics dealing with the properties and behavior of energy, especially the movement (dynamics) of heat (thermal energy).[22] The first two laws of thermodynamics are the important ones for our purposes. The first, phrased in popular terms, is that energy is neither created nor destroyed. Energy doesn't disappear and the universe has a fixed amount of it.

Energy can, however, be transformed or converted in numerous ways, many of which are relevant to economic growth. For example, we use wind turbines to convert wind energy to electrical energy. We use furnaces to convert the chemical energy of coal into thermal energy. We use bongo drums to convert the kinetic energy of a moving drumstick into a form of wave energy called "sound."

The energy transformation process ecological economists emphasize more than neoclassical economists is the process of photosynthesis, by which plants convert electromagnetic energy (light) into chemical energy with the help of a little water and soil. This is the most widespread energy transformation on Earth and supports virtually all life. Economic growth interferes with photosynthesis because it tends to replace plants with pavement (or other less-than-natural features). Not every economic activity precludes photosynthesis, but only the agricultural, silvicultural and pastoral sectors incorporate substantial amounts of photosynthesis directly in the production process. Even in many of these cases, activities like poor ranching practices in arid regions result in a negative net effect on photosynthesis.

There is another sort of energy transformation almost as profound as photosynthesis. It was identified by Albert Einstein: "It followed from the special theory of relativity that mass and energy are both but different manifestations of the same thing—a somewhat unfamiliar conception for the average mind. Furthermore, the equation E is equal to mc^2, in which energy is put equal to mass, multiplied by the square of the velocity of light, showed that very small amounts of mass may be converted into a very large amount of energy and vice versa."[23]

"Very large," indeed. For example, there are approximately 30 grams (slightly more than an ounce) of hydrogen atoms in a kilogram (2.2 pounds) of water. Einstein's formula tells us that converting those 30 grams of hydrogen would yield 2,700,000,000,000,000 joules of energy. This is the amount of energy emitted in the combustion of 270,000 gallons of gasoline!

Because energy and mass are "different manifestations of the same thing," we can restate the first law of thermodynamics: "Neither matter nor energy are created or destroyed," although matter may be *transformed* into energy. Apparently energy may be transformed into mass, too, such as when a high-energy photon passes near an atomic nucleus and is converted into an electron and a positron.

In any event, the first law of thermodynamics puts a cap on the global economy. The economy cannot be larger than what is made possible by the available matter and energy. At first glance this may seem like a highly theoretical point, yet it is an extremely important point, because it refutes the claim that there is no limit to economic growth. The only argument left standing that even resembles the no-limit claim is, "There may be a limit to economic growth, but it is so far off that we need not consider it for purposes of policy and management." Hopefully, Chapter 1 sufficed to show that the time is now to get serious about the limits to growth. If not, the rest of Part 3 should do it.

There is but one other argument remotely supporting the claim of no limits, and it goes like this: "Of course there is a limit to the production and consumption of goods and services, but there is no limit to the *value* of those goods and services. Therefore, there is no limit to economic growth after all." We shall deal with this reddest of red herrings in Chapter 7. For now, a few more observations on Einstein's discovery are in order.

$E = mc^2$ opened a lot of doors, some of hope, some of horror. Unfortunately, the doors of hope are still largely theoretical, while the doors of horror swung open immediately. If we could pry open the theoretical doors of hope, we would enter a world where the awesome potential of the atom has been harnessed to do our economic bidding *and* pose little risk to our health. The doors of horror, on the other hand, were blasted open in the New Mexico desert and the hallways led to Hiroshima and Nagasaki. There is no going back, either; only vigilant effort to prevent going further.

Nuclear technology may be used in peace and war alike, but we should remember the bomb came first. It wasn't until the 1950s when peaceful purposes of nuclear fission were developed. The United States, United Kingdom, Russia, China, France, Israel, India, Pakistan and North Korea are known to have nuclear bombs. Today there are approximately 450 nuclear reactors among 30 nations.

When it comes to $E = mc^2$, the United States can't seem to pry open the doors of hope and it can't seem to guard the horrible doorknobs from newcomers such as Iran and Libya. To add to the confusion, no one knows for sure what the United States hopes to accomplish with its nuclear technology. Self-defense? Or GDP growth in an economy that is 85 percent fossil-fueled? Self-defense would help justify the American government seeking out and destroying weapons of mass destruction, even if it seems hypocritical to most of the world. Nuclear-powered GDP growth in a full-world economy, on the other hand, is actually a *threat* to national security and international stability.

I came to the subject of energy availability in the 1990s during my PhD research. While conducting a policy analysis of the Endangered Species Act,

I was analyzing the causes of species endangerment in the United States, which turned out to be a *Who's Who* of the American economy.[24] It struck me that the constant search for more energy to fuel more economic growth would simply lead to more endangered species and less biodiversity. As I suggested in *Shoveling Fuel for a Runaway Train*, when you're riding a runaway train you'd be better off running *out* of fuel, not finding a more plentiful source.

But then, some will say, we could have more powerful brakes, or could more quickly straighten the tracks ahead, if only we had more fuel to power the brakes or fix the tracks. This is akin to saying that, if only the obese had a more plentiful food supply, they could devote the extra calories to studying methods of dieting. Surely all that extra food could be used to lose weight! Do you believe it? Likewise, more energy for economic growth wouldn't be devoted to applying the brakes. To put it in less metaphorical terms, energy for economic growth, *by definition*, is used for increasing the production and consumption of goods and services in the aggregate.

Howard T. Odum, known as "H.T.," was a brilliant systems ecologist who passed away in 2002. He gradually focused on the energetic limits to economic growth as his career at the University of Florida progressed. His work on this topic culminated in *A Prosperous Way Down*, published in 2001. Despite editorial help from Charlie Hall, Odum's one-time star pupil and a tell-it-like-it-is professor at the State University of New York (Syracuse), *Prosperous Way Down* is esoteric and remains somewhat obscure even among ecological economists. Odum builds his theory around a concept he calls "emergy," which opens the linguistic door to jargon such as "emcalories," "emjoules," and even "emdollars." The basic concept is quite simple, however. Emergy is defined as the energy "that has to be used up directly and indirectly to make a product or service."[25] In other words, emergy is the sum of *all* energy embodied in a good or service. It is sometimes referred to as "energy memory." A wooden table's emergy, for example, is equal not only to the watts of electricity that ran the table saw and lathe used in forming the wooden parts of the table, but also the solar power required to grow the tree that produced the lumber. Plus the solar power required by the ancient life that was eventually fossilized and became fuel for the chainsaw that cut down the tree and the electric plant that ran the sawmill and the shop tools. And the solar power required for growing the amount of food that gave the logger, miller, and furniture-maker the calories to do the work required in the production of the table, and so on. Screws, drills, and the associated miners who extracted the metals for screws and drills would all be accounted for in a thorough calculation of the wooden table's emergy.

As with all goods and services, ultimately it is solar energy that accounts for virtually all the energy that went into the production of the wooden table. Therefore, Odum invented the term "solar emcalories" as the common currency of embodied energy. While the sun's supply of energy may seem practically limitless to the neoclassical economist, Odum's emergy concept helps to illuminate just how energy-intensive, and limited, today's industrial economy is. We can't keep pumping out higher quantities of goods such as tables, Hummers, and Metrodomes, or services such as massages, love cruises, and Super Bowls using only our annual allowance of solar energy. We have to go to the well—the oil well—again and again, deeper and deeper, burning up the solar energy that drenched the earth those millions of years ago, burning up emergy. What happens when the well runs down, way down? This is precisely what Odum's "prosperous way down" addresses.

In Chapter 1 we briefly considered the "Olduvai theory" of energy production, the scary scene in which per capita energy production plummets after teetering at the edge of a steep gorge.[26] Odum held out hope that the social and economic adjustments to a world with dwindling oil supplies could occur gradually and gracefully enough to be, in some holistic sense, "prosperous." This "prosperous way down" would entail a gradual return of self-sufficiency and resourcefulness to the American lifestyle, with similar adjustments required in Europe, Japan, and (by now) much of China, plus all of the motor-driven megalopolises of the world. For example, instead of mass markets of groceries shipped from afar, people would tend little gardens and establish little trading cooperatives.

As I write from the midst of the Washington, DC, metropolitan area, where millions of people live in apartments, townhouses, and condos, and knowing the Atlantic seaboard is increasingly covered by such metropoli, I have serious doubts about Odum's hopeful scenario. What we *can* be certain of is this: assuming a prosperous way down is even possible, it is not going to happen as long as nations are hell-bent on economic growth. Hell-bent nations take hand-carts to hell, not prosperous ways down. Virtually by definition, the prosperous way down will require reduced production and consumption of goods and services: less trucking, less packaging, less marketing, etc. In Odum's terms, this means less emcalories per foodstuff, less emcalories per wooden table, and certainly less emcalories spent on Hummers and NASCAR. Lest that word "spent" go unnoticed, we are talking about less GDP.

Odum went so far as to propose a new monetary currency to assist in the ironically named "prosperous" way down: the "emdollar." The amount of emdollars paid for a good (or a service) would reflect the amount of solar energy embodied. For example, consider the amount of money paid for two tables, each identical in materials, appearance, and utility. The first table is produced using chainsaws, trucks, and electric lathes. The second table is produced using handsaws, horses, and carving tools. In today's American dollars, the first table costs less because with fossil fuels not yet burned up by Escalades and NASCAR, chainsaws and trucks are cheap to run. Also, much less labor is required to use such machinery than to use hand saws, horses, and carving tools. We may think of this labor as being subsidized by cheap gas.

In emdollars, on the other hand, the hand-sawn, horse-drawn, carved-leg table would cost less. There may be more labor required to build this table, but the calories burned by the sawyer and horsedriver and leg-carver are trumped by the enormous amount of solar energy embodied in the fossil fuels that run the chainsaw, truck, and lathe.

Economists should immediately recognize Odum's proposal as an attempt to advance an "energy theory of value." Philosophers will point out that such a theory proposes that goods and services have intrinsic, inherent values. Historians will add that ever since Aristotle intrinsic value has been distinguished from "value in exchange," or the worth of a commodity in terms of its capacity to be exchanged for other commodities.

Meanwhile value in exchange is expressed as "price." What determines price became a major topic of debate among the classical economists. Adam Smith thought the major determinant of price was utility, Ricardo thought it was labor and Marx thought it was the profit motive of the capitalist. Finally the neoclassical economists, led by Alfred Marshall, developed the theory that prices are determined in a free market by supply and demand at the margin. And for us as consumers, price is an everyday practical concern as we manage our income and budget.

Nevertheless, intrinsic properties do have a major influence on price. Gold, for example, is highly priced not only because of the high demand for it, but because it is rare. The supply is low and the effective supply is much lower yet. If all the gold on Earth consisted of large nuggets sitting on the seashore, its effective supply would be much higher than if the gold were far below the Earth's surface. It would cost much less, too, because it would take *much less energy* to extract. How much do you think an ounce of gold would cost if we had to mine a mile into the Earth to find it? Why would it cost so much? Largely because of the *energy* it would take to extract it.

The neoclassical scissors of supply and demand don't quite cut it. It takes energy for the invisible hand to do the cutting. The more energy it takes, the less slicing will be done. The invisible hand wields its scissors along the paths of least resistance, but lots of supplying and demanding takes lots of energy.

In more technical terms, energy requirements are inversely related to supply. The more energy it takes to extract or otherwise produce goods or services, the lower the supply effectively becomes. If it took *no* energy to produce goods or services, presumably supplies would be limited only by the amount of *materials* required to produce the goods and services. Because all goods or services do require energy for their production, however, we see there can be no such thing as an unlimited supply of goods and services.

What are the implications of all this to Odum's work? The short answer is that Odum was a utopian if he thought the emdollar would be adopted as a medium of exchange in the face of free-market ideology. In a free market, energy requirements do affect prices because they influence effective supplies, but prices are also affected by demand. Emdollars would do a reasonably good job of reflecting supply but not of demand. Therefore, the emdollar would have to be foisted onto the market, past the invisible hand. It could be done if citizens really, really wanted things priced that way. But when entire states such as Arizona require their high school students to take courses in "free enterprise" rather than ecology, the emdollar won't make it off page one of Odum's book.

The long answer, on the other hand, will come out of our struggles to develop the policies required for the grandkids' security, because Odum's work provides some of the necessary conceptual groundwork. We may never adopt the emdollar, but we will need to develop other policy tools (for example, higher energy taxes in American dollars) that do help us get the prices right.

Odum seemed a rather wise fellow, and perhaps getting the prices right—even if in regular American dollars—is what he intended all along.

But even getting the prices right isn't going to save the day with economic growth at the crossroads. Proper pricing is a microeconomic approach to a macroeconomic problem. We're getting there ...

References

Czech, Brian, *Supply Shock: Economic Growth at the Crossroads and the Steady State Solution*, New Society Publishers, 2013.

Czech, Brian, "Julian Simon Redux." *Conservation Biology*, 16 (2002): 570-571.

Czech, Brian, "American Indians and Wildlife Conservation." *Wildlife Society Bulletin*, 23 (4) (1995): 568-573.

Czech, Brian, "Big Game Management on Tribal Lands," in Stephen Demarais and Paul R. Krausman, eds., *Ecology and management of Large Mammals in North America*, 277-289, Prentice Hall, 1999.

Daly, Herman, *Ecological Economics and the Ecology of Economics: Essays in Criticism*, Edward Elgar, 1999.

Diamond, Jared, *Guns, Germs, and Steel: The Fate of Our Most Precious Resource*, Houghton Mifflin, 2001.

Ferguson, Niall, *The Ascent of Money: A Financial History of the World*, Penguin, 2008.

Geist, Valerius, *Buffalo Nation: History and Legend of the North American Bison*, Voyageur Press, 1996.

Hall, Charles and John Day, "Revisiting the Limits to Growth after Peak Oil," *American Scientist*, 97 (2009): 230-238.

Klein, M. J., "Thermodynamics in Einstein's Universe," *Science*, 157 (1967): 509-516.

Lasswell, Harold D., *Politics: Who Gets What, When, and How?* McGraw-Hill, 1936.

McDaniel, Carl and John M. Gowdy, *Paradise for Sale: A Parable of Nature*, University of California Press, 2000.

Meadows, Donella, et. al, *The Limits to Growth*, Signet, 1972.

Michener, James A., *Poland*, Fawcett, 1984.

Norgaard, Richard B., "Intergenerational Commons, Economism, Globalization, and Unsustainable Development," *Advances in Human Ecology*, 4 (1995): 141-171.

Odum, Howard T. and Elizabeth C. Odum, *A Prosperous Way Down: Principles and Policies*, University Press of Colorado, 2001.

Oelschlaeger, Max, *Caring for Creation: An Ecumenical Approach to the Environmental Crisis*, Yale University Press, 1994.

Rees, William, ed., *Herman Daly Festschrift* (e-book), The Encyclopedia of the Earth, 2013, http://www.eoearth.org/view/article/153492/.

Stannard, David E., *American Holocaust: The Conquest of the New World*, Oxford University Press, 1992.

Turner, Graham, "A Comparison of the Limits to Growth with Thirty Years of Reality," CSIRO Working Paper Series 2008-2009, 2008.

NOTES

1. The ISEE is far from a perfect representative for ecological economics. In its attempts to "reach across the aisle," the ISEE has numerous neo-classical and other pro-growth economists. This is an underlying theme of the book—the predominance of neoclassical and other perpetual-growth economics, which permeates even the ecological economics movement. For over a decade, despite the efforts of ISEE members, the ISEE Board of Directors ahs refused to adopt a position statement on the trade-off between economic growth and environmental protection, even though that trade-off is one of the central concepts of ecological economics.

2. See Turner, *A Comparison of The Limits to Growth with Thirty Years of Reality*. Turner found that data from 1970-2000 corroborated the "standard run" scenario described in *Limits to Growth*. This scenario reflects "business as usual" with population and economic growth resulting in "overshoot and collapse" in the mid-21st century. Turner also described how earlier critiques of *Limits to Growth* were faulty and based on mischaracterizations that were widely circulated and perpetuated. See also Hall and Day, "Revisiting the Limits to Growth after Peak Oil."

3. One source of this often-cited quote of Einstein is Klein, "Thermodynamics in Einstein's Universe," 509.

4. Although Daly is retired from the University of Maryland, he is on the Board of Directors of the Center for the Advancement of the Steady State Economy (CASSE) and writes a regular column for CASSE's *Daly News*, a blog named after Daly and devoted to steady state economics and policy.

5. *Herman Daly Festschrift* (e-book), *Encyclopedia of the Earth*, National Council for Science and the Environment, eoearth.org/article/Herman_Daly_Festschrift (e-book).

6. See, for example, Daly, *Ecological Economics and the Ecology of Economics*, 17.

7. Daly, *Ecological Economics*, 60.

8. Lasswell, *Politics.*

9. Norgaard, "Intergenerational Commons, Economism, Globalization, and Unsustainable Development."

10. Czech, "Julian Simon Redux."

11. George Will, opinion columnist for *The Washington Post*, has long been loose with the facts on environmental issues, denying the causes and effects of resource scarcity, pollution and climate change. However, he finds a receptive audience on environmental matters because of the adverse reactions to "doomsday" prophecies. (See steadystate.org/george-will.)

12. With the quotation, "Natural resources originate from the mind...," Bradley was describing one of Julian Simon's "energy themes." Clearly he agreed with these themes; the quotation comes from Bradley's acceptance speech of the Julian Simon Award. See heartland.org/policybot/results/10298/Robert_Bradley_receives_Julian_Simon_ Award.

13. See senate.ucsf.edu/tobacco/executives1994congress.

14. Czech, "American Indians and Wildlife Conservation;" Czech, "Big Game Management on Tribal Lands;" Diamond, *Guns, Germs, and Steel*.

15. Michener, *Poland*.

16. Ferguson, *The Ascent of Money*.

17. McDaniel and Gowdy, *Paradise for Sale*.

18. Czech, "Big Game Management."

19. Diamond, *Guns, Germs, and Steel*. See also, for the North American case especially, Stannard, *American Holocaust*.

20. Geist, *Buffalo Nation*.

21. Oelschlaeger, *Caring for Creation*.

22. Types of energy include kinetic, potential, thermal (heat), chemical, electrical, electro-chemical; electromagnetic (light), sound and nuclear.

23. One may hear Einstein's pronouncement at aip.org/history/Einstein/voice1.

24. Czech, et al., "Economic Associations among Causes of Species Endangerment in the United States."

25. Odum and Odum, *A Prosperous Way Down*, 67.

26. Less than a year after I wrote chapter I, a three-part series was published in the 2003 volume of *New Scientist*. [See Brian Czech. 2013. *Supply Shock: Economic Growth at the Crossroads and the Steady State Solution*. Gabriola Island, Canada: New Society Publishers.] The first paragraph summed up the predicament: "Civilization is at a turning point. In the next 50 years, we will experience the biggest surge in energy demand in history. Yet a growing number of experts are warning that the rate at which we are able to pump oil from the ground is likely to peak within a few years. If we want to keep our cars on the roads and the lights on in our homes, we need to find a new source of energy, and fast." Newscientist.com/article/mg17924061.000-power-struggle-html; accessed July 21, 2012.

Mission Statements and Music Lessons: Educators Raise the Bar for Students

6

Hal Marcovitz

At The Gray Charter School in Newark, New Jersey, the kindergarten kids learn about careers, Shakespeare is taught to eight-year-olds, the school year begins in the third week of August, Thanksgiving break is three days only, and parents attend classes on how to organize their lives at home. Oh, and 85 percent of the school's graduates go on to college—about three times as many as the Newark public schools send to college.

"We start in the third grade with Shakespeare," says Verna Gray, the founder and principal of The Gray Charter School, who adds that the purpose of teaching Shakespeare to young children is more about making them understand the moral lessons found in the plays than in unraveling the mysteries of iambic pentameter. *Hamlet*, Gray says, offers important lessons in character development and self-reliance. "To thine own self be true," says Gray, quoting Polonius. "You have to decide for yourself whether you are going to be a good person. You have to look at yourself in the mirror and say, 'I am a good person. I help people.'"[1]

At The Gray Charter School, developing character is regarded as important as developing minds, because Gray is convinced that young people will learn more if they don't fight in the hallways, if they don't bully their classmates, if they don't do drugs—in other words, if they come to school *wanting* to learn. That is the concept Gray employed when she founded the school in 2000, after spending 24 years as a Newark public school teacher.

Gray's concept has proven value. Ten years after first opening its doors, The Gray Charter School was selected as a National Blue Ribbon School by the U.S. Department of Education.

Mission Statements

Located on busy Liberty Street just blocks from the Passaic River, The Gray Charter School is by now a well-known institution in the tough urban world of Newark. The school is able to accommodate 328 students—and has a waiting list of more than 900. In fact, only about 30 slots open a year—most, of course, in kindergarten. In a typical year, The Gray Charter School receives about 100 applications for those slots and—as most charter schools do—fills them through a lottery. For the Newark parent looking for a quality education for a child, and a chance for that child to excel and attend college, The Gray Charter School represents a rare oasis in the all-too-often limited world of inner-city education.

What is the school day like at The Gray Charter School? Students wear uniforms. Classes begin at 7:30 a.m., promptly. At the beginning of each year, students have to submit Mission Statements listing their goals, such as a desire to earn high grades. "They are supposed to write the Mission Statements with their families," says Gray. "What is their goal for life? Do they want to be good students in school? Are they going to be nice to people and try to help people? We want achievable goals. If they don't have a goal, they are doing their own thing, and that's not good."[2]

As for the staff, before classes begin in August each teacher is handed a stack of cards containing the academic records of their students—including comments about the students—that were filled out by the previous year's teachers. Gray tells the teachers to put the cards aside and not look at them—at least for months. She believes teachers often stress the negative qualities about their students when they fill out the cards, and she doesn't want the new teachers forming preconceived notions about the students in their classes. "You are not made of stone," she tells teachers. "Those negative comments will affect how you think, act, and talk to your students, and conduct your class."[3]

Walk through the hallways of The Gray Charter School and you will hear music everywhere—violins and handbells as well as wood recorders, among other instruments. Typically, more than 200 of the 328 students learn to play musical instruments and those who don't still have to learn to read music. Reading musical notes is, in fact, the way children at The Gray Charter School learn to read their schoolbooks.

For starters, Gray likes the way each note in music includes a phonic value: After all, to sing *do re mi* the new reader must first learn how to pronounce the notes. And there are vowel sounds in each of those notes and others as well, so vowels are introduced to young readers as they learn music. Music, like English, is read left to right. A musical note stands for a certain sound, just as letters of the alphabet represent sounds. Songs have beginnings and ends—so do sentences and paragraphs. Songs tell stories, just as books do. Song lyrics often stress cause and effect, just as paragraphs in a story often illustrate.

In stressing education in music, and other arts as well—drama classes are also an element of the curriculum at The Gray Charter School—Gray is bucking a national trend. When budget-strapped schools look for places to cut, they usually start with arts education. That is particularly true in inner-city schools that usually have fewer resources to begin with. Arne Duncan, the U.S. Secretary of Education, has called on schools to preserve the arts, recognizing how important they are to nurturing talent in young people. Citing a recent study by the National Endowment for the Arts titled "The Arts and Achievement in At-Risk Youth," Duncan pointed out that low-income students who had arts-rich experiences in high schools were more than three times as likely to earn a B.A. as low-income students without those experiences. The NEA report found that 100 percent of high-poverty secondary schools offered music instruction a decade ago, while only about 80 percent did as of 2009. As Duncan noted, "Research suggests that arts education not only boosts academic outcomes, but that neighborhood-based arts and cultural activities can build stronger cities and communities and boost civic engagement."[4]

Aside from what a student might see on a sheet of music, or a page of printed type, Gray finds other elements in learning to read music that serve as important tools in helping young students learn how to read books. For example, learning to play a song on a violin takes a lot of concentration—so does reading a story. Music requires students to hone their memorization skills—an obvious benefit when it comes to reading comprehension. "The kindergarten kids start reading in August when school opens," she says. "By November 1 they are reading really well. These are kindergarten kids; they can't read at all when they first come to school."[5]

As for those students who do take up a musical instrument and stay with it for the duration of their enrollments at The Gray Charter School, Gray says they generally get better grades than the students who do not.

Parent Academy

At home, the parents of The Gray Charter School students are expected to be involved with their children's schoolwork—helping them learn to read, or complete their school projects, or looking over their homework. Gray learned long ago many parents are not very good at helping their children with schoolwork. They may be too busy to help their children with their homework—a fact of life in many single-parent homes. Or, even in homes with both parents, Gray has found many of them maintain an aloof attitude when it comes to taking an interest in their children's schoolwork.

That is why Gray makes the parents of the children in her school attend what she calls Parent Academy. The purpose of Parent Academy not only helps parents become involved with their children's schoolwork, but it also helps them become, well, better parents. Parent volunteers teach the classes, and cover such topics as how to discipline children and how to teach life skills to children. There is also a network of parents who reach out to other parents who may need help. For example, if somebody's car breaks down and they can't drive their child to school, a volunteer in the parents' network will provide the ride.

Some parents visit the homes of other parents to help them with organizing their households. Gray says there are many parents who don't understand the importance of getting their children out of bed the same time each morning, making sure breakfast is served on time, and making sure they get out the door on time. Such help may involve simply hanging a whiteboard in the kitchen and writing down the tasks parents have to accomplish each day: Make breakfast, drive to school, help with homework, attend school recital, and so on.

The Gray Charter School ends after the eighth grade, at which time the students must find charter high schools, or enter the Newark public school system. But Gray does make efforts to keep track of the students and many do keep in touch. One boy, she reports, is now an undergraduate at the University of Chicago, hoping to attend medical school. According to Gray, he started planning a career in medicine after a physician spoke in front of his class. After the class, the boy told Gray he hoped to become a neurosurgeon.

How old was the child when he decided to pursue a career in medicine? Says Gray, "He told me that when he was in the first grade."[6]

The Academic Middle

Sally Wagner has a far different task than Verna Gray. Wagner is a faculty member for the Humble Independent School District near Houston. Humble Independent is a suburban school district serving a population of mostly middle-class Texans. The district includes some 38,000 students who attended 27 elementary schools, eight middle schools and six high schools. Unlike Gray, who convinces children from lower-income families that they have the talents and skills to attend college, Wagner's job requires her to convince suburban, middle-class underachievers that they are also college material.

Wagner is facilitator for the AVID program at Humble Independent—AVID stands for Advancement Via Individual Determination. The program was founded in 1980 by Mary Catherine Swanson, a teacher at a San Diego high school that had just been desegregated. As students from lower-income homes and underperforming schools entered her high school she realized they would need extra help to have any chance of gaining admissions into colleges. AVID has since grown into a national program, organized and supported by a foundation in San Diego.

Everybody knows the type of student who fits the profile of an AVID participant: The student's parents expect him or her to go to college, and the student truly wants to go to college, but the student's schoolwork is sub-par. The student would seem to have the intelligence and talent to perform college-level work, but the grades don't reflect the student's abilities. Perhaps the student doesn't know good study habits, perhaps the student isn't receiving support at home, perhaps the student has an after-school job that takes her away from study time, perhaps the student simply doesn't realize the work that is required to get into college. Says Wagner, "It may be a time management issue. When granddad picks you up at school and you go to work with him, or you go to soccer practice, and then you go to your sister's soccer practice until 10 o'clock at night, are you going to study anything after an exhausting day? On that time frame, do you have thirty minutes to sit down and study? Did you do that when you were at work with granddad? What's the situation like at granddad's work? Is there a place where you can sit down where it is quiet?"[7]

Humble Independent, like most school districts, features Advanced Placement classes for the bright kids and overachievers, but it also has what the district calls its "Level" classes—these are classes that require the least amount of effort from the students. And so to find students for AVID, faculty members at

Humble Independent look for the kids who have enthusiasm and are achieving good grades—but they are doing it as students in the Level classes.

Says Wagner, "The kids don't really know how they are being identified, but we do send emails out to teachers that basically say, 'Recruiting for our next school year and we're looking for students who are academically in the middle.' That is the No. 1 requirement—that they be academically in the middle, and that they have a desire to do more. . . . We look in our Level classes for students making high B's or low A's, and we see if they are receiving the help that they need.

"We look for students who have the potential to achieve. That's what we ask the teachers for. . . . We look for kids with high grades on tests, but maybe they aren't turning in homework, so sometimes their grades are not as high."[8] At Humble Independent, more than four thousand students are enrolled in the AVID program, which begins in the sixth grade.

Study in Groups

When students enter the AVID program, they leave their Level classes behind and are seated in AP classes or pre-AP classes. To help them with their AP work, Humble Independent recruits local college students to work as tutors. AVID tutoring sessions are a bit different than the image of a college math major sitting across a table from a high school kid, helping the kid with his algebra homework. The AVID students attend the tutoring sessions together. It is the job of the tutor to lead the students to the right answer rather than just correct papers and show them what they did wrong. Says Wagner, "With AVID it is not only our goal to get kids to college; our goal is to get our kids through college. We don't want them going for one year then dropping out. A lot of times the way you do that is to work in study groups. Nobody wants to be in a study group with a kid who won't contribute. All of our tutoring is Socratic . . . it would be much easier to tell the kids the answers, but the next time they do a problem like that they are going to need somebody to give them the answer. It's basically torture for them, they have to stand there and work together. The [tutors] in the group can't give them answers—they have to ask them questions to lead them to the answers.

"It's hard for them, but kids don't ask questions—not in middle schools and high schools; they certainly do at younger levels. When they are young they ask you questions about everything but by the time they get into middle school the only thing they want to know is 'Why can't I do this?' We really push them to question and make them responsible for their own learning."[9]

The notion that students study better in groups is often attributed to Uri Treisman who, in 1981, worked as a teaching assistant at the University of California at Berkeley. Treisman is now a professor at the University of Texas and a member of the AVID board of directors. At Berkeley, Treisman noticed the overachieving Asian students all studied in groups while African American students, many of whom were scoring lower grades, tended to study alone. So Treisman organized study groups among the African American students, and their scores soon improved.

True Mission of AVID

AVID is about more than just finding ways to push underachievers through AP classes. The AVID students meet together each week to talk about their frustrations, challenges and achievements and lend support to each other. To build teamwork, they get involved in community service projects—at Humble Independent, AVID students have picked up litter along roads and staged fund-raisers to help pay for field trips. (The 2012 middle school air guitar competition was a major success.) AVID students take college tours together. They fill out college financial aid forms together. They prepare for the PSAT, SAT, and ACT tests together. It is all about making them believe they are no different than other college-bound students.

Wagner says the first graduates of the Humble Independent AVID program reached their final year in college in 2014, so it is still too early to gauge the success of the program. But some individual stories do make it back to Humble Independent. She says, "We had 27 students in that [first] class and I know that four of them graduated a semester early. Two of those kids decided to go into the military and one of them is in culinary arts school in Paris."[10]

There is another message that has emerged through the AVID concept. Even if young people ultimately elect not to go to college, they must still leave high school with a level of skills that would otherwise make them eligible for university admission. High school graduates need to read on a higher level than may have been necessary a generation ago. They must possess math skills. Local employers in the Humble Independent district have been telling that to educators for years, Wagner says.

73

Wagner says she came to realize the importance of providing high school graduates with a higher set of skills after attending a lecture in 2011 by Dr. Willard R. Daggett, founder and president of the Utah-based International Center for Leadership in Education. The center is dedicated to moving schools toward teaching more rigorous and relevant skills to students. Daggett's message is that unless schools start doing a better job of preparing young people for college and the workplace, more and more young people will find themselves leaving high school adrift in the economy with few prospects. In other words, the number of young people who do excel and are prepared for prosperous careers and lives will decline. From a societal point of view, the ramifications can be significant: When it comes to paying for social services, the few will support the many.

Says Wagner, "Dr. Daggett is an education guru and he told us...that by 2020, 20 percent of the population would be supporting 80 percent of the population. At first I laughed and thought that was insane, but I think that is a very realistic possibility. It's one of those things where my district said, 'Absolutely not.' We can't have these children for thirteen years and put them on the street without the skills necessary to survive. It's scary and horrible to think that."[11]

NOTES

1. Interview with the author, Dec. 1, 2014.
2. Ibid.
3. Verna Gray, *How To Run A Successful Public School In America*. Charleston, SC: BookSurge, 2010, p. 35.
4. Quoted in U.S. Department of Education, "U.S. Secretary of Education Arne Duncan Reinforces Importance of the Arts in Schools," Aug. 18, 2009, www.ed.gov/news/speeches/prepared-remarks-us-secretary-education-arne-duncan-report-arts-education-public-eleme. Accessed Dec. 9, 2014.
5. Interview with the author, Dec. 1, 2014.
6. Ibid.
7. Interview with the author, Dec. 4, 2014.
8. Ibid.
9. Ibid.
10. Ibid.
11. Ibid.

7

A Well-Educated Workforce Is Key to State Prosperity*

Noah Berger and Peter Fisher

What can state governments do to boost the economic well-being of their people? That is the central question of state economic policy. Incomes and wages can increase across an economy when productivity—production per capita—increases. States have many tools in their arsenal to increase productivity, including investments in public infrastructure, in technological innovation at public universities and other institutions, and in workers through the education and training systems. But many states have been retreating from their responsibility to ensure state economic growth that benefits all residents in favor of a short-sighted approach to economic development. In these states, the focus is on luring employers from other states with strategies that do not lead to rising incomes because they do not make the workforce more productive. Even worse, the focus drains resources from the most important, proven path to increasing productivity: investments in education.

Major findings of this report include the following:

- Overwhelmingly, high-wage states are states with a well-educated workforce. There is a clear and strong correlation between the educational attainment of a state's workforce and median wages in the state.
- States can build a strong foundation for economic success and shared prosperity by investing in education. Providing expanded access to high

* This chapter is a shortened version of Noah Berger and Peter Fisher, *A Well-Educated Workforce Is Key to State Prosperity* (2013). The complete report is available at http://www.epi.org/publication/states-education-productivity-growth-foundations/.

quality education will not only expand economic opportunity for residents, but also likely do more to strengthen the overall state economy than anything else a state government can do.

- Cutting taxes to capture private investment from other states is a race-to-the-bottom state economic development strategy that undermines the ability to invest in education.
- States can increase the strength of their economies and their ability to grow and attract high-wage employers by investing in education and increasing the number of well-educated workers.

Investing in education is also good for state budgets in the long run, since workers with higher incomes contribute more through taxes over the course of their lifetimes.

Introduction: Education Suffers as State Economic Development Wars Escalate

Historically, U.S. economic growth and prosperity have been achieved through an implicit partnership of federal, state, and local governments. The federal government provided overall economic stability and sought to ensure that the economy never veered too far from full employment.[1] State and local governments assumed primary responsibility for the education system that produced a more skilled and productive workforce. Federal and state governments both invested in infrastructure, and in basic research that provided enormous long-term benefits for the private sector. The end result was a long period of postwar productivity growth, the prerequisite for growth in the standard of living.

During the 1970s and 1980s, state and local governments across the country became convinced that they should play a more aggressive and expansive role in economic policy (Fisher and Peters 1998). Economic development became accepted as a major function of state and local government, and came to mean the direct promotion of private investment within the borders of a state or city. This led to escalating competition for a limited supply of private capital investment through increasingly generous incentive packages.

While cutting costs to business has become the principal focus of economic development policy in many states, more and more states are cutting programs across the spectrum to lower state taxes. In many cases these ideas are promoted as a way to attract employers from other states. But the preponderance of evidence has shown that in the long run these strategies are inefficient and ineffective (Fisher 2013; Mazerov 2013; Lynch 2004). State and local taxes on business are simply too small a share of total business costs to play a significant role in location decisions; other factors—labor skills, wages, access to inputs and markets—are much more important. Yet business tax breaks are expensive, and take money from investments in education and infrastructure that increase productivity and support growth. And as public resources are squandered on unproductive state efforts to capture private investment at the expense of other states, inadequate investments in education weaken the ability of a state to develop, grow, and attract businesses that offer high-skilled, high-wage jobs.

Strong state education systems are good not just for the national economy; they are good for the citizens of the state. The connection between education and income is strong. A high school diploma, technical college certificate, or college degree not only increases one's skills and productivity, but signals to employers that the individual is motivated and completes tasks. A more educated individual is more likely to participate in the job market, to have a job, to work more hours, and to be paid more, and less likely to be unemployed (French and Fisher 2009). But the benefits of education go beyond the economic returns. Higher levels of education also correspond to improved health and lower rates of mortality, and lower rates of crime (Grossman and Kaestner 1997; Lleras-Muney 2005; Lochner and Moretti 2004).

And the benefits of a more educated population accrue not just to the more educated workers, but to future generations (Wolfe and Zuvekas 1995; Haveman and Wolfe 1995; Smith, Brooks-Gunn, and Klebanov 1997; French and Fisher 2009; Duncan, Kalil, and Ziol-Guest 2008).

The Productivity-Education Link

The best way to measure whether an economy is working is to look at whether the incomes of average people are increasing. To achieve rising incomes for average people, two things need to happen: productivity needs to increase (creating more income overall), and new income generated from their increased productivity needs to be returned to workers in the form of higher wages.

Ensuring the fair distribution of the rewards of productivity growth is primarily a federal responsibility, through such things as strong labor laws, fair trade policies, and monetary and fiscal policies that encourage full employment. There are some steps states can take in this area, such as maintaining strong labor standards, including minimum wage laws that protect the lowest paid workers.

Where states have the greatest role to play, however, is in making sure that all of their people—and particularly in those from the most disadvantaged backgrounds—have the tools to be highly productive. Education is the key to that, as are other things that make learning possible, such as making sure children have decent health care and sufficient nutrition. Reducing poverty itself has also been shown to improve the ability of children to thrive (Marr, Charite, and Huang 2013).

Evidence suggests that states that increase the level of education of their workforce see greater productivity. As shown in **Figure A**, between 1979 and 2012, states in which the share of adults with at least a college degree experienced greater increases in productivity, measured as gross state product per hour worked.

There is also evidence that greater productivity is associated with higher wages. **Figure B** shows that between 1979 and 2007, states with larger increases in productivity experienced larger increases in median worker compensation.

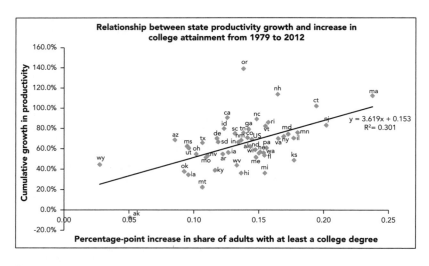

Figure A

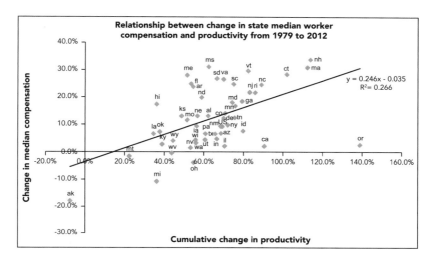

Figure B

Education, Wages, and State Economic Success

The previous section established the link between education and productivity, and productivity and wages. We can further test the assumed link between education (and, alternatively, tax rates) and wages by reviewing correlations between certain characteristics and high-wage state economies.

Our analyses allow us to answer several important questions. First, "are high-wage economies more common in low-tax states?" The answer, as shown in **Figure C**, is "no."

The figure shows no clear relationship between state taxes (as a share of state personal income) and median wages. Higher-tax states appear to have slightly higher median wages, but that correlation is not significant.

One conclusion from this chart could be that it is very unlikely that we would ever see a clear pattern when looking at wages across all 50 states—because states are so different in so many ways.

Testing the accuracy of this conclusion leads to our second question: "Is there a factor that does show a strong correlation with high-wage economies?" The answer is "yes."

Overwhelmingly, high-wage states are states that have a well-educated workforce, evident in **Figure D**. The correlation is very strong and there are very large differences between median hourly wages in states with well-educated

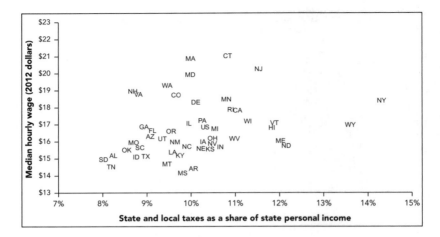

Figure C

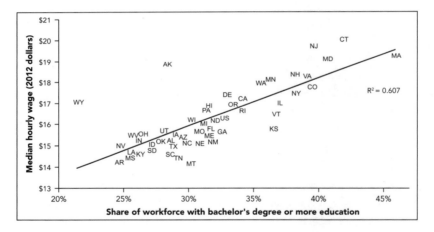

Figure D

workforces and hourly wages in states with less-well-educated workforces (as measured by the share of workers who have at least a bachelor's degree). In the 22 states with the least-educated workforces (30 percent or less with a bachelor's degree or more education), median wages hover around $15 an hour, the only exceptions being Alaska and Wyoming. In the three states where more than 40 percent of the population has a bachelor's or more education, median wages are $19 to $20 an hour, nearly a third higher.

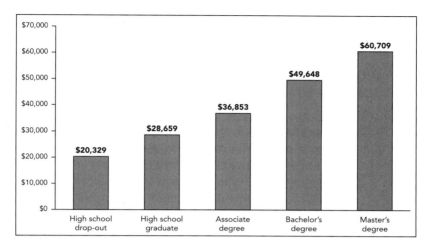

Figure E

In some ways, the correlation between wages and education should not be surprising. For an individual, annual earnings rise with increasing education, as shown in **Figure E**. Higher median annual earnings for those with more education reflect not just higher hourly pay, but more stable employment and fewer periods of unemployment.

It makes sense that if an individual's wages increase with education, then wages across an economy likely increase as more people have higher levels of education. Businesses that need well-educated workers, and pay the wages such workers earn, will grow and prosper in states that have such workers and may be forced to leave states that don't.

While this correlation between education and high-wage jobs is not surprising, what perhaps should be surprising is how often policymakers ignore it and pursue other quick fixes, such as special tax breaks or other subsidies for businesses. Looking at the correlation between education and wages, there is little indication that states have found a way to create a high-wage economy without a well-educated workforce.

Education as Smart Economic Development Policy

Does the correlation between education and earnings necessarily mean that states can strengthen their economies in the long run by adopting policies that increase the number of well-educated workers? Recent academic work suggests that the answer is, "Yes." A study by Federal Reserve economists examined the factors contributing to greater state prosperity over a 65-year period and found that a state's high school and college attainment rates were important factors in explaining its per capita income growth relative to other states between 1939 and 2004 (Bauer, Schweitzer, and Shane 2006).

Increasing educational attainment can be achieved by a variety of policies and programs, including those that increase access to postsecondary education by restraining tuition growth or increasing financial aid, reduce high-school drop-out rates, move people without high school degrees through GED and associate degree programs, increase the quality of K–12 education to improve success of high school graduates in postsecondary education, and offer pre-school programs that lead to long-term improvements in educational outcomes.

An evaluation of the effectiveness of alternative education strategies is beyond the scope of this report. But there is evidence that state expenditures on primary and secondary education improve school performance and raise state per capita income. For example, investments in school facilities led to improvements in student test scores (Cellini, Ferreira, and Rothstein 2010). And over a 34-year period, states that improved their position relative to other states on real per-capita education spending improved their relative position in real per-capita income, and the direction of causality was from education spending to income (Bensi, Black, and Dowd 2004). Also, the long-term benefits of early childhood education programs have been well documented (Lynch 2007).

Conclusion

Ultimately, the wealth of a society can increase only if the economy becomes more productive. A more productive economy can support both higher wages and higher profits, as well as shorter work weeks and a higher quality of life. So the question of how to increase productivity needs to be at the center of any debate about state economic development.

As this paper shows, moving jobs from one state to another state does nothing to increase productivity. Rather, productivity rises with investments in infrastructure and workers, with investments in education that raise educational achievement providing a major boost. Thus, investing in education is a core contribution states can make to the well-being of their residents and the national economy overall.

States can build a strong foundation for economic success and shared prosperity by investing in strategies that make their people more productive, chief among them education. Providing expanded access to high quality education and related supports—particularly for those young people who today lack such access—will not only expand economic opportunity for those individuals, but will also likely do more to strengthen the overall state economy than anything else a state government can do.

References

Bauer, Paul W., Mark E. Schweitzer, and Scott Shane. 2006. "State Growth Empirics: The Long-Run Determinants of State Income Growth." Federal Reserve Bank of Cleveland Working Paper 06–06. http://www.clevelandfed.org/research/workpaper/2006/wp0606.pdf

Bensi, Michelle, David Black, and Michael Dowd. 2004. "The Education/Growth Relationship: Evidence from Real State Panel Data." *Contemporary Economic Policy*, vol. 22, no. 2. http://onlinelibrary.wiley.com/doi/10.1093/cep/byh020/abstract

Bureau of Economic Analysis. National Income and Product Accounts. Various years. *National Income and Product Account Tables* [data tables]. http://www.bea.gov/iTable/index_nipa.cfm

Bureau of Economic Analysis. State/National Income and Product Accounts public data series. Various years. *Annual State Personal Income and Employment* [data tables]. http://www.bea.gov/iTable/iTable.cfm?reqid=70&step=1&isuri=1&acrdn=1#reqid=70&step=1&isuri=1

Bureau of Labor Statistics. Current Population Survey Outgoing Rotation Group microdata. Various years. Survey conducted by the Bureau of the Census for the Bureau of Labor Statistics [machine-readable microdata file]. Washington, D.C.: U.S. Census Bureau. http://www.bls.census.gov/ftp/cps_ftp.html#cpsbasic

Bureau of Labor Statistics. Current Population Survey basic monthly microdata. Various years. Survey conducted by the Bureau of the Census for the Bureau of Labor Statistics [machine-readable microdata file]. Washington, D.C.: U.S. Census Bureau. http://www.bls.census.gov/ftp/cps_ftp.html#cpsbasic

Bureau of Labor Statistics. Labor Productivity and Costs program. Various years. *Major Sector Productivity and Costs* and *Industry Productivity and Costs* [databases]. http://bls.gov/lpc/#data (unpublished data provided by program staff at EPI's request)

Bureau of Labor Statistics. Local Area Unemployment Statistics. Various years. http://www.bls.gov/lau/

Cellini, Stephanie Riegg, Fernando Ferreira, and Jesse Rothstein. 2010. "The Value of School Facility Investments: Evidence from a Dynamic Regression Discontinuity Design." *The Quarterly Journal of Economics*, vol. 125, no. 1, 215–261. http://qje.oxfordjournals.org/content/125/1/215.short

Current Population Survey Annual Social and Economic Supplement. *Historical Income Tables* [data tables]. Various years. www.census.gov/hhes/www/income/data/historical/index.html

Duncan, Greg J., Ariel Kalil, and Kathleen Ziol-Guest. 2008. *Economic Costs of Early Childhood Poverty.* Washington, D.C.: Partnership for America's Economic Success.

Fisher, Peter. 2013. *Corporate Taxes and State Economic Growth.* The Iowa Policy Project. http://www.iowafiscal.org/2011docs/110209-IFP-corptaxes.pdf

Fisher, Peter S., and Alan H. Peters. 1998. *Industrial Incentives: Competition Among American States and Cities.* W.E. Upjohn Institute for Employment Research, p. 5. http://www.upjohn.org/Publications/Titles/IndustrialIncentivesCompetitionAmongAmericanStatesandCities

French, Lily, and Peter S. Fisher. 2009. *Education Pays in Iowa: The State's Return on Investment in Workforce Education.* The Iowa Policy Project. http://www.iowapolicyproject.org/2009docs/090528-ROI-educ.pdf

Grossman, Michael, and Robert Kaestner. 1997. "Effects of Education on Health" in *The Social Benefits of Education,* eds. J.R. Behrman and S. Nevzer. Ann Arbor: University of Michigan Press.

Haveman, Robert, and Barbara Wolfe. 1995. "The Determinants of Children's Attainments: A Review of Methods and Findings." *Journal of Economic Literature,* vol. 33, no. 4, 1829–1878.

Lleras-Muney, Adriana. 2005. "The Relationship Between Education and Adult Mortality in the United States" *Review of Economic Studies,* vol. 72, no. 1, 189–221.

Lochner, Lance, and Enrico Moretti. 2004. "The Effect of Education on Crime: Evidence from Prison Inmates, Arrests, and Self-Reports." *The American Economic Review,* vol. 94, no. 1, 155–189.

Lynch, Robert. 2004. *Rethinking Growth Strategies: How State and Local Taxes and Services Affect Economic Development.* Washington, D.C.: Economic Policy Institute. http://www.epi.org/publication/books_rethinking_growth/

Lynch, Robert G. 2007. *Enriching Children, Enriching the Nation: Public Investment in High-Quality Prekindergarten.* Washington, D.C.: Economic Policy Institute. http://www.epi.org/publication/book_enriching/

Marr, Chuck, Jimmy Charite, and Chye-Ching Huang. 2013. *Earned Income Tax Credit Promotes Work, Encourages Children's Success at School, Research Finds.* Center on Budget and Policy Priorities. http://www.cbpp.org/cms/?fa=view&id=3793

Mazerov, Michael. 2013. "Academic Research Lacks Consensus on the Impact of State Tax Cuts on Economic Growth: A Reply to the Tax Foundation." Center on Budget and Policy Priorities, June 17. http://www.cbpp.org/files/6–17–13sfp.pdf

Smith, Judith R., Jeanne Brooks-Gunn, and Pamela K. Klebanov. 1997. "Consequences of Living in Poverty for Young Children's Cognitive and Verbal Ability and Early School Achievement." Pages 132–189 in *Consequences of Growing up Poor,* eds. G.J. Duncan and J. Brooks-Dunn. New York: Russell Sage Foundation.

Tax Policy Center. Various years. *State Tax Facts* [data tables]. http://www.taxpolicycenter.org/taxfacts/listdocs.cfm?topic2id=90

Wolfe, Barbara, and Samuel Zuvekas. 1995. *Nonmarket Outcomes of Schooling.* University of Wisconsin, Institute for Research on Poverty, discussion paper no. 1065–95.

NOTES

1. An economy has reached full-employment when any further increases in aggregate demand would fail to reduce the unemployment rate. Note that this, of course, does not mean the unemployment rate will be zero—some degree of "frictional" unemployment (temporary unemployment as workers move between jobs and move from out of the labor force into paid employment) and "structural" unemployment (a mismatch between workers demanded by employers and those available in any given local labor market) will always persist. The Employment Act of 1946 called for the federal government to maintain full employment, and fiscal and monetary policy in the ensuing postwar period was used to attain that goal while keeping inflation low. In more recent decades, concern with inflation has often taken precedence over unemployment in Federal Reserve monetary policy, and the effectiveness of fiscal policy to stimulate the economy has been challenged by those who would shrink government at all costs.

8 Smaller Soft Pretzels: Learning to Live a Healthy Life

Hal Marcovitz

Bettyann Creighton is the type of person who tosses out adjectives like "fabulous," "brilliant" and "phenomenal." These type of words come easily to her, which is something of an accomplishment considering the huge task she faces every day: finding ways to help Philadelphia's 130,000 public school students grow up with good health and nutrition habits.

Creighton's philosophy is to teach these habits early, to the youngest students. She wants to immerse them in healthy lifestyles just as their English teachers instruct them in good grammar or their math teachers drill them in the fundamentals of arithmetic. Take, for example, the program known as Movement Breaks that Creighton brought to city schools in 2006.

"The Movement Breaks are fabulous," she says. "In the grand scope of things we wrote a wellness policy for the school district and part of our wellness policy was that after two hours of seat time kids needed to get up and move even if it was just right next to their desks. And then when we revised it in 2011 we ramped it up to every ninety minutes. The cool thing about it is that it gave schools permission to do this. Up until that point it could have been frowned upon as lost instruction time."[1]

Here's the philosophy behind the Movement Breaks: Sitting behind desks all day isn't healthy—any denizen of cubicle life in his or her mid-40s suffering from lower back pain or carpal tunnel syndrome is well aware of that. Chances are that when they were young people, nobody told them to stand up and stretch every hour or so, or even more often than that. Now, these workers and their insurance companies spend a lot of money on doctors and physical therapists while their employers pay higher insurance premiums and lose money due to absenteeism.

These workers owe their jobs at least in part to their elementary school educations—the educations that provided them with the basic tools they used to learn higher skills and, certainly, employable skills. Creighton, director of physical education, health and safety for the Philadelphia School District, believes that while young people are receiving the foundations on which to build their careers, they should also be receiving the foundations on which to build and maintain healthy lifestyles.

Population Health Management

What is happening in the Philadelphia schools is part of a national trend. Schools as well as other institutions—state and local governments, universities, corporations, and foundations and similar organizations are developing new ideas about health care that go beyond the old model that essentially says if a person gets sick they should go to the doctor or the hospital emergency room. In recent years the trend has been changing to a model known as "population health management." In other words, how can society keep people from getting sick so they don't have to go to the doctor? Says Denise Koo, senior advisor for health systems at the U.S. Centers for Disease Control and Prevention, "The United States spends more than twice as much as any other country in the world on health care, yet the life expectancy in the U.S. is shorter than in many other high-income countries. Recent analyses also show that "improvements in population health...life expectancy, years lived in good health...in the United States have not kept pace with advances in population health in other wealthy nations," despite what we spend on health care. Maybe our traditional emphasis on individual patient care needs to be better complemented with efforts directed at populations."[2]

One organization that is charting these efforts is the Duke University Department of Community and Family Medicine, which provides examples of some of the more innovative programs on a website, PracticalPlaybook. org. One of the innovations cited by Duke is the 2003 decision by officials in Benton County, Oregon, to locate a county-sponsored primary health care clinic in the same office as the county's Department of Public Health, assuming that public and primary health are intimately linked. If people are getting sick, it could be any number of issues. It could be environmental, and should be addressed by the county's Health Department. It could be a leaky sewer pipe nearby; or a local factory filling the air with smog, causing asthma patients to wheeze. These are the type of issues a public health agency could explore, and if workers at a public health agency see an abundance of wheezing asthma patients sitting in their common waiting room with the clinic, they may be more prone to investigate why.

Duke also cites an outreach program aimed at young asthma patients sponsored by Boston Children's Hospital. A 2005 study by the hospital found that a large number of its emergency room patients were young asthma sufferers from low-income neighborhoods. Under the Community Asthma Initiative, following a child's initial emergency room visit the hospital assigns a staff member to visit the patient in the community to monitor the steps taken at home to minimize the child's asthma symptoms. By 2014, the hospital reported, asthma-related emergency room visits had dropped by 58 percent.

In Montana, a state with few doctors and often many miles between patients, the state Health Department initiated the Telehealth Program. The program was established in 2009, specifically aimed at helping the states' 58,000 type 2 diabetes patients manage their symptoms. Hospitals that joined Montana Telehealth assign staff members to contact diabetes patients by phone; during the calls, staff members discuss diet, medications and life-style issues encountered by patients. By 2014, Montana Telehealth reported a 20 percent decline in hospital visits by diabetes patients.

Another innovative diabetes program was established in Lake County, Illinois, where the county Health Department partnered with NorthShore University HealthSystems in 2010 to provide food assistance to diabetic patients. Consuming good food is an integral component of controlling blood sugar, but many diabetes patients lack knowledge about good nutrition or, in some cases, can't afford to buy the right foods. (In Lake County, 7 percent of adults are diabetic.) And so the Health Department started a community garden, tilled by the patients. Anybody who helps out at the garden can take the produce home, free of charge. By 2014, more than 150 families were active participants, harvesting eggplants, tomatoes, green beans, zucchini, and peppers. In addition, the Health Department holds nutrition classes for the participants, and part of the curriculum includes cooking lessons led by dieticians. So not only do diabetes patients learn about good nutrition, but they help produce good food and then learn how to prepare meals for the table.

Life in Mingo County

And then there is the story of the rural Mingo County, West Virginia, where a lot of ordinary people looked around and decided their community of some 26,000 people was literally dying. How bad was it in Mingo? A study by Harvard University found the average life expectancy in the county— a mere 67 years, according to 2006 statistics—placed Mingo among the bottom 1 percent of U.S. counties.

A 2008 screening performed in Mingo schools by West Virginia University found 35 percent of fifth-graders were obese and 32 percent suffered from hypertension. Indeed, it was hard to find good nutritional habits in Mingo because it was often hard to find good food. By 2008, there was no grocery store to be found in or around the town of Williamson, the Mingo County seat.

A study underwritten by the Robert Wood Johnson Foundation ranked Mingo among the worst counties in West Virginia in such categories as poor physical health days, poor mental health days, low birth weight and preventable hospital stays. Mingo is in West Virginia coal country, which means people in Mingo have had to endure all the ills associated with mining. According to a West Virginia University study, these ills include cancer, birth defects, and heart disease. (In 2011, Massey Energy settled a lawsuit by some five hundred residents of Mingo who alleged that coal company contamination of their water led to cancer and other ills.)

A lot of people reacted to life in Mingo and started making changes on their own. Dino Beckett, a local doctor, provides free health care in his office on Fridays. Bill Richardson, the West Virginia University agricultural extension agent for Mingo County, wanted to help people in Mingo start eating right by establishing a local farmers market. Vicki Lynn Hatfield suspected many people in Mingo County suffered from diabetes but didn't know it. In 2008, she started the Mingo County Diabetes Coalition. The group's first project was organizing a fitness walk. The Coalition hoped for 70 participants; 180 signed up. In the second year, participation nearly doubled.

Sustainable Williamson

By 2010, these individual efforts had coalesced into a community-wide program known as Sustainable Williamson. The Diabetes Coalition is one of its most active organizations and has since expanded its services to include a two-tier program that includes a clinical team that visits high-risk diabetes patients in their homes, and a community outreach team that helps make Mingo County a healthier place to live.

Jennifer Hudson, the current director of the Diabetes Coalition, says the clinical team is composed of a nurse and nursing assistant. The team receives referrals from about twenty physicians in Mingo County who identify high-risk diabetes patients—those who may need extra attention. The clinical team visits the patients in their homes, either weekly or biweekly. Team members monitor their diets and exercise habits, and determine whether they are taking their medications properly. "You can see things in the home you can't see in the doctor's office," says Hudson. "A patient might say to the nurse, 'I try to take my insulin but it keeps dripping out.'"[3]

And by that, Hudson means, patients may simply be having trouble with the self-injection procedures, and in need of some reminders from the nurse on how to administer their medications. Or, the clinical team may be able to tell whether diabetes symptoms are worsening between doctors' visits and alert physicians that patients need their medications adjusted. Most doctors see their diabetes patients every three months, but as the Diabetes Coalition's clinical team has learned, a lot can go wrong in three months.

The clinical team goes beyond fundamental medical checkups. Team members question the patients on the foods they eat. Since many patients live in low-income households (30 percent of Mingo residents live below the poverty line), they may not have access to healthy foods because they can't afford them. And so the clinical team may help link patients with local food pantries.

Since the Diabetes Coalition established its clinical team, diabetes has become something less of a problem in Mingo County. According to Hudson, since 2008 blood sugar readings among Mingo County diabetes patients have been in decline.

Writing Prescriptions for Vegetables

The Diabetes Coalition has also been working with doctors to use their prescription pads to write "prescriptions" for their patients to eat nutritious foods or take walks. It is psychological—a patient is more likely to follow doctor's orders if she sees if it written on a prescription pad. "If you see an Rx beside it you'll do it,"[4] says Hudson.

The Diabetes Coalition's other focus is to involve the community in improving the overall health of Williamson and Mingo County. For example, the Diabetes Coalition provides grants to encourage businesses to sponsor healthy projects for the community—from making their work environments healthier for their employees to performing community service projects. The local farmers market, for example, won a grant from the Diabetes Coalition to help buy a vehicle to make the market mobile—to drive good food to the most rural corners of the county where people may not have access to the standing market in Williamson.

One Diabetes Coalition project has worked with volunteer groups to plant more gardens and create walking paths around Williamson. Hudson's group concluded that more people would take walks if there were more walking paths and gardens to walk through, and so creation of these areas has been a community-wide project. "You can see a real difference in Williamson—a change for the better," says Hudson. "I see more people walking and I hear more people talking about taking walks. And I can see more people eating healthy foods."[5]

Circles, Squats, and Stretches

Back in those Philadelphia classrooms, the Movement Breaks started out simply with instructions to teachers to have the children get up from their desks. And then, for ten minutes, the lesson on social studies or math or English would continue—nothing changed, except the kids were now standing, giving their muscles opportunities to stretch, their blood opportunities to flow to new places, and their hearts opportunities to beat at different rates. Then everybody sat down and the lesson moved on until the next Movement Break. But Creighton thought the schools could do better, so the program was refined. Students were asked to do little exercises: twenty repetitions of arm circles, ten squats, a minute of pretend jump rope and then ten stationary forward lunges. Sitting exercises were added next: ten sets of marching feet, ten toe touches, ten leg lifts, and ten abdominal stretches.

In the meantime, Creighton wondered whether there were actual programs that had been established by physical fitness experts designed specifically for classroom time. While attending a conference, she learned about Activity Works, a twelve-minute classroom exercise program developed in 2007 by North Shore LIJ Health System, a Long Island, New York company. "It is a video put up on a Smart Board or screen," says Creighton. "There are three kids, actors and actresses, doing movements while they are exploring the rainforests or outer space, wonders of the world, or capitals of the United States. In the classroom, the kids get up from their desks and follow along with these actors and actresses. They are walking, they are marching, they are reaching, they are stretching. The science behind Activity Works is that it gets the heart rate up, takes it down a little, gets it back up, and brings it down.

"It is brilliant, just brilliant. Not only are the kids moving and getting their heart rates up and back down again but they are also learning something interesting while they are doing it."[6]

Pharmaceutical company Johnson & Johnson stepped forward to offer funding, and, by 2015, elementary school students in some 800 Philadelphia classrooms were engaged in Activity Works exercises. Johnson & Johnson also offered staff time, providing data collection on the progress of the students. "That has been phenomenal,"[7] says Creighton.

Campaign for Healthier Schools

Activity Works was added to the Philadelphia schools as Creighton and her department inaugurated Campaign for Healthier Schools, a comprehensive health and nutrition program. Making use of government, corporate, and foundation grants that have totaled some $10 million, the Campaign for Healthier Schools was inaugurated in 2010.

A major component of the Campaign was to establish Wellness Councils at each school, which would set goals to make their students healthier. Creighton found that the groups, working independently, thought of some 800 goals.

One goal that all Wellness Councils shared was to improve nutritional habits among the students. In other words, how would they convince students to change their eating habits from snacking on junk foods to eating fruits and other healthier snacks? Creighton says some building principals took a no-nonsense approach, banning unhealthy snack foods from schools for at least one day a week. Staff members stationed at the school entrances with grocery bags collected unhealthy snacks as the students entered the buildings. (Those snacks were traded for fruits.)

Creighton thought there could be more effective approaches. For starters, she thought parents should be engaged. Teachers were encouraged to limit classroom birthday celebrations to once a month, and to discourage parents from sending cupcakes or other treats to school on birthday party day. Instead, the parents were asked to send in healthy snacks or, instead, donate books to the classroom. Or, send nothing at all. Instead of holding a birthday party in the classroom, why couldn't the teacher take the kids outside to celebrate the birthday with playtime?

But kids were eating unhealthy snacks at other times as well. A lot of teachers rewarded students for good work with candy. "We have asked teachers to think about fancy pencils or erasers or little trinkets," she says. "They have done a good job with that."[8]

Fundraisers in schools are often food-based: In exchange for a donation, the student may receive a soft pretzel. (For the education of non-Philadelphians, the Philadelphia staple known as the soft pretzel is a large and doughy snack food, covered in salt and mustard, and—depending on the age of the consumer—contains certain and undisputable artery-clogging qualities.) Creighton realized the hopelessness of telling Philadelphians to give up soft pretzels and so, when the treat is offered at fundraisers, organizers are encouraged to offer smaller versions of the snack. "We don't think soft pretzels are going to go away—not in Philadelphia—but what we recommend is going to the smaller soft pretzel,"[9] she says.

Bicycles and Basketball Stars

One of the key successes in the Campaign for Healthier Schools has been the involvement of corporations, institutions, and other groups. For example, Microsoft donated Xboxes to three Philadelphia middle schools that health educators use to help lead exercise classes by running exercise-themed games. "These students can't use Activity Works because it is juvenile. But the Microsoft Xbox is right up their alley," Creighton says. "One of our mantras here at school district for the past 12 or 15 years is that video games are not going away and we need to embrace the technology and use it to our advantage. We use the games to make the kids move. The [Xboxes] are really, really doing a fabulous job of integrating in Movement Breaks for the older kids."[10]

Philadelphia-based Drexel University and Einstein Healthcare Network, also based in the city, provide nutritionists to lead classes in good eating habits under a program titled Eat Right Now. The Philadelphia Bicycle Coalition provides instructors who lead bicycle safety classes in the schools. Independence Blue Cross Foundation, an institution sponsored by a major city health insurer, underwrites the Healthy Futures program in the schools. Targeted toward fourth-grade students—an age in which experts find young people are very open to new ideas—the program provides nutrition, exercise, and disease prevention education in elementary schools.

Eatiquette is an example of a Healthy Futures program. As part of Eatiquette, school cafeterias are transformed from places where kids simply line up to eat, as though they are in assembly lines, into nontraditional school environments where students gather around tables, passing plates of nutritional foods to one another. In this environment, social skills and teamwork are emphasized as much as good eating habits. Another Healthy Futures program is Get Fit, in which players and coaches from a number of local professional sports franchises—among them the Philadelphia 76ers basketball team, Philadelphia Union soccer team, and Philadelphia Freedoms tennis team—visit physical education classes and actually participate as teachers. The thinking here is that words of encouragement and instruction from a local sports star may make more of an impression on a young mind than what the gym teacher may have said—a thousand times or so.

Across the Curriculum

Of course, basketball and soccer stars and Xbox games can be found in physical education classes. To make health and fitness truly a part of the lives of all Philadelphia public school students—particularly for older students who are not following the Activity Works actors into rainforests—Creighton says educators must find ways to integrate healthy living across the curriculum. As health education moves into the future, she says, healthy living must be integrated wholly into a student's life. At this point, Creighton isn't sure how to do that, but she is sure that, given time, innovators will find new ways to cross curriculum lines when it comes to preparing young people for healthy lifestyles. (Would it be, for example, asking too much for the history teacher to ask the class to pause for a moment to reflect on the health consequences faced by Henry VIII, who weighed 320 pounds when he died at the age of 56? And then there is the story of that most famous Philadelphian of all, Benjamin Franklin, who despite his admonition that, "Early to bed and early to rise, makes a man healthy, wealthy, and wise," nevertheless suffered from gout and bladder stones—clear consequences of an unhealthy diet. What would it take for the teacher to dwell on Franklin's ill health for a few minutes of class time?)

"That is what I would love most to see," says Creighton. "There is a lot of literature, novels, fiction, whatever for young adults, young teens, preteens, and tweens where there are always health concepts. For teachers to integrate healthy lifestyles and wellness into their work, whether it would be math or science or social studies or English—that is a dream."[11]

NOTES

1. Interview with the author, Oct. 28, 2014.
2. Denise Koo, "A New Tool for Improving Health," National Academy for State Health Policy Weekly Insight, May 13, 2014, www.statereforum.org/weekly-insight/new-tool-for-improving-health. Accessed Nov. 4, 2014.
3. Interview with the author, Nov. 5, 2014.
4. Ibid.
5. Ibid.
6. Interview with the author, Oct. 28, 2014.
7. Ibid.
8. Ibid.
9. Ibid.
10. Ibid.
11. Ibid.

9 Workplace Wellness Programs Can Generate Savings

Katherine Baicker, David Cutler, and Zirui Song

Abstract

Amid soaring health spending, there is growing interest in workplace disease prevention and wellness programs to improve health and lower costs. In a critical meta-analysis of the literature on costs and savings associated with such programs, we found that medical costs fall by about $3.27 for every dollar spent on wellness programs and that absenteeism costs fall by about $2.73 for every dollar spent. Although further exploration of the mechanisms at work and broader applicability of the findings is needed, this return on investment suggests that the wider adoption of such programs could prove beneficial for budgets and productivity as well as health outcomes.

Cost of Health Care Health Promotion/Disease Prevention

In an environment of soaring health care spending, policymakers, insurers, and employers express growing interest in methods of improving health while lowering costs. Much discussion has taken place about investment in disease prevention and health promotion as a way of achieving better health outcomes at lower costs. President Barack Obama has highlighted prevention as a central component of health reform, as have major congressional reform proposals.[1,2] Workplace-based wellness programs, which could affect prevention, have been showcased in these reform proposals, the popular press, and congressional hearings.[3,4]

This enthusiasm for workplace programs stems in part from the fact that more than 60 percent of Americans get their health insurance coverage through an employment-based plan,[5] as well as from the recognition that many employees spend the majority of their waking hours in the workplace, which makes it a natural venue for investments in health. There are several reasons that employers might benefit from investments in employee wellness. First, such programs might lead to reductions in health care costs and thus health insurance premiums. Second, healthier workers might be more productive and miss fewer days of work. These benefits may accrue at least partially to the employer (such as through improved ability to attract workers), even if the primary benefits accrue to the employee.

These factors may motivate the increasing interest in such programs among employers—and especially large employers. In 2006, 19 percent of companies with 500 or more workers reported offering wellness programs, while a 2008 survey of large manufacturing employers reported that 77 percent offered some kind of formal health and wellness program.[6–8] Consistent with the evidence presented below, small firms seem slower to offer such programs, and many of the programs offered are still quite limited in scope.[9]

Several well-publicized case studies have suggested a positive return to employers' investment in prevention. For every dollar invested in the program, the employer saves more than the dollar spent. The Citibank Health Management Program reported an estimated savings of $4.50 in medical expenditures per dollar spent on the program.[10] Studies from the California Public Employees Retirement System (CalPERS), Bank of America, and Johnson and Johnson have similarly estimated sizable health care savings from wellness programs.[11–13] Despite this anecdotal evidence of high returns, however, most employers do not engage in wide-scale workplace wellness promotion practices. The 2004 National Worksite Health Promotion Survey showed that only 7 percent of employers offered comprehensive programs[14] of the type specified in the recommendations of the influential Institute of Medicine report Healthy People 2010.[15] These include health education, worksite screenings linked to appropriate medical care, and the integration of the program into corporate or organizational structure.

Some empirical studies attempt to estimate the return on investment for employer wellness programs more systematically, but shortcomings in this literature leave the question unresolved.[16] In particular, most studies lack an adequate comparison or control group, and are thus not able to account for possible unobserved variables or alternative pathways that might be responsible for observed differences in costs between wellness program participants and nonparticipants (rather than those differences being attributable to the wellness program itself). This leaves open the possibility of selection bias—for example, if the healthiest employees were most likely to enroll in voluntary wellness programs, a comparison of participants and nonparticipants might suggest that the programs are improving health more than they really are.

Low response rates, inexact case-control matching, and potential publication bias (studies finding high returns may be more likely to be published) also call into question the evidence of high returns. In addition, Sean Nicholson and colleagues show that common methods used by employers to calculate costs and benefits of health-related investments might not reflect the true impact of these programs.[17] These shortcomings mean that even the limited evidence available might not be robust or generalizable.

In this study we conducted a meta-analysis of the literature on costs and savings associated with employer-based wellness promotion policies. We began by screening existing studies for analytical rigor, and then we compiled standardized estimates of return on investment from those studies. We focused on studies for which there was a comparison group of nonparticipants, and we examined effects of wellness program interventions on health care costs and absenteeism.

We found a large positive return on investment across these rigorous studies, which suggests that the wider adoption of such programs could prove beneficial for budgets as well as health. That they have been implemented so selectively, however, necessitates further research into the likely effects of broader adoption.

Study Data and Methods

We conducted a primary literature search from prior peer-reviewed meta-analyses of employee wellness programs, as well as a computerized search of MEDLINE, Lexis-Nexis, and other health and social science databases. Search terms included "employee," "wellness," "workplace," "disease management," and "return on investment." This produced an initial sample of more than 100 peer-reviewed studies of employee wellness programs spanning the past three decades.

Among these peer-reviewed studies, we restricted our analysis to studies that satisfied the following criteria: (1) they had a well-defined intervention; (2) they had a well-defined treatment and comparison group, even if the comparison group was not strictly randomly assigned; and (3) they represented analysis of a distinct new intervention, rather than further analysis of an intervention already examined in one of the other studies. We performed additional analysis on the subset of these studies that reported "difference-in-difference" estimates of the study outcome (comparing the change in the outcome from before the program to after the program in the treatment group to the change in the outcome over the same period for the comparison group), or the raw data allowing for this calculation.[18]

Applying these criteria narrowed our sample to thirty-two original publications. These studies are listed in Appendix Table 1.[19] Two of these studies reported results of multiple separate interventions; we treated these as separate studies. Several other studies reported the results of multiple interventions, but because participants were allowed to self-select into intervention arms, we treated these as a single case each. Thus, the thirty-two original publications gave us an effective sample of thirty-six studies. Of these, twenty-two looked at employee health care costs, and twenty-two looked at employee absenteeism (eight examined both).

We catalogued the characteristics of the firms that undertook these employee wellness programs and the qualitative dimensions of the programs themselves. We analyzed the health care cost and absenteeism studies separately, but we also converted the absenteeism results into dollar cost units using a uniform wage rate to construct comparable estimates of return on investment.

Study Results

Sample characteristics

More than 90 percent of employee wellness programs in our sample were implemented in large firms (those with more than 1,000 workers). One-fourth examined wellness programs at employers with more than 10,000 workers. A number of industries were represented: 25 percent of sampled employers were in financial services; 22 percent in manufacturing; and

16 percent in school districts, universities, and municipalities. Other industries represented included utilities, telecommunications, energy, pharmaceuticals, and makers of consumer products. Ten studies took place across multiple locations, often the employer headquarters and satellite locations; some were implemented across multiple employers.

Characteristics of Wellness Programs

We can characterize the employee wellness programs in the study sample along two dimensions: the method of delivery and the focus of intervention (Exhibit 1). The method of delivery characterizes how the intervention was carried out. By far the most frequently used method of delivery is the health risk assessment—a survey that gathers baseline self-reported health data from the employee, which are in turn used by the employer to tailor the subsequent intervention.[20] The health risk assessment is used in 80 percent of the studies in our sample; it most commonly serves as the initial intervention or requirement for participation in the wellness program.

Exhibit 1 Summary of Characteristics of Worksite Wellness Programs Studied

Method of delivery	Percent of firms
Health risk assessment	81
Self-help education materials	42
Individual counseling	39
Classes, seminars, group activities	36
Added incentives for participation	31
Focus of intervention	
Weight loss and fitness	66
Smoking cessation	50
Multiple risk factors	75

Source: Authors' calculations based on 36 studies described in Appendix Table 1, available online at http://content.healthaffairs.org/ cgi/content/full/29/2/hlthaff.2009.0626/DC1

Summary of Characteristics of Worksite Wellness Programs Studied

Participation is almost always voluntary among employees at the treatment site, making selection bias a major concern. Assessments are commonly used in conjunction with a clinical screening of risk factors, including blood pressure, cholesterol, and body mass index (BMI). Importantly, the assessment tool provides the employee with information on risk factors that motivate participation. The majority of programs that did not use the assessment method featured an on-site gymnasium or workout facility, which employees were encouraged to use.

The second most common wellness intervention mechanism was the provision of self-help education materials, individual counseling with health care professionals, or on-site group activities led by trained personnel. In our sample, about 40 percent of studies included the use of self-help materials; 40 percent offered individual counseling; and 35 percent featured on-site group activities, classes, or seminars. Most programs offered a combination of these interventions.

The use of incentives to motivate participation was seen in 30 percent of programs. Incentives were most commonly bonuses and reimbursements for program participation, but they also included the payback of down payments prior to participation. Such cases may involve an employer's withholding a small portion of employee compensation until program participation occurs. Incentives have become more common in recent interventions.

The most common foci of the programs were obesity and smoking, the two top causes of preventable death in the United States. More than 60 percent of the programs explicitly focused on weight loss and fitness. All but three of the remaining programs focused on either multiple risks or risks specific to the participant. Half of the programs focused on smoking, often in conjunction with obesity. Seventy-five percent of programs focused on more than one risk factor, including stress management, back care, nutrition, alcohol consumption, blood pressure, and preventive care, in addition to smoking and obesity.

Impact of Programs on Medical Spending

Twenty-two studies reported on the impact of wellness programs on employee health care costs (Exhibit 2). The average sample size of intervention groups exceeded 3,000 employees, and the size of comparison groups averaged about 4,500 employees. Although the studies examined programs for three years on average, most wellness programs continued (often indefinitely) beyond the study duration.

Exhibit 2 Summary of Employee Wellness Studies Analyzed

		Average sample size					
Study focus	Number of studies	Treatment	Comparison	Average duration (years)	Average savings[a]	Average costs[a]	ROI[b]
Health care costs	22	3,201	4,547	3.0	$358	$144	3.27
Absenteeism	22	2,683	4,782	2.0	$294	$132	2.73

Source: Authors' calculations based on studies described in Appendix Table 1, available online at http://content.healthaffairs.org/cgi/content/full/29/2/hlthaff.2009.0626/DC2 [a]Per employee per year, costs in 2009 dollars. [b]Average of the individual return-on-investment (ROI) figures for each study.

Summary of Employee Wellness Studies Analyzed

We grouped the studies into three types: those that had a randomized controlled trial or matched control group and pre- and post-intervention data; those that had a nonrandomized or unmatched comparison group and pre- and post-intervention data; and those that had post-intervention data only but met our other inclusion criteria (Exhibit 3). We standardized the costs and benefits of each program to annual figures in 2009 dollars, assuming a linear distribution of both costs and benefits over time. We calculated savings as the difference between treatment and comparison groups after the intervention subtracted by the differences between the groups before the intervention (when available). Using reported figures for program costs, we calculated a return on investment for each study.[21]

Summary of Findings from Studies of Employee Health Care Costs, Pre- and Post-Intervention

Averaging across all programs in which they were reported, the interventions produced $358 in savings through reduced health costs per employee per year, while costing the employer $144 per employee per year. The average calculated return on investment across the fifteen studies that reported

Exhibit 3 Summary of Findings From Studies of Employee Health Care Costs, Pre- and Post-Intervention

Study number	Years	Sample size Treat	Sample size Control	Health care costs ($), treatment group (T) Pre	Health care costs ($), treatment group (T) Post	Health care costs ($), control group (C) Pre	Health care costs ($), control group (C) Post	Change in health care costs ($), T−C Change, pre	Change in health care costs ($), T−C Change, post
Group A									
1	4.0	1,890	1,890	1,531	2,907	1,427	3,429	−522	−626
2	2.0	340	340	1,739	1,459	1,198	1,107	351	−189
3	3.2	11,194	11,644	2,736	3,411	2,896	4,136	−724	−563
4	5.0	8,451	2,955	247	655	253	1,234	−579	−573
5	1.0	919	867	2,171	1,695	1,881	1,995	−300	−590
6	1.0	21,170	719	2,336	2,937	2,048	2,905	32	−255
7	1.5	301	412	1,891	1,621	1,970	1,710	−89	−11
8	1.5	180	412	2,036	1,283	1,970	1,710	−427	−493
9	1.5	295	412	1,986	1,485	1,970	1,710	−225	−242
Group B									
10	1.0	392	142	294	296	295	396	−100	−99
11	0.5	2,586	50,576	1,616	1,185	500	419	766	−351
12	6.0	1,272	244	2,140	2,337	1,825	2,908	−571	−886
13	3.0	3,993	4,341	1,620	2,008	1,647	2,596	−588	−561
14	5.0	388	355	1,159	2,397	825	1,701	696	363
15	5.0	667	892	695	1,687	605	1,977	−290	−380
Group C									
16	4.0	1,275	2,687		3,222		3,909		−687
17	5.0	13,048	13,363		4,176		4,454		−278
18	4.0	337	321		2,078		1,672		406
19	4.0	367	343		1,772		1,346		426
20	4.0	183	184		1,128		979		149
21	2.0	221	296		1,256		2,424		−1,168
22	2.5	950	6,640		1,413		1,396		17

Source: Authors' calculations based on studies described in Appendix Table 1, available online at http://content.healthaffairs.org/cgi/content/full/29/2/hlthaff.2009.0626/DC2

Notes: Table has been abridged because of space constraints. The full exhibit is available as Supplemental Exhibit 3 in the online Appendix. All figures denote health care costs per employee per year, in 2009 dollars. Group A: Randomized controlled trial or matched control group. Group B: Nonrandomized or unmatched comparison group. Group C: Post-intervention data only.

program costs was 3.37 (that is, for every dollar spent, $3.37 was saved).[22] An additional seven studies reported savings but not costs, which made a direct calculation of return on investment for these studies impossible.

If we were to assume that they had the same average cost of $144 as the studies that did report costs, that would imply a slightly lower average return on investment of $3.27 (although given that these studies reported somewhat lower savings, we have no reason to assume that their costs were the same). Only two studies reported that employer wellness programs did not save money.

Studies with random assignment to treatment and control groups or with carefully matched comparison groups are perhaps the most persuasive. In a typical randomized study, employees were randomly assigned to the program and control group, or in several cases to different intensities of the wellness program. In matched comparison studies, the comparison group typically comprises age- and sex-matched nonparticipants from the same employer identified through a retrospective review of participation.

Nine of the studies in Exhibit 2 had such designs. This matching is an effort to limit the bias introduced by voluntary self-selection of potentially healthier employees into wellness program participation. However, self-selection remains an important limitation in these studies. The average program savings reported in these studies was $394 per employee per year, and the average program cost was $159 per employee per year. The average calculated return on investment for this group was 3.36.

Six studies used comparison groups that were neither randomized nor matched, yielding $319 saved per employee per year and $132 spent per employee per year (average return on investment of 2.38). Seven studies did not report baseline data, thus allowing only for calculation of post-intervention cost differences (averaging $162 per employee per year).[23] Study numbers 4, 10, and 15 reported lower health care costs overall than the other studies, but they are among the earliest studies in the group—all published in the 1980s, when average spending (even accounting for inflation) was substantially lower than it is now.

Impact of Programs on Absenteeism

The twenty-two studies that examined employee absenteeism had, on average, smaller treatment groups and slightly larger comparison groups compared with those that did not, although the size is generally similar (Exhibit 2). These studies were carried out for only two years on average, compared to three for health care cost studies. We monetized absentee days using the average hourly wage rate in 2009 of $20.49.[24,25]

The average program savings across the studies was a more modest $294 per employee per year, while program costs were $132 per employee per year (Exhibit 4). Twelve of these twenty-two studies reported program costs. The average calculated return on investment for these twelve studies was 3.27.[26] As above, we could assume that the programs that did not report costs had similar average costs to those who did, which would imply a lower average return on investment of 2.73. All but one of the studies showed some reduction in absentee days.

As with the studies on medical costs, the average savings was relatively similar in the subset of studies with rigorous control groups. Among the nine studies with random control groups or matched comparison groups, the average number of absentee days saved was 1.7 per employee per year, estimated to cost $274 per employee per year. The next eleven studies had average program savings of 1.9 absentee days or roughly $309 per employee per year. Taken together, they represent slightly more modest program savings than the health care cost studies suggest.

Discussion

Our review of the evidence suggests that large employers adopting wellness programs see substantial positive returns, even within the first few years after adoption. Medical costs fall about $3.27 for every dollar spent on wellness programs, and absentee day costs fall by about $2.73 for every dollar spent. Although these benefits surely accrue in part to the employee, it is also likely that they accrue in part to the employer—in the form of either lower replacement costs for absent workers or an advantage in attracting workers to the firm. We discuss only two dimensions of potential benefits (reduced health care costs and reduced absenteeism), but there are likely many other benefits as well, including improved health, reduced turnover, and lower costs for public programs such as disability insurance and Medicare.

Our results show more modest return on investment than prior meta-analyses by Larry Chapman, which had more lenient inclusion criteria and reported an average gross return on investment of 5.81 across twenty-two studies,[27] and by Steven Aldana, which reported gross return on investment of 3.48–5.82 across seven studies.[28] We believe that our more systematic treatment of intervention and comparison groups pre- and post-intervention and calculation of equivalent costs and benefits has resulted in more comparable and reliable figures.

Limitations

There are clearly limitations in the broader generalization of these findings. First, the firms implementing these programs are likely those with the highest expected returns. Second, it is difficult to gauge the extent of publication bias, with programs seeing high return on investment most likely to be written about and studies with significant findings of positive returns most likely to be published.

Exhibit 4 Summary of Findings From Studies of Employee Absenteeism

| Study number | Years | Sample size | | Absentee days, treatment (T) | | Absentee days, control (C) | | Difference in absentee days, T−C | | Savings in wages ($)[a] |
		Treat	Control	Pre	Post	Pre	Post	Difference, pre	Difference, post	
Group A										
1	1.0	919	867	36.0	34.4	36.0	38.8	0.0	−4.4	721
2	1.5	301	412	5.0	4.7	5.1	4.8	−0.1	−0.1	0
3	1.5	180	412	5.2	3.2	5.1	4.8	0.2	−1.5	280
4	1.5	295	412	5.2	4.1	5.1	4.8	0.1	−0.7	131
5	1.0	266	1,242	4.6	4.2	7.0	9.1	-2.4	-4.9	413
6	2.0	597	645	18.0	13.5	19.1	18.2	−1.1	−4.7	590
7	2.0	1,406	487	5.9	5.6	5.3	6.0	0.6	−0.4	173
8	2.0	29,315	14,573	5.7	4.9	5.2	4.9	0.5	0.0	82
9	1.0	2,546	7,143	5.6	5.5	6.0	6.2	−0.4	−0.8	70
Group B										
10	1.0	392	142	0.3	0.1	0.1	0.5	0.1	−0.4	92
11	0.5	2,586	50,576	3.9	3.0	1.6	1.5	2.3	1.5	123
12	4.0	1,275	2,687	3.1	2.3	3.1	3.3	0.0	−1.0	167
13	2.0	221	296	8.7	9.0	10.0	12.4	−1.3	−3.4	342
14	6.0	2,596	1,593	6.6	17.2	6.6	23.3	0.0	−6.1	1,000
15	2.0	450	1,178	29.2	27.8	33.2	38.1	−4.0	−10.3	1,033
16	1.0	469	415	12.4	11.0	14.3	14.2	−2.0	−3.2	203
17	4.0	3,122	1,850	9.1	10.2	9.1	10.8	0.0	−0.6	88
18	2.0	7,178	7,101	3.2	3.0	2.9	2.9	0.3	0.1	33
19	2.0	2,232	5,863	4.4	3.7	5.6	5.5	−1.2	−1.8	102
20	2.0	688	387	2.5	2.6	2.9	4.3	−0.4	−1.7	225
Group C										
21	3.0	727	1,950							115
22	2.0	1264	4,982							492

Source: Authors' calculations based on studies described in Appendix Table 1, available online at http://content.healthaffairs.org/cgi/content/full/29/2/ hlthaff.2009.0626/DC2

Notes: Table has been abridged because of space constraints. The full exhibit is available as Supplemental Exhibit 4 in the online Appendix. Absenteeism figures denote absenteeism days per employee per year. Group A: Randomized controlled trial or matched control group. Group B: Nonrandomized or unmatched comparison group. Group C: Missing group-level data. 'Using uniform wage rate of $20.49 per hour, Bureau of Labor Statistics, 2009 (assuming eight hours per day).

Third, almost all of the studies were implemented by large employers, which are more likely than others to have the resources and economies of scale necessary both to implement and to achieve broad savings through employee wellness programs. Whether smaller employers can achieve positive return on investment through wellness programs is an important policy question.[29] These factors may help explain why such programs have not (yet) been adopted more widely, although they are clearly gaining rapidly in prominence.

Our analysis does not account for the time profile of cost incurred and benefits accrued within programs, and the studies included extend through only a limited time window. This is important because wellness program costs are likely to be front-loaded—that is, more costly at the start—while health benefits are likely to accumulate gradually. Therefore, to the extent that program costs decrease over time and benefits increase over time, we may be understating the true return on investment.

Our analysis cannot address the important question of which attributes of wellness programs are most important, and how such programs should be optimally designed. Well-designed field experiments that compare the effectiveness of program components such as patient education and professional counseling across different industries and populations are needed to answer it.

Indeed, the answer might not be the same everywhere. A manual laborer in a manufacturing plant is likely to have different underlying health risks, and may respond to employee wellness programs differently, than an office-based clerical worker in a financial institution. Corporate culture, the structure of program incentives, and the diffusion of program participation or health behavior through employee social networks are all likely to affect return on investment.

Further study is also needed to elucidate the time path of return on investment—in particular, the relative cost-effectiveness of a program's first years compared to its later years. Only a few of the studies in our sample provided data on costs and savings for each year of the program, which made it difficult to describe the average time path of return on investment. The assumption of a linear trend in savings from the beginning to end of program evaluation may not reflect the reality of behavior change within organizations.

Emerging Patterns

Still, some patterns are emerging. A growing literature suggests that building incentives into wellness programs helps to raise participation among employees.[30,31] In the 2004 National Worksite Health Promotion Survey, 26 percent of worksites used incentives to increase employee participation. Recent studies by Kevin Volpp and colleagues used both lotteries and financial commitments by participants to show that financial incentives are effective at motivating weight loss and smoking cessation.[31,32] These and similar approaches, borrowing from psychology and behavioral economics, may provide creative solutions to employers aiming not only to increase participation, but ultimately to modify behavior that is resistant to change.[33]

These intriguing findings suggest that adding provisions that promote wellness initiatives might be a promising component of comprehensive health reform. Such measures might include direct subsidies (such as the tax credits for small employers that have been proposed in some legislation by Sen. Tom Harkin [D-IA] and others) or an easing of regulatory barriers, including an exploration of the legal implications of Health Insurance Portability and Accountability Act (HIPAA) nondiscrimination rules and the Americans with Disabilities Act (ADA) for program design.[34] The current reform debate has incorporated active discussion of wellness promotion (including testimony from witnesses on the success of particular employers' programs) and the hope that such programs will be a key component in slowing health care cost growth, but it is difficult to evaluate how realistic these hopes are.

Conclusion

Health insurance in the United States is likely to continue to be employment-based. Our critical review of the existing evidence suggests that employer-based wellness initiatives may not only improve health, but may also result in substantial savings over even short-run horizons. Encouraging (or even subsidizing) such programs also seem to have broad political appeal, perhaps in part because they operate with less direct government oversight and fewer government dollars and in part because they hold the promise of slowing health care cost growth without the specter of rationing care. Understanding the factors that make them most successful and the barriers to their wider adoption could help smooth the path for future investments in this very promising avenue for improving health and productivity.

NOTES

1. Pear R. Congress Plans Incentives for Healthy Habits," *New York Times.* 2009 May 9.

2. Steinbrook R. Health care and the American Recovery and Reinvestment Act. *New England Journal of Medicine.* 2009;360(11):1057–60.

3. "Text: Obama's Speech on Health Care Reform," *New York Times.* 2009 Jun 15 [cited 2009 Dec 28]. Available from: http://www.nytimes.com/2009/06/15/health/policy/15obama.text.html?_r=1=policy

4. "Getting Healthy, with a Little Help from the Boss," *New York Times.* 2009 May 22.

5. Blumenthal D. Employer-sponsored health insurance in the United States—origins and implications. N Engl J Med. 2006;355(1):82–8.

6. Consulting MHR. National survey of employer-sponsored health plans: 2006 survey report. New York: Consulting MHR; 2007.

7. Capps K, Harkey JB. Employee health and productivity management programs: the use of incentives [Internet]. Lyndhurst (NJ): National Association of Manufacturers,

ERISA Industry Council, and IncentOne; 2008 [cited 2010 Jan 8]. Available from: http://www.incentone.com/files/2008-SurveyResults.pdf.

8. There is no broadly accepted definition of a wellness program, which makes comparisons of figures across studies difficult. Disease management, such as the disease management pilots incorporated the Medicare program and recently (unfavorably) reviewed by the Congressional Budget Office (CBO), is generally viewed as distinct from wellness initiatives.

9. McPeck W , Ryan M, Chapman LS. Bringing wellness to the small employer. *American Journal of Health Promotion.* 2009;23(5):1–10.

10. Ozminkowski RJ, Dunn RL, Goetzel RZ, Cantor RI, Murnane J, Harrison M. A return on investment evaluation of the Citibank, N.A., health management program. Am J Health Promot. 1999;14(1):31–43.

11. Bly JL, Jones RC, Richardson JE. Impact of worksite health promotion on health care costs and utilization. Evaluation of Johnson & Johnson's Live for Life program. *Journal of the American Medical Association.* 1986;256(23):3235–40.

12. Fries JF, Harrington H, Edwards R, Kent LA, Richardson N. Randomized controlled trial of cost reductions from a health education program: the California Public Employees' Retirement System (PERS) study. Am J Health Promot. 1994;8(3): 216–23.

13. Leigh JP, Richardson N, Beck R, Kerr C, Harrington H, Parcell CL, et al. Randomized controlled study of a retiree health promotion program. The Bank of America Study. *Archives of Internal Medicine.* 1992;152(6):1201–6.

14. Linnan L, Bowling M, Childress J, Lindsay G, Blakey C, Pronk S, et al. Results of the 2004 National Worksite Health Promotion Survey. Am J Public Health. 2008;98(8):1503–9.

15. Culyer AJ, Newhouse JP. *Handbook of Health Economics,* 1st ed. Amsterdam; New York: Elsevier; 2000.

16. Goetzel RZ, Ozminkowski RJ. The health and cost benefits of work site health-promotion programs. *Annual Review of Public Health.* 2008;29:303–23.

17. Nicholson S, Pauly MV, Polsky D, Baase CM, Billotti GM, Ozminkowski RJ, et al. How to present the business case for healthcare quality to employers. *Applied Health Economics and Health Policy.* 2005;4(4):209–18.

18. Although in the case of random assignment "before" data would not be necessary for the construction of causal estimates (since difference between the treatment and control groups after the intervention would reflect the effects of the intervention), in practice all of the studies with randomized assignment reported both before and after data. In the case of non-randomly assigned comparison groups, the "before" data are necessary to net out any existing differences between the groups in estimating the effect of the intervention.

19. The Appendix is available online at http://content.healthaffairs.org/cgi/content/full/29/2/hlthaff.2009.0626/DC1

20. Huskamp H, Rosenthal MB. Health risk appraisals: how much do they influence employees' health behavior?. *Health Affairs* (Millwood). 2009;28(5):1532–40

21. An alternative metric to return on investment would be net present value. In this context we prefer return on investment because it allows us to compare normalized results across studies

(as internally calculated ratios, rather than dollar figures) and allows us to compare our results to those of other studies (the majority of which calculate return on investment). There is unfortunately a paucity of information about the time path of investments and returns.

22. Fourteen studies reported their own return on investment, which did not always exactly match ours, because they were not always calculated over the same time period. The average of the fourteen reported returns on investment yields an almost identical 3.36.

23. As noted above, in nonexperimental settings, baseline comparisons are a useful way to gauge existing differences in non–randomly assigned treatment and comparison groups.

24. Bureau of Labor Statistics. Employer costs for employee compensation summary. Washington (DC): BLS; 2009 Jun 10.

25. The share of these costs borne by the firm in the form of increased replacement worker costs depends on how many sick days workers are entitled to and whether workers are able to convert unused sick days to other days of leave or pay.

26. In this case the average return on investment of 4.71 reported by these twelve studies is much higher than that we calculated directly using reported costs and benefits.

27. Chapman LS. Meta-evaluation of worksite health promotion economic return studies: 2005 update. Am J Health Promot. 2005;19(6):1–11.

28. Aldana S. Financial impact of health promotion programs: a comprehensive review of the literature. Am J Health Promot. 2001;15(5):296–320.

29. Some insights can be gained from the magnitude of the return on investment seen in large firms, however. For the firms studied here, with roughly 50,000 employees, on average, the benefits in lower medical costs are about 3:1. Even in the extreme case where all of the costs of wellness programs are fixed costs, those costs could be spread over only one-third the number of employees and still be cost-neutral.

30. Serxner S, Anderson DR, Gold D. Building program participation: strategies for recruitment and retention in worksite health promotion programs. Am J Health Promot. 2004;18(4):1–6.

31. Volpp KG, John LK, Troxel AB, Norton L, Fassbender J, Loewenstein G. Financial incentive-based approaches for weight loss: a randomized trial. JAMA. 2008;300(22):2631–7.

32. Volpp KG, Troxel AB, Pauly MV, Glick HA, Puig A, Asch DA, et al. A randomized, controlled trial of financial incentives for smoking cessation. N Engl J Med. 2009;360(7):699–709.

33. Loewenstein G, Brennan T, Volpp KG. Asymmetric paternalism to improve health behaviors. JAMA. 2007;298(20):2415–7.

34. Mello MM, Rosenthal MB. Wellness programs and lifestyle discrimination—the legal limits. New Engl J Med. 2008;359(2):192–9.

10

Work and Training Opportunities: Integrating the Disabled into the Workforce

Hal Marcovitz

A quarter-century ago Congress passed the Americans with Disabilities Act, a law with the noble intention of, among other goals, ending discrimination against disabled people in the workplace. In fact, Title I of the ADA says, "No [employer] shall discriminate against a qualified individual on the basis of disability in regard to job application procedures, the hiring, advancement, or discharge of employees, employee compensation, job training, and other terms, conditions, and privileges of employment."[1]

Memo to Congress: It hasn't worked. According to the U.S. Bureau of Labor Statistics, the unemployment rate among disabled people in 2013 stood at a staggering 82.4 percent—that was the same year in which the unemployment rate for the nondisabled stood at 7.1 percent. In other words, the unemployment rate among the disabled is 11 times that of everyone else.

The problem isn't that employers are intentionally excluding disabled people from the workforce—under the ADA, they are prohibited from even asking whether a job applicant is disabled. Therefore, employers aren't supposed to know whether a prospective employee may be disabled. Rather, the problem can be found more in the way society prepares disabled people for the workforce. In fact, society doesn't do a very good job of it: Disabled people leave school with very few skills employers require. Therefore, when disabled people compete with others for jobs, they find themselves at a disadvantage. The ADA did a very good job of prohibiting discrimination on the basis of a disability, but did little to help disabled people prepare for competing in a world that is told it has to look the other way and not see a disability.

"If you check the demographics of unemployment, people with disabilities have hugely higher rates of unemployment then our economy at large," says Nancy Gurney, president of Opportunity Services in Minneapolis, Minnesota. "There are all kinds of factors that keep people with disabilities from working. They can't engage in the workforce the way you and I do. In other words, if I need to find a job I have a strong resume, I've got a lot of work experience, I have a college education, I have a network. If you think of all the ways that you find a job and then you think of the way a person with Down syndrome or a person with attention deficit disorder or a person with autism is going to find a job, they need other resources."[2]

The End of Sheltered Workshops

Opportunity Services provides occupational training for some 1,500 disabled clients per year in Minnesota as well as Florida and Massachusetts. Gurney founded the organization in 1973 at a time when most people with disabilities—if they found employment at all—worked in what are known as sheltered workshops. Typically, disabled people are bused, or make their way on their own, to workshops where they work side by side, making simple household goods such as screwdrivers or loose-leaf binders or key chains. Or they apply labels to jars or glue cardboard sheets together to make boxes. While on the job they do not interact with nondisabled people save for, perhaps, their supervisors. In many cases they are paid for piecework—in other words, they don't make at least minimum wage but, instead, are compensated according to how many key chains or screwdrivers they make, or how many cardboard boxes they assemble. A provision of an archaic 1938 law allows nonprofit organizations to pay disabled employees less than the minimum wage. In 2013, the news media reported that some employees of Goodwill Industries earn the equivalent of 22 cents per hour. (At the time, top executives of Goodwill were reported to be earning $1 million or more a year.)

Congress has recognized this disparity and in 2014 passed the Workforce Innovation and Opportunity Act, which established limits on who can work in sheltered workplaces—specifically employees under the age of twenty-four. The law says these younger employees can't earn less than the minimum wage unless they have also received vocational training in their schools. And since vocational training for disabled students in public schools is, by most accounts, sorely lacking, it appears the Act will help keep young disabled people out of sheltered workshops.

Gurney says the Act will help phase out sheltered workshops, which she favors. Disabled people should not be segregated together in workshops, she says, but making their ways in the real world of work. "We kind of want to protect them in our culture and we don't let them engage in a normal work development process," she says. "We need to do that. They should have jobs when they exit from high school. They should have a sound transition. They deserve public education and those years should be spent in a lot of job trials and work experience so that they have the skills sets that businesses need to engage in employment."[3]

Job Coaches

It is hard to argue with Gurney but because there is relatively little vocational training provided by schools to disabled people they often lack the skills businesses require. "Some schools are very good at [vocational training] but most schools are not; they tend to be involved in classroom training," Gurney says. "They'll call it 'living skills' where you learn how to manage your apartment. Well, you are not going to have your own apartment if you don't have a job. We are self-sufficient in our country if we have work."[4] Gurney says it is not unusual for her organization to accept clients who have been out of high school for four or five years or more and have never worked a day in their lives.

And the reason nobody will hire them is not because the local supermarket has a discriminatory policy, but rather because the disabled applicant isn't prepared to work in the aisles of a supermarket. Shop for groceries and you will invariably see a clerk working with one of those hand-held scanners that performs a number of functions, such as changing prices on products, or taking inventory, or even making sure the items are in the correct places on the correct shelves. Of course, the right buttons need to be pushed to make sure the right information has been passed from scanner to product and back again. The supervisor in the supermarket probably expects to spend no more than a few minutes teaching a new clerk how to use the scanner. For somebody who may have Down syndrome or is hearing-impaired or autistic, that might not be the case.

That's where organizations like Opportunity Services step in. The agency provides job coaches who teach clients how to use tools like supermarket scanners. The coach will actually go to the job site and spend hours, or for as long as it takes, to make sure the client can use the scanner, and carry out all the other functions of his or her job as well, the way the store expects the employee to perform. Moreover, the job coach will check back—sometimes periodically, sometimes every day. Says Gurney, "We have everything from what we call inattentive placement where you are just hired by a company and you hold the job. You need a little bit of support, maybe not much. Maybe you are pretty independent; you just need a little jumpstart to get you ready. We call that supported employment.

"We also have what we call scattered site employment where you are doing pretty good. You are hired directly by the company but you need more support on a daily basis. We might have a job coach out there to get you started, and then check in with you at the end of your shift. You need more support and more frequently than someone who might need short-term support or no support."[5]

Supermarkets and other businesses tend to make a lot of changes, though. They move the stock around the store. A deli owner may concoct a new sandwich. A hotel may buy new vacuum cleaners for the housekeeping staff. For everybody else at the company, the changes may be covered in a quick meeting and brief tutorial. Disabled clients need more time and retraining, which means the job coach has to return to the job site and work with the client to learn the new tasks and duties. Says Gurney, "We just had a situation where a job coach walked into my office and said, 'All of the people are going to have to be retrained at the Wyndham Hotel.' Great, that's OK, but it's a day of training for a person with a hearing impairment there. That means we have to have an interpreter. The hearing-impaired person can't take notes; if you don't have your eyes and your ears to retain information you can't take notes. So the job coach will likely have to attend that day of training and work with him and make sure there are written materials so that person will have reinforcement and training and can implement whatever they will be trained to do. The job coach will spend the full day with the staff. That is an additional function; you and I would not need that."[6]

Still, Gurney insists, it is far easier for Opportunity Services to send a job coach back to the Wyndham Hotel to spend a day with a hearing-impaired employee than to find that employee another job. According to Gurney, on average it takes her organization forty-five days once a new client joins her program to provide vocational training and find that person a job. Opportunity Services would much rather send a job coach to a supermarket to spend a few hours showing the client which buttons to push to reduce the price of the canned peas on sale.

Remote-Control Car Soccer

At the Prospector Theater in Ridgefield, Connecticut, the job coaches are already on staff. They work alongside the disabled employees, selling tickets, making popcorn, filling beer and soda cups, showing audience members to their seats. In fact, at the Prospector Theater the job coaches aren't even called job coaches. If their jobs on a particular day require them to take tickets, they are called ticket-takers. If their jobs on a particular day call on them to pop the popcorn, they are called popcorn poppers. The disabled people who work at the theater have the same job titles. The Prospector Theater employs ninety-five people, all but twenty of whom are disabled.

The theater was founded by Valerie Jensen, who used to teach art to disabled people before she decided that her clients needed jobs more than they needed crafting skills. So she raised $30 million to convert an old bank on Prospect Street into a multiplex movie theater specifically to employ disabled people. She describes the Prospector Theater, which opened in November 2014, as something of a hybrid—not quite a sheltered workshop, and not quite a business where disabled people are mainstreamed into the workforce. The theater is, certainly, anything but sheltered—hundreds of ticket-buying patrons come and go every day. They interact with the employees (Jensen prefers to call them "prospects"), buy their popcorn from them, and even play games with them.

In 2015, when ticket sales for *Fast & Furious 7* were lagging—Jensen says the action flick couldn't seem to find the right demographic in Ridgefield—she hoped to boost sales by staging a game for theater patrons. So she bought some remote-control model cars and staged a game of "remote-control car soccer" in a courtyard next to the theater. Some of the prospects played on the same team as the ticket buyers. "I invented a game, remote-control car soccer. We played that. My coaches and I wrote out all the soft skills you are doing while you are playing and interacting with remote-control cars. It is really remarkable the teamwork and frustration at having to problem-solve. If you think about what that game represents—if you are playing with remote control cars and you have sclerosis you are on as close to a level playing field as you can be because it is more than just sitting down and watching a screen and playing video games. You are really up and cheering and watching a whole sporting event. The kind of camaraderie, teamwork, compassion, and energy that formed among the people on the teams, it is something that they will take away with them as a meaningful interaction. It happened very naturally and quickly in an authentic way."[7]

Employers Need to Ask

Jensen agrees with Gurney in believing that the ADA hasn't lived up to expectations and needs to be retooled. Specifically, she would like to see the employer given permission to ask specific questions about a job candidate's disabilities. Rather than leading to discrimination, she believes most employers are forward-thinking and would use that information to figure out how to fit the employee into its workforce.

Jensen believes that if she knew a little more about what each prospect is capable of doing—and not doing—she could do a better job of finding them meaningful work. And a better job of making sure they aren't doing the wrong things.

"I have a real world example of this that I encountered a couple weeks ago," she says. "We have a young gentleman who is high school age and he joined our Clean Team. He is happy. Our Clean Team is not just janitorial; they work at our dances. It is a lot of fun. He's doing a good job, and we are training him to be an usher. But he had a terrible seizure out of absolutely nowhere. We brought the medics in. He came back to work the next day, and he had another huge seizure. So I got the mother on the phone and I said, 'Is there something you want to tell me? Every once in a while he has seizures.' I dragged out of her that he has epilepsy. I said to her, 'Why wouldn't you tell me that he has epilepsy? I could've had him on the ladder or I could have had him up on a stage or I could have had him in a really dangerous position.' I still would've hired him; I have other people with epilepsy.

"We have to look back and kind of dissect why a mother would not tell. I guess it is that historically, people think employers just won't hire people with disabilities. I told the mother, 'Look, to me that would be child abuse. My son is type 1 diabetic and if I didn't tell any of his teachers or his coaches—that could have catastrophic results. That is a real world example—it signals that the whole system is crazy. If you know what somebody's disability is then really you can help accommodate him and you can make the adjustments."[8]

Moreover, Jensen doesn't think most disabled people mind talking about their disabilities. When a blind prospect started work at the theater, Jensen asked him—she admits somewhat awkwardly—whether he prefers the term "visually impaired." "He said, 'Val, that's offensive to me.' I said, 'I'm trying not to be offensive, tell me what should I say?' He said, 'Visually impaired would mean I have some sort of vision. I am completely blind, lights out. Don't bother calling me visually impaired or something like that. Call me blind because I am blind.' I said, 'Oh my God, isn't that rude?' He said, 'Why would that be rude? It is a fact of life. I am blind.' If more people had that kind of attitude we would be on such a more even playing field."[9]

Jensen's ideas for how to employ disabled workers are gaining traction. For starters, when the Prospector held a job fair prior to opening, more than three hundred applicants responded—all on a single day. Within months after the theater opened, hundreds more applied for jobs. "We get hundreds and hundreds of applications every month," she says. "It's heartbreaking, people are begging for the jobs. People are saying, 'You don't even have to pay me, I'll just come.' And we say, 'Look we can't do that.' It's sad, but it raises up a signal: All those applications are an indicator that we have a problem here."[10]

Moreover, she constantly receives inquiries from other advocates for the disabled asking for advice on starting their own movie theaters. She counsels them to think carefully about the idea before committing themselves. The Prospector was a good fit for Ridgefield, she says, because the town lacked a move theater. Jensen advises the advocates who contact her to look hard at their own communities, decide what their communities are lacking, and then move forward on their projects with an eye toward filling two needs: one need for the disabled people who need jobs, the other for the community which may be lacking a service. "Everybody has what they need in front of them, they just have to connect the dots in their own world,"[11] she says.

The Day after Graduation

Certainly, though, at this point the Prospector Theater is still a unique experiment in employing the disabled. Not every community has an advocate of the caliber of Jensen who saw a need and was able to raise $30 million and build a theater—all within three years. And so it appears that although the future of sheltered workshops might be cloudy, there may still be a need for job coaches and organizations like Opportunity Services.

Or maybe not. Gurney sees change, particularly in the corporate world. She points to McDonald's as one company that has accepted the idea that disabled people are a good fit for places in the organization. In fact, McDonald's has structured its job training with the disabled in mind. "McDonald's has targeted people with disabilities and they have a McJobs training program. They have made a corporate event out of this," she says. "In order for somebody with a disability to learn how to make a Big Mac they will provide puzzle pieces. They created a wooden puzzle with all those pieces to make a Big Mac."[12]

Even Gurney concedes that, under ideal circumstances, there wouldn't be a need for organizations like Opportunity Services. If the schools did their jobs, if companies seized the moment and structured their organizations with disabled employment in mind, if Congress made changes in the ADA and mandated more vocational training for the disabled, it would be possible for disabled people to be more prepared than they are now to enter the workforce, and the unemployment rate among the disabled would not be more than eleven times that of everyone else.

Paraphrasing Richard Luecking, the noted expert on transitioning students to jobs, Gurney says, "In a perfect world the day after your graduation is the same day as your first day on the job. In other words when you exit your public school program you have a job. A different culture picks up your support but it doesn't look any different to you if you are a person with a disability. There would be a seamless transition from school to work and we would all cooperate. That to me would be wonderful."[13]

NOTES

1. U.S. Equal Employment Opportunity Commission, "Titles I and V of the Americans With Disabilities Act of 1990 (ADA)," July 26, 1990. www.eeoc.gov/laws/statutes/ada.cfm.

2. Interview with the author, April 22, 2015.

3. Ibid.

4. Ibid.

5. Ibid.

6. Ibid.

7. Interview with the author, April 26, 2015.

8. Ibid.

9. Ibid.

10. Ibid.

11. Ibid.

12. Interview with the author, April 22, 2015.

13. Ibid.

11

Gender, Race, and the Business Case for Diversity

Matt L. Huffman

There is little doubt that ascriptive characteristics such as gender and race remain key axes of inequality in the U.S. labor market. Race and gender inequality are manifest in many ways including the segregation of workers across jobs, occupations, and workplaces (see Bygren & Kumlin, 2005; Charles & Grusky, 2004; Huffman & Cohen, 2004); restricted access to managerial and high-status jobs within firms (see Huffman, Cohen, & Pearlman, 2010; Presidential Glass Ceiling Commission, 1995); and the pay gap (see Blau & Kahn, 2004; Grodsky & Pager, 2001). Importantly, these dimensions of inequality are mutually reinforcing; for example, the gender wage gap is driven largely by women's concentration in lower-paying jobs (Petersen & Morgan, 1995). Questions about the specific mechanisms that undergird inequalities along these and other dimensions have fueled an enormous body of research spanning many disciplines. My purpose in this chapter is neither to review nor adjudicate between various perspectives on the sources—or extent—of race and gender inequality. Rather, I attend to the question of the potential benefits to more fully opening up the labor market to women and racial/ethnic minorities. This "opening up" can be broadly interpreted to mean—alone or in combination—the reduction of employment discrimination, the use of policies to increase labor force participation rates, programs to reduce work-family conflict, or other efforts to more fully utilize available labor pools. As such, the utility of this exercise does not depend on one's views about the sources of inequality. That is, it does not matter if one thinks that the gender wage gap, for example, is driven by discrimination on the part of employers or the fair and efficient operation of labor markets in conjunction with rational choices made by workers.

What are the benefits to opening up the labor market opportunities of women and other groups, and what are the mechanisms that might account for these benefits? To answer these closely related questions, I review empirical and theoretical work on the implications of organizational diversity, especially by gender and race. My focus assumes that many of the benefits of increased employment opportunities for women and other groups would accrue primarily through their contributions to for-profit companies, as this is the proximate arena in which their inclusion would generate measurable benefits. I note, however, that there are certainly other ways that one could dissect the question.

Workplace Diversity: More Than Just Buzzwords?

The 1990s saw a sharp rise in diversity rhetoric in organizational management (Edelman, Fuller, & Mara-Drita, 2001). For some, the diversity movement was an easy target, especially because there was little rigorous empirical research to back claims that promoting diversity was a worthy goal for anyone, let alone organizations. Additionally, and perhaps more troubling to some, the promotion of gender and racial diversity in employment was conflated with Affirmative Action, and worst of all, employment quotas. Thus, although widely accepted, views on organizational diversity run the gamut—from harmless but ineffective to an assault on the operation of efficient labor markets that ultimately hurt employers, and by extension, the economy.

Subsequently, scholars of varied disciplinary stripes begin seriously examining the effects of diversity at multiple levels; for example, in workgroups, on corporate boards, and in organizations' work forces more generally. Following Cox (1993) and others (for example, see Presidential Glass Ceiling Commission, 1995), advocates often take the tack of promoting the "business case," arguing that the increased diversity that flows from more fully opening employment opportunities to women and others "pays." That is, diversity positively affects companies' bottom line by broadening employee perspectives and offering increased resources for problem solving (Cox, 2001). Diverse groups, it is argued, exploit members' individual and distinct social networks for information and knowledge, which combined with diversity in members' knowledge, abilities, skills, and experiences makes them better problem solvers and decision makers (DiTomaso, Post, & Parks-Yancy, 2007; Jehn, Northcraft, & Neale, 1999). Findings reported by Chua (2011) also underscore the positive relationship between network cultural heterogeneity and creativity, which has implications for the functioning of a multicultural workforce. Relatedly, Phillips, Liljenquist, and Neale (2009) found an increased willingness among members of a majority group to critically evaluate task-relevant information and offer unique perspectives when there is more social diversity present compared to when there is not. Additionally, this relationship holds even when those who are "different" in the group do not offer their own opinion; it appears that the very presence of social diversity encourages people with varied viewpoints more willing to offer those perspectives. Owing to these and other mechanisms, it is argued that diversity leads to a more efficient and optimal use of available labor. Therefore, it is argued that increasing workplace diversity is simply good business.

But, are claims about the business case for diversity borne out by empirical research? What does the evidence suggest? The question remains somewhat elusive, as data limitations have to some extent stunted the development of a focused, coherent body of research testing the good-for-business perspective on organizational diversity. That said, the cumulative evidence in this area is solidifying in its support for the business case for organizational diversity. In what follows, I offer a brief overview of some work in this area; due to space limitations, the review is not exhaustive.

Two recent studies explore the link between organizational diversity and firm performance. In one study, Herring (2009) examined several outcome measures taken from approximately 500 for-profit businesses from the National Organizations Survey, a random sample of work establishments in the U.S. He found diversity (by race and gender) to be associated with increased sales revenue, more customers, greater market share, and greater relative profits. Notably, Herring's (2009) statistical models rule out likely alternative explanations; for example, perhaps larger firms are more diverse and also more profitable. The effects of diversity reported by Herring (2009) were net of firm size and other potentially confounding variables.

Similarly, findings from Nielson and Nielson (2013) support the business case argument. They analyzed longitudinal data from 146 firms and found that firm performance (measured by a firm's total return on assets) is positively associated with diversity among top management teams. They argued that group diversity leads to a heightened ability to solve complex tasks relative to more homogeneous groups. This provides a comparative advantage with respect to strategic decision making.

Other notable recent analyses have linked firm performance—variously measured—and the demographic diversity of the workforce. A series of studies by the nonprofit organization Catalyst also further supports the "diversity pays" perspective. These studies often focus on the effect of gender and racial diversity at the top of organizational hierarchies, such as in managerial positions or on corporate boards or other organizational leadership positions. In one analysis, Catalyst (2011) examined three measures of firms' financial performance: return on sales, return on invested capital, and return on equity (ROE). The findings suggest a strong positive relationship between women's presence on the companies' boards of directors and the three financial performance indicators. The findings of the 2011 Catalyst study mirror those reported in 2007 (see Catalyst, 2007). Although the Catalyst studies focus on the bivariate relationship between gender and racial representation on corporate boards and firm performance, while not considering other potential factors that could account for the relationship, their findings are nonetheless consistent with the business case for diversity.

My brief review of recent empirical work highlights some of the growing evidence demonstrating positive effects of racial and gender diversity in organizations across a range of measures and at different levels. As such, these findings suggest that opening up opportunities to women and other groups—either by easing work-family conflict, reducing artificial barriers to advancement, or by other means, is likely to have positive effects that will extend throughout the economy. To the extent that the "business case" for diversity is supported by this growing corpus of rigorous research, promoting fuller participation by women and other protected groups will have economy-wide benefits. Importantly, these studies examine the association between diversity and various outcome measures, so variation in diversity is taken for granted. But where does diversity come from? Of course, whether the commonly used policies and programs used by organizations to promote diversity—such as mentoring programs and diversity training—actually work to increase diversity is an empirical question, and we have less good evidence than many commonly assume. Employers, human resource professionals, attorneys, and others often assume that organizational diversity policies work as intended. What does the research say? Perhaps the best evidence on the effectiveness of these programs is found in Kalev, Dobbin, and Kelly (2006). Their findings suggest that some methods effectively increase diversity, while others do not. Therefore, we should not assume that commonly used methods used to promote diversity are effective, and we need much more research on what actually works and what does not.

Organizational Diversity: A Bed of Roses?

The relationship between the demographic composition of groups and various group-level processes is complicated, with heterogeneity having some well-documented negative effects. Recognizing this, Herring (2009:209) notes that organizational diversity may have dual outcomes, with some beneficial to companies and others simultaneously "costly to group functioning." Skerry (2002), for instance, points out that racial and ethnic diversity is linked with conflict, especially emotional conflict among coworkers. And, diverse work teams may be characterized by lower satisfaction among their members (Tsui, Egan, & O'Reilly, 1992) and heightened communication problems, even as they enjoy enhanced creativity and innovation and a broader range of contacts and information sources (DiTomaso, Post, & Parks-Yancy, 2007). It should be noted that it is entirely possible that, as Herring (2009:209) notes, diversity may be valuable to a company's bottom line even if changes in an organization's demographic composition make incumbent members uncomfortable or even unhappy. Of course, arguments about the bottom line hinge on effects on firm performance, competitive advantage, and efficiency. As such, findings regarding negative effects of diversity on other, non-bottom line outcomes, such as workers' distaste for working with nontraditional group members, do not undermine key findings about profits, returns on investments, and market position. Of course, the importance of the bottom line is frequently cited by employers to justify policies and practices that may be held in similarly low regard by their employees.

Conclusions

Labor market inequalities linked to gender and race continue to be a persistent feature of the U.S. economy. Regarding gender, compelling evidence suggests that progress toward gender equality stalled in the 1990s after several decades of marked improvement on many indicators (Blau & Kahn, 2004; Cohen, Huffman, & Knauer, 2009; Cotter, Hermsen, & Vanneman, 2004). One way to think about the ramifications of reducing inequality on major indicators, such as the underrepresentation of women on corporate boards or other high-status positions in organizations, is to consider what we know about the "business case" for diversity. That work makes a strong case for increasing the labor market opportunities of women and protected groups by underscoring that associated increases in organizational diversity can improve firms' performance on a host of outcomes. The positive economy-wide implications are clear by extension. Of course, increasing diversity is not just a matter of reducing bias on the part of employers. Indeed, other approaches, such as policies that ease work-family conflict, can also have positive effects. For example, work-family conflict has been linked to depression and marital dissatisfaction (Allen, Herst, Bruck, & Sutton, 2000). And, other work shows that boundary-spanning work demands (such as receiving work-related contact during nonworking hours) can have detrimental mental health consequences, especially among women (Glavin, Schieman, & Reid, 2011). It would be hard to argue that employers do not have an interest in having workers who are not depressed and are otherwise healthy. Thus, "opening up" employment opportunities for women and minority workers, broadly conceived, can be accomplished at many levels. It is clear that the associated increase in workplace diversity is good for individuals' careers, which are enhanced by the potential of upward mobility, new opportunities, and increased work-related benefits. However, these positive effects ripple outward, cascading from individuals to firms, and ultimately to the entire U.S. economy.

REFERENCES

Allen, T. D., Herst, D. E. L., Bruck, C. S., & Sutton, M. (2000). Consequences associated with work-to-family conflict: A review and agenda for future research. *Journal of Occupational Health Psychology*, 5: 278–308.

Blau, F., & Kahn, L. (2004). The U.S. gender pay gap in the 1990s: Slowing convergence. NBER Working Paper no. 10853, National Bureau of Economic Research, Cambridge, MA.

Bygren M., & Kumlin, J. (2005). Mechanisms of organizational sex segregation: Organizational characteristics and the sex of newly recruited employees. *Work and Occupations*, 32: 39–65.

Catalyst. (2011). *The bottom line: Corporate performance and women's representation on boards, 2004–2008.* Catalyst.

Catalyst. (2007). *The bottom line: Corporate performance and women's representation on boards, 2007.* Catalyst.

Charles, M., & Grusky, D. B. (2004). *Occupational ghettos: The worldwide segregation of women and men.* Stanford, CA: Stanford University Press.

Chua, R. Y. (2011). Innovating at the world's crossroads: How multicultural networks promote creativity. *Harvard Business School Working Paper 11–085.*

Cotter, D. A., Hermsen, J. M., & Vanneman, R. (2004). *Gender inequality at work.* New York: Russell Sage Foundation.

Cox, T. (2001). *Creating the multicultural organization: A strategy for capturing the power of diversity.* San Francisco, CA: Jossey-Bass.

Cox, T. (1993). *Cultural diversity in organizations: Theory, research, and practice.* San Francisco, CA: Berrett-Koehler.

DiTomaso, N., Post, C., & Parks-Yancy, R. (2007). Workforce diversity and inequality: Power, status, and numbers. *Annual Review of Sociology, 33:* 473–501.

Edelman, L., Fuller, S. R., & Mara-Drita, I. (2001). Diversity rhetoric and the managerialization of law. *American Journal of Sociology,* 106: 1589–1641.

Glavin, P., Schieman, S., & Reid, S. (2011). Boundary-spanning work demands and their consequences for guilt and psychological distress. *Journal of Health and Social Behavior,* 52: 43–57.

Grodsky, E., & Pager, D. (2001). The structure of disadvantage: Individual and occupational sources of the black-white wage gap. *American Sociological Review,* 66: 542–567.

Herring, C. (2009). Does diversity pay? Race, gender, and the business case for diversity. *American Sociological Review,* 74: 208–224.

Huffman, M. L., & Cohen, P. N. (2004). Racial wage inequality: Job segregation and devaluation across U.S. labor markets. *American Journal of Sociology,* 109: 902–936.

Huffman, M. L., Cohen, P. N., & Pearlman, J. (2010). Engendering change: Organizational dynamics and workplace gender desegregation. *Administrative Science Quarterly,* 55: 255–277.

Jehn, K. A., Northcraft, G. B., & Neale, M. A. (1999). Why differences make a difference: A field study of diversity, conflict and performance in workgroups. *Administrative Science Quarterly,* 44: 741–763.

Kalev, A., Dobbin, F., & Kelly, E. (2006). Best practices or best guesses? Assessing the efficacy of corporate affirmative action and diversity policies. *American Sociological Review,* 71: 589–617.

Nielsen, B. B., & Nielsen, S. (2013). Top management team nationality diversity and firm performance: A multilevel study. *Strategic Management Journal,* 34: 373–382.

Petersen, T., & Morgan, L. A. (1995). Separate and unequal: Occupation-establishment segregation and the gender wage gap. *American Journal of Sociology,* 101: 329–365.

Phillips, K. W., Liljenquist, K. A., & Neale, M.A. (2009). Is the pain worth the gain? Advantages and liabilities of agreeing with socially distinct newcomers. *Personality and Social Psychology Bulletin,* 35: 336–350.

Presidential Glass Ceiling Commission. (1995). *A solid investment: Making full use of our nations' human capital.* Washington, DC.

Skerry, P. (2002). Beyond sushiology: Does diversity work? *Brookings Review,* 20: 20–23.

Tsui, A. S., Egan T. D., & O'Reilly, C. A. (1992). Being different: Relational demography and organizational attachment. *Administrative Science Quarterly,* 37: 549–579.

Peer Counseling, Relationships, and Activism: Engaging Young People to Prevent Teen Pregnancy

12

Hal Marcovitz

For most African American teenagers living in the Bronx, New York City's Stop-and-Frisk program has been, understandably, invasive, racist, and a violation of their civil rights. To Estelle Raboni, Stop-and-Frisk offered an opportunity for young people in the Bronx to become activists. Her aim was to encourage young people to organize themselves, speak with a common voice, reach out to others, and find ways to feel as though they had achieved a set of goals.

"One of the reasons they [protested against Stop-and-Frisk] is that a young person had been shot and killed approximately one block away from their school," says Raboni. "They said as African American kids they were constantly being harassed by police on their way to school and they felt, given the recent murder of this young man...they really wanted to do something around this issue.

"They invited the New York City Civil Liberties Union in to talk about Stop-and-Frisk and what their rights are as young people. [The students helped provide] education among their peers in their schools, and they also did a petition drive and presented it to their local city council member who represented their district."[1]

It should be pointed out here that Raboni heads the Bronx-based program Changing the Odds, which is not primarily concerned with ensuring that the civil rights of African American teenagers are protected. Rather, the goal for Changing the Odds is to make sure teenage girls do not get pregnant.

More Responsive Citizens

So what does organizing a petition drive against an unpopular city ordinance have to do with making sure teenagers know the dangers of unprotected sex? In recent years, adolescent pregnancy experts like Raboni have embraced a new concept in the prevention of teen pregnancy. They have learned that it is no longer good enough for a teacher to stand in front of a group of young people and tell them to be abstinent, or teach them about birth control, or the dangers of sexually-transmitted diseases, or the limited opportunities in life they can expect as teenage parents. They have learned that teenagers are at their best, and most receptive to positive ideas, when they are engaged, involved, and part of the learning process.

And so organizing a petition drive against Stop-and-Frisk helped the young people enrolled in Changing the Odds learn how to be better and more responsive citizens. It gave them an opportunity to feel a part of their community and—more importantly—to act maturely and responsibly. And by becoming more mature and more responsible as they work together in a community service project, it is very likely that young people will treat sex the same way: With maturity and responsibility. "The community service part is one of the most attractive parts of the program," says Raboni. "We don't really pitch the program as a social work type of program...we don't market it like, 'This is going to save you.' This is just an after-school program of community service and you get to talk about a bunch of different things—things that you wouldn't normally talk about at school."[2]

Each Changing the Odds participant is required to provide twenty hours of community service a year, although Raboni says it is not unusual for the teens to exceed that number. Here are some other community service projects in which Changing the Odds members have participated: They have raised money for animal shelters, raised money to buy food for people in need, and conducted a toy drive. "They collected toys that had been gently used, cleaned them up, wrapped them up, and delivered them to a homeless shelter where there was a very large population of homeless children," says Raboni. "They had a Christmas party for them."[3]

Does it work? From a statistical point of view, it is too early to tell. The community service program at Changing the Odds was established in 2011 and Raboni says the statisticians want to see a few more years of data before they can proclaim that, yes, getting teenagers involved in community service is directly linked to a decline in the teen birth rate. However, there are some early indications that, overall, the tactics employed by Changing the Odds are having the desired effect.

Relating to Teens

Changing the Odds is a program sponsored by the Morris Heights Health Center in the Bronx. The students who participate meet after school with an adult facilitator who leads discussions on relationships, values, decision-making skills, and sexual health. There is a lot of give-and-take in the discussions, and facilitators are selected for their communications skills and how they relate to the teens. In other words, Raboni learned early on that some guy wearing a white shirt and a tightly-knotted polka dot tie would probably have some communication hurdles to overcome if he expected to reach the young people sitting before him. "Ideally, I like to look for people who grew up in the Bronx who conceivably graduated from a Bronx high school or a Bronx middle school who have similar backgrounds," says Raboni. "Some of our facilitators are African American or Latino and it's helpful to have people speak similar languages and have similar experiences to demonstrate to young people that yes, it is possible to complete high school and finish college....

"There is also a certain social aspect that a facilitator should have.... We really have a mix of people. The most important aspect is what kind of effect does that person have when they walk into a room full of young people? Are they judgmental? Or do they come into it really enjoying young people and wanting to work with young people and that's really the most important factor."[4]

More than seven hundred Bronx teenagers at a dozen high schools are enrolled in Changing the Odds. At all but one of the schools, Changing the Odds members have higher attendance rates than students who are not a part of the program. Also, 65 percent of Changing the Odds students report that after three years in the program they are more likely to use birth control than they were before they joined.

The Second Decade

You probably can't find a community more unlike the Bronx than Gaston County, North Carolina. The county is far from rural—more than 200,000 people do live in Gaston County, and most live in the county seat, Gastonia. Gaston County can be found in the southern Piedmont. Standing on West Franklin Boulevard in Gastonia, you can see the type of hills and greenery that are unknown on East Tremont Avenue in the Bronx.

But Gastonia and the Bronx may not be as different as they seem. Gaston County has a high percentage of low-income families—the type of families in which teenage girls are considered at a high risk for pregnancy. And regardless of their race or their family's income level or their housing situations, Sally Swanson says teenagers in Gaston County—and everywhere else for that matter—have the same thing in common: They are in the second decade of life. "It's a particular decade—the second decade—and that's the way we like to talk about it for educational and for clinical services," she says. "It's a pretty rapidly changing time and what is appropriate for an eleven-year-old is not appropriate for a thirteen-year-old and is not appropriate for a fifteen-year-old and is not appropriate for seventeen-year-old. You really have to be responsive to those changing needs in the second decade."[5]

Like Raboni, Swanson heads a teen pregnancy prevention program. Sponsored by the Adolescent Pregnancy Prevention Campaign of North Carolina, Swanson heads Gaston Youth Connected, which serves more than eight hundred young people in Gaston County. And as in the Bronx, the philosophy in Gastonia is one of engagement: Nobody preaches to young people at the program's headquarters. Discussions are give-and-take and young people are made to feel engaged.

Indeed, young people are so engaged at Gaston Youth Connected that they helped design the place. The headquarters has a clinical function, but not just for pregnancy testing: Young people can receive other types of medical services there, such as physicals for their school sports teams. But administrators didn't want the clinic to look like, well, a clinic. So they invited the teens to participate in the design—to give certain rooms a teen-friendly atmosphere. And so in the rooms set aside for teen programs, the furniture is colorful and funky and the art work on the walls tends toward the surreal.

"It's a demarcated area in the main health center designed with the help of teens," says Swanson. "They came in and gave their opinions on what it should look like so that it would actually have the feel of a place that is designed for adults but trying to fit what teens might look for. The only people who are in there are teens and the people who serve them and they will serve anybody from twelve to nineteen in there. It's not just for reproductive health; it's for an age group."[6] Moreover, in the clinical portion of the center there are separate waiting rooms for teens and their parents. Swanson says her group has concluded that when a young person needs to see a doctor—whether it is for a pregnancy test or any other procedure—teens are much more comfortable if they can be with people their own ages.

Peer Counseling

Gaston Youth Connected reaches out to young people in other ways—ways which are particularly effective when it comes to, well, communicating the way teenagers like to communicate. Part of the wider Adolescent Pregnancy Prevention Campaign of North Carolina program is the Birds & Bees Text Line in which young people can text their questions about sex to staff members who answer them truthfully, frankly, and anonymously. Some sample questions:

> *"If you take a shower before you have sex, are you less likely to get pregnant?"*
> *"Does a normal penis have wrinkles?"*
> *"If my BF doesn't like me to be loud during sex but I can't help it, what am I supposed to do?"*
> *"Why do guys think it's cool to sleep with a girl and tell their friends?"*[7]

Actually, Swanson says, teenagers who ask specific questions about sex are in the minority. Most young people, she says, ask knotty questions about relationships. Gaston Youth Connected also supports a Facebook page where teens can post questions and comments, and the Adolescent Pregnancy Prevention Campaign of North Carolina has established a youth-friendly website, The Playbook (teenplaybook.org), that provides answers to questions in ways in which teens can relate. For example, here is how The Playbook describes male condoms. (Keep in mind this description may have been prompted by an Adolescent Pregnancy Prevention Campaign study indicating that just one in four teenagers knows how to use a condom).

> Male condoms are one of the most popular forms of birth control out there. They slip over a guy's penis to prevent pregnancy and lower the risk of STIs by keeping the guy's sperm inside the condom and out of the girl's vagina. There are hundreds of shapes and sizes to choose from, with lube and without.
>
> Effectiveness: 98 percent when used correctly, no side effects (unless you are allergic to latex). Cost is about $1 per condom but free condoms are available at health centers. They can be bought at grocery stores and drug stores. Other notes: You MUST use a condom every time you have sex.[8]

The study contained no similar statistics about oral contraceptives, although it did cite one participant's assertion that she doesn't use the pill because it would make her gain weight. Here is how The Playbook explains oral contraception:

> "The pill" is a pill (how's that for stating the obvious). Some people call it "oral contraception." You take it once a day, at the same time every day. There are lots of different kinds of pills on the market, and new ones come out all the time. They all work by releasing hormones that keep your ovaries from releasing eggs. The hormones also thicken your cervical mucus, which helps block sperm from getting to the egg in the first place.
>
> Average cost, up to about $90 a month. Side effects are sore breasts, nausea, spotting, and a decreased sex drive. Where to get them: You gotta get a prescription. Effectiveness: The pill's really effective when taken perfectly, but most don't take if perfectly. Frequency: You gotta take it at the same time everyday.[9]

Abstinence Skills

As with Changing the Odds, there is a community service element to Swanson's program. In this case, though, Gaston Youth Connected does aim squarely at prevention of teen pregnancy. Some of the teen participants are selected to serve on the Teen Action Council where they work as peer counselors. They are given stipends that, basically, pay them to give out good advice.

For example, Swanson says, counselors in her program know very well that boys like to talk among themselves about sex—that's just what boys do. It is the job, then, of the young peer counselor to be the positive voice in the conversation—to say the right things and give good counsel to his friends. "They are there to intervene when something is wrong," says Swanson. "They have even had to do it with teachers if there is something that is not quite right—there have been episodes when they have had to correct teachers. We encourage that—to correct it when it is happening. Why let it go on? The [peer counselors] are very well-trained in reproductive health and sexual health."[10]

There are other components to Swanson's program. There are adult facilitators who lead discussions on sex education that are all inclusive—they talk about everything from birth control to abstinence. And when it comes to talking about abstinence—and make no mistake, abstinence is still taught as the best way to avoid teen pregnancies—Gaston Youth Connected applies a strategy of engagement. According to Swanson, it is simply not good enough to advise young people to be abstinent—they have to be trained in what can only be called abstinence skills.

For girls, that might include strategies about how to tell their boyfriends they are not ready to go all the way. (And, Swanson is quick to add, the adult facilitators are also finding that many boys need to employ similar strategies when their girlfriends insist on going further than they may be willing.) Boys must also be provided with strategies on how to conduct themselves among their girlfriends. A big part of the message, she says, is that sex is really an adult activity and most adults treat sex with an attitude of respect. Says Swanson: "Most of the programs deal with helping young people how to decide. Role-playing can be a part of it: You ask young people what they want in their lives and what would get in the way of that. This skill-building piece enables them to practice having an alternative—like if something gets a little too heated for you and you need to get out of the situation how would you do that? Do you have a conversation? Do you just say no?"[11]

But young people are similar to adults in that their relationships are important to them. Boys do care about the girls they are dating, and the girls care about the boys. They want to please each other—and they don't want to hurt each other. "People are in relationships that they care about," she says. "We sometimes slight teenage relationships, like they are not real. Teens have very real feelings. They are often in relationships they care a lot about and hopefully they are healthy relationships.

"So we may tell them, 'Here is how you say, in a caring way, you are important to me and I'm not just saying no, go fly a kite, but here is what I want for myself and here is what I want from you and this is why I am waiting.' We hope they do something that shows care for the relationship. That to me strikes home and makes much more of an impression on a young person than just saying no. They are real people and they have real relationships and they care deeply about them. They are respecting [their relationships] but are also learning there are some good choices they can weave into them. So we practice that. It may be role-playing where you get them to pretend they are in a situation they don't want to be in. You may get them to write down goals they have for themselves, write down their own boundaries or limits they want to go by. Things like that would be considered skill-building."[12]

Healthy Choices

Gaston Youth Connected has collected some statistics indicating that its philosophy is effective. Over the past several years—due, Swanson insists, to the federal government's acknowledgment that abstinence-only programs don't generally work—the national teen pregnancy rate has dropped. In 2007, the national teen pregnancy rate was about 40 per 1,000 girls; in 2012 the rate dropped to about 29 per 1,000 girls. North Carolina lags behind the national average, with about 60 per 1,000 girls in 2007 and about 40 per 1,000 girls in 2012. Gaston County lags behind the North Carolina average, but it is making progress. The county's 2007 teen pregnancy rate was about 80 per 1,000 girls, but in 2012 the rate was recorded at about 43 per 1,000 girls. Therefore, it would appear that programs like Swanson's are helping young people in Gaston County avoid pregnancies.

Says Swanson, "For me I'm very driven by the notion of using what works I think you have to provide accurate education and it's no surprise that if you replicate programs that increase knowledge and change behavior—healthy choices—you are going to do better. That's our premise. I come from a human rights framework; I think it is unconscionable not to give kids information that they clearly need as they develop through adolescence. They are developing physically, intellectually and sexually during that second decade.

"I think it's a human rights issue. I think many people would feel that way so I think you should provide that information but there is also evidence that it actually works. There is a corollary between offering better and more complete education and having better choices made. People are making better choices because of it."[13]

NOTES

1. Interview with the author, July 22, 2014.
2. Ibid.
3. Ibid.
4. Ibid.
5. Interview with the author, July 29, 2014.
6. Ibid.
7. Jan Hoffman, *New York Times*, "When the Cellphone Teaches Sex Education," May 1, 2009, www.nytimes.com/2009/05/03/fashion/03sexed.html?pagewanted=all&_r=0. Accessed July 30, 2014.
8. Adolescent Pregnancy Prevention Campaign of North Carolina, The Playook, www.teenplaybook.org. Accessed July 30, 2014.
9. Ibid.
10. Interview with the author, July 29, 2014.
11. Ibid.
12. Ibid.
13. Ibid.

13 The Benefits of Declining Teenage Childbearing

Robert D. Plotnick

Policy makers and the public have long considered teen childbearing to be an important social problem. There are at least four reasons for their concern. First, the time required and the financial and emotional demands of raising young children may create adverse consequences for teenage parents such as obtaining less schooling and work experience, and, consequently having lower earnings and greater poverty. Other possible consequences may include greater marital instability and higher lifetime fertility. Second, children of teenage parents may suffer consequences such as poorer health, impaired cognitive and behavioral development, higher likelihood of maltreatment, early sexual activity and parenthood, and longer term adverse effects on educational attainment, earnings, crime, and marriage. Third, government spends billions of dollars on health care, income support, and other services for teenage families and collects fewer taxes to the extent that teenage parents and their children have lower earnings. Last, because for many years a high proportion of teen births have been to unmarried parents, there are moral concerns among many Americans and policy makers.

If these concerns are well founded, recent decades have brought very good news. The teen birth rate in the United States has fallen dramatically, as shown in the graph. In 1991, the birth rate was 61.8 (births/1,000 teenage women).[1] By 2013 it was 26.6—a remarkable decline of 58 percent, reflecting major changes in teenage sexual behavior. The absolute number of teen births similarly plummeted from 520,000 to 275,000 (47 percent), even as the number of female teens *increased* by about 2 million, or 23 percent.

Every state experienced a significant decline though naturally there was considerable cross-state variation. In 40 states the rate fell between 40 and 59 percent. In four (CA, CT, MA, and NJ) and Washington, DC, the rate fell 60 percent or more. In six (KS, MT, NE, SD, WV, and WY), it fell between 24 and 38 percent.

The decline in teen childbearing occurred for both unmarried teens, whose birth rate fell 40 percent (from 44.6 to 26.7) and married teens, whose rate fell fully 66 percent (from 410.2 to 137.8). It declined for all major racial and ethnic groups—53 percent for non-Hispanic whites, 63 percent for non-Hispanic blacks, 56 percent for Hispanics, 64 percent for Asians/ Pacific Islanders, and 59 percent for Native Americans.

If there was one off-note, it was that the share of teen births to unmarried women rose from 69 to 89 percent over the same period. This increase happened because the decline in births to married teens was faster than that for unmarried teens. The absolute number of births to unmarried women fell 32 percent.

This chapter examines the consequences for American society of this welcome demographic change. It addresses three questions that reflect the concerns discussed earlier:

- What social and economic outcomes are better for persons who avoid teenage parenthood?
- How much better off are children of non-teenage parents compared to children of teenage parents?
- What are the financial benefits of the improved social and economic outcomes attributable to less teenage childbearing?

The analysis leads to the conclusion that the financial benefits are remarkably large—an average of more than $80,000 for each fewer birth.

What social and economic outcomes are better for persons who avoid teenage parenthood?

The simple facts are clear. Teenage mothers have worse social and economic outcomes than women who delay parenthood. They are more likely to drop out of high school, remain unmarried, earn less, be overweight or obese, be poor, and receive cash and in-kind government assistance. While less information on teenage fathers is available, it suggests that they similarly fare worse than other men: having less schooling, lower long term employment and earnings, greater poverty, and lower odds of later marriage.

But simple comparisons of teenage and older parents can be misleading because the two groups differ in important characteristics that also affect future outcomes. For example, teenage mothers are more likely to have been raised in low income families, and low income itself is associated with lower education and earnings and greater chances of relying on government assistance. Young women strongly intending to graduate from college are likely to be more committed to avoiding pregnancy. So, to properly understand the adverse consequences of teenage parenthood, we need to adjust as fully as possible for the many ways in which teenage parents differ from teenagers who delay parenthood. Doing so yields more accurate estimates of the *causal* effects of teenage childbearing on later outcomes, and hence, of the benefits of having less of it.

Intuition and common sense suggest to most people that the financial and time pressures on teenage parents greatly compromise their future prospects. A balanced reading of the best evidence, which gives greater weight to studies of teens who became parents in the 1990s, when teen births started their rapid decline and a much higher proportion of them were to unmarried mothers, indeed finds important adverse impacts.[2] This means that the decline in teenage childbearing has large benefits. At the same time, these studies do not support the popular perception that teenage childbearing has devastating impacts.

Teenage *motherhood* has important negative impacts on education. It reduces the likelihood of earning a high school diploma by about eight percentage points, and of obtaining postsecondary education by 19 percentage points. Some studies find that teen mothers are more likely to complete the GED; others do not. The adverse impact on total years of schooling appears to be no more than one year.[3]

Evidence about teen motherhood's effects on labor market and financial outcomes is ambiguous. One study (Fletcher and Wolfe 2012) based on data from the 1990s reports large negative impacts on earnings and family income. So does one study using earlier data (Hoffman 2008). The other two studies using earlier data do not. On net, we assess this evidence as supportive of a negative impact. Two studies examine work hours. One (Ashcraft et al. 2013) finds that teenage mothers work about 17 percent fewer hours as adults while the other (Hotz et al. 2005) finds they work 21 percent more. The studies all agree that teen childbearing does not lead to greater use of welfare.

We have less information about teenage motherhood's effects on marriage and later fertility. Two studies using earlier data find no impact on later marriage or divorce. One finds that teenage mothers have more total children; the other finds no relationship. Unfortunately, findings for more recent cohorts of teenage mothers are lacking.

While early fertility may affect a woman's health, only one study has examined this issue. It reports a strong negative relationship between teenage motherhood and adult weight. Other things being equal, teen mothers are 7 percentage points more likely to be overweight (35 versus 27 percent) and 12 percentage points more likely to be obese (42 versus 30 percent).[4]

Teenage *fatherhood's* effects have been examined in only two high quality analyses. One (Fletcher and Wolfe, 2012) focuses on the short-term effects of becoming a teenage father in the 1990s and reports mixed results. The serious negative effects are that teenage fathers are less likely to graduate from high school and attain three-quarters of a year less schooling. On the positive side, they are more likely to earn a GED and to be married. They are more likely to have ever cohabited and to be in the military. Teenage fatherhood shows no significant relationship with short term employment, earnings and total income.

The longer term adverse effects of teenage fatherhood may be larger (Dariotis et al. 2011). By age 37, men who were teenage married fathers had 1.6 years fewer years of schooling and $7,000 lower annual earnings compared to married men who postponed fatherhood until their mid to late 20s.[5]

What are the benefits of not being born to a teenage parent?

Here again, the simple facts are clear. Children born to teenage women have worse outcomes than children of women who delay parenthood. They are more likely to have behavior problems, suffer maltreatment and be placed in foster care, attain less education, initiate sex before age 16, become teenage parents themselves, remain unmarried, have worse health, be incarcerated, be poor, and receive government assistance.

And here again, simple comparisons between children of teenage mothers and other children can be misleading because the two groups differ in important characteristics that also affect future outcomes. For example, teenage parents are more likely to have low incomes, and there is compelling evidence that being raised in a low income family with parents of any age leads to lower education and earnings, earlier childbearing, and greater reliance on government assistance. Hence, estimates that adjust as fully as possible for differences in children's family background provide the most persuasive evidence of the *causal* impact of being born to a teenage mother.

The study with the best evidence (Levine et al. 2007) uses two advanced techniques to examine diverse outcomes for children under age 14 and for adolescents and young adults. The findings are mixed. With one technique, being born to a teenage mother is strongly related to the likelihood of repeating a grade in elementary school, weakly related to truancy and surprisingly, related to a lower likelihood of using marijuana. The other technique finds no such relationships. Neither finds that having a teenage mother is related to the likelihood of early sexual activity or fighting. Counter to conventional wisdom, neither technique shows significant relationships with academic test scores, a result consistent with earlier research that used advanced methods.

Levine et al. (2007) does not examine other important outcomes such as high school completion, post-secondary education, adult earnings, early childbearing, marriage, and criminal activity. Future research may uncover adverse impacts of being born to a teenage mother for these or other outcomes. Still, the strongest current evidence suggests skepticism about claims that children born to teenagers suffer serious disadvantages *because* their mothers are young.[6] Yes, children of teenage mothers are disadvantaged, but it appears the reason is mainly because their mothers are disadvantaged, not because their mothers are young.

Financial Benefits of Declining Teenage Childbearing

In 2013 there were 257,000 (47 percent) fewer births to teenage women than in 1991. Since about three percent of births are multiple, the number of teenage mothers declined by 249,000. The decline in teenage fathers was about 125,000, because many of the partners of teenage mothers were age

20 or older. Rough but plausible back-of-the-envelope calculations suggest that the annual financial benefits of less teenage childbearing are substantial. These benefits accrue both to the teenagers who avoid parenthood and to taxpayers who finance the government costs incurred by teenage births.

Consider first the benefits of the increase in education attributable to less teenage parenthood. Based on evidence discussed above, suppose that young women and men who avoided parenthood respectively obtained 0.5 and 0.75 more years of schooling. Census Bureau estimates of earnings for different levels of education (Julian and Kominski 2011) suggest that this extra schooling would increase total earnings over the work-life by $23,700 for each woman and $69,800 (in 2013 dollars) for each man. Multiplying the increases by the number of women and men who avoided teenage parenthood projects to $14.63 billion of higher lifetime earnings for just this one year of reduced teen childbearing. The teenagers enjoy higher private incomes as adults and society benefits from increased tax revenues.

Many teenage mothers rely on Medicaid and other government programs to pay the costs of their births and health care for their infants. Following birth, they and their children also receive benefits from other public programs such as the Earned Income Tax Credit, Temporary Assistance for Needy Families (TANF), Supplemental Nutrition Assistance Program (food stamps), SCHIP, subsidized child care, and WIC. A second large benefit of less teen childbearing is that public agencies do not have to pay these costs for teenagers who avoid parenthood.

The avoided costs are substantial. A rigorous study estimated that the public costs for a teenage mother's prenatal care, delivery and postpartum care and one year of infant medical care are $4,670 (in 2013 dollars). This estimate implies public savings of $1.20 billion from 257,000 fewer teenage births. Including five years of benefits from other public programs that assist young children increases the cost per birth to $22,190 and overall savings to fully $5.70 billion.[7]

Together, the benefits to teens and public agencies from one fewer teenage birth sum to $80,900. The total benefits from the decline in childbearing in 2013 relative to 1991 accrue to fully $20.33 billion. Possible savings in medical costs from any decline in obesity attributable to fewer teen births would slightly increase this figure.

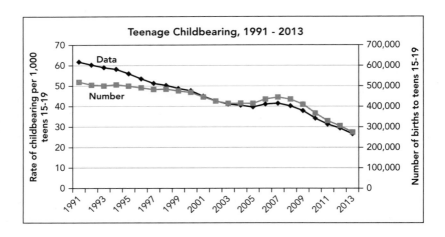

It is important to note one caveat. The estimates reflect the average cost savings of avoiding a teen birth. But it is likely that teens who did not become parents in 2013 compared to 1991 were relatively advantaged among the teens at high risk of parenthood. For such teenagers becoming a parent may have had below average adverse impacts, so the benefits from them avoiding parenthood would correspondingly have been below average. If this is the case, the $21.16 billion estimate is too high. We do not have nearly enough information to assess the extent of overstatement. Still, even if it is double the real amount, the benefits from reduced childbearing in 2013 would have been a substantial $10.6 billion.

Conclusion

The dramatic decline in teenage childbearing over the past quarter century is a welcome development. Because teenagers who become parents face diminished life chances, the decline has meant important benefits to the thousands of young persons who would have become parents in the past. It has also produced large savings for the public agencies that would have provided health care, income support and other programs to teenage parents and their children. Further declines in teen childbearing will bring further dividends to the young women and men who avoid parenthood and to society at large.

References

Ashcraft, A., I. Fernández-Val, and K. Lang. 2013. "The consequences of teenage childbearing: Consistent estimates when abortion makes miscarriage non-random," *Economic Journal* 123 (September), 875–905.

Chang, T., H. Choi, C. Richardson, and M. Davis. 2013. "Implications of teen birth for overweight and obesity in adulthood," *American Journal of Obstetrics & Gynecology* 209 (2) 110.e–110e7.

Dariotis, J., J. Pleck, N. Astone and F. Sonenstein. 2011. "Pathways of early fatherhood, marriage, and employment: A latent class growth analysis," *Demography* 48(2), 593–624.

Fletcher, J. and B. Wolfe. 2009. "Education and labor market consequences of teenage childbearing: Evidence using the timing of pregnancy outcomes and community fixed effects," *Journal of Human Resources* 44(2), 303–325.

Fletcher, J. and B. Wolfe. 2012. "The effects of teenage fatherhood on young adult outcomes," *Economic Inquiry* 50(1), 182–201.

Hoffman, S. 2008. "Updated estimates of the consequences of teen childbearing for single mothers," Pp. 74–118 in Hoffman, S. and R. Maynard (Eds.) *Kids Having Kids: Economic Costs and Social Consequences of Teen Pregnancy*. Washington DC: The Urban Institute press.

Hotz, V.J., S. McElroy and S. Sanders. 2005. "Teenage childbearing and its life cycle consequences: Exploiting a natural experiment," *Journal of Human Resources* 40(3), 673–715.

Julian, T. and R. Kominski. 2011. "Education and synthetic work-life earnings estimates," *American Community Survey Reports*, ACS–14. Washington, DC: U.S. Census Bureau

Kane, J., S. Morgan, K. Harris and D. Guilkey. 2013. "The educational consequences of teen childbearing," *Demography* 50(6), 2129–2150.

Levine, J., C. Emery and H. Pollack. 2007. "The well-being of children born to teen mothers," *Journal of Marriage and Family* 69(February), 105–122.

Monea, E. and A. Thomas. 2011. "The public cost of pregnancy," Brookings Working Paper, Center on Children and Families, The Brookings Institution, March.

Ventura, S., M. B. Hamilton, and T. Mathews. 2014. "National and state patterns of teen births in the United States, 1940–2013," National Center for Health Statistics, National Vital Statistics Reports 63(4, August 20).

Notes

1. This is the rate for women age 15–19. I ignore births to girls younger than 15 because they are very infrequent (a birth rate of 0.3 in 2013) and account for merely 1.1 percent of all births to women under age 20 in 2013. Data are from Ventura et al. (2014).

2. Most of the findings for women are based on the 5 studies that use the best empirical methods: Hotz et al. (2005), Hoffman (2008), Fletcher and Wolfe (2009), Ashcraft et al. (2013) and Kane et al. (2013). Many earlier studies that reported worse consequences did not adjust for preexisting differences between parents and nonparents as well as these studies. Teen births in the studies by Fletcher and Wolfe and Kane et al. occurred

in the 1990s, when about 75 percent were non-marital. Teen births in the other three studies occurred in the 1970s and 1980s, when nonmarital births accounted for about 47 percent. Also, labor market conditions and welfare policy in the 1990s had changed substantially from the 1970s and 1980s. Hence, findings from those two studies merit greater weight.

3. The high school impact is from Fletcher and Wolfe (2009). Hoffman (2008) reports a larger effect while the other two studies of this outcome find no effect. The postsecondary impact is from Hoffman (2008), the only study to examine this outcome. Kane et al. (2013) finds negative impacts of a teen birth on years of schooling. Three other studies examine this variable and report no significant impact.

4. Chang et al. (2013) uses weaker methods and fewer controls than the other studies so the impacts are very likely overstated.

5. The study does not report findings for teenage unmarried fathers. It did not adjust for preexisting differences between fathers and non-fathers as well as Fletcher and Wolfe (2012) and the best studies of teen mothers, so the impacts are probably overstated.

6. Earlier research using simpler methods found adverse effects for a variety of outcomes, including worse cognitive development, lower educational attainment, increased risk of problem behavior, maltreatment, and placement in foster care, and greater incarceration. Such findings have helped shape the perception that being born to a teen mother puts a child at severe disadvantage, but their validity is highly questionable.

7. See Monea and Thomas (2011) for details. The estimates assume that 29% of avoided teenage births would never have occurred and 71% would have been delayed until the woman was in her early to mid-20s. The estimates of costs per birth are for women below 200 percent of the federal poverty line, which overstates public costs since some teenage mothers live in families with higher incomes. The estimates ignore out-of-pocket medical expenses, which understates private costs. On net, since about 75% of teen births have recently been covered by Medicaid, the estimates probably are slightly inflated.

Listening to Termites: Businesses Move to Reduce Their Carbon Footprint

14

Hal Marcovitz

What's not to like about Ben & Jerry's? Anybody who has sampled the company's nomenclature-rich ice cream flavors, such as Hazed & Confused or Karamel Sutra or Wayne'Swirled or Boom Chocolatta, usually goes back for more.

As an American corporation, Ben & Jerry's is well-known for its progressive agenda. The company, headquartered in Vermont, actively pursues Fair Trade in procuring its ingredients. Ben & Jerry's has celebrated marriage equality by changing the name of its chocolate chip cookie dough-flavored ice cream to "I Dough, I Dough." And the company has protested a U.S. Senate vote opening the Arctic National Wildlife Refuge to oil exploration by delivering a 900-pound Baked Alaska to the Capitol steps.

But Ben & Jerry's has also looked at itself and often hasn't liked what it has learned. Each year, the company produces a Life Cycle Analysis, taking a hard look at its business practices. Among the areas examined in the annual study are diversity, volunteerism, whether the company pays living wages to its employees, and corporate support for nonprofit organizations. One major area of study in the LCA is the company's environmental impact. (To produce the 2014 environmental report, Ben & Jerry's retained CoClear, a New York consulting firm that looked at such factors as greenhouse gas emissions, use of landfills, and so on.)

The 2014 report examined the company's carbon footprint, and found this interesting fact:

> The LCA showed that 41 percent of Ben & Jerry's total carbon footprint is traceable back to the cows that create the common ingredient in every Ben & Jerry's flavor—cream. When it comes to climate change, the methane from the front and back ends of cows is approximately 21 times more potent than CO2, making manure management a major opportunity for improvement. The nitrous oxide associated with fertilizers doesn't appear in the same quantities as methane, but clocking in at 300 times more potent than CO2, this gas is another area where we need to help farmers reduce their use.[1]

A Few Words about Manure

A few words here about manure and how it is managed. Big cattle farms store manure (and urine, too) in manure lagoons. If it sounds like a messy business, well, it is. After sitting for months in the lagoons, the water evaporates which leaves the, uhh, solid matter behind. The solids are used as fertilizer on crops.

It's not quite a perfect system. The New York environmental advocacy group GRACE Communications Foundation has studied manure lagoons, and concluded that American dairy cows produce much more manure than is needed to fertilize American farm fields. The group cites U.S. Agriculture Department statistics finding that cows generate 335 million tons of "dry" manure a year, roughly a third of the total residential and commercial output of municipal waste. Indeed, about 2,500 cows produce the same amount of waste as a city of some 400,000 people. GRACE Communications cited studies that American dairy cows (and hogs, too) produce much more manure than is needed for fertilizer. The rest is piling up, so to speak, but it is also leaking out of the lagoons into streams and groundwater and other places, too.

But the real mess can be found not in the lagoons, but in the air above the lagoons. As Ben & Jerry's acknowledged, the gasses that are emitted by the lagoons are toxic. In 2001, the Natural Resources Defense Council and Clean Water Network studied gasses emitted from manure lagoons, and concluded,

Organic matter in livestock manure is converted to carbon dioxide and methane during the anaerobic decomposition process that occurs in lagoons. The most abundant gas produced during this process is carbon dioxide, although oceans, plants and soils are constantly absorbing it from the atmosphere. Carbon dioxide is not highly toxic itself, but contributes to oxygen deficiency, or asphyxiation. Health problems associated with elevated levels of carbon dioxide include respiratory problems, eye irritation, and headaches. Carbon dioxide is also a greenhouse gas ...

Methane generated during anaerobic decomposition is released from lagoons into the air. Methane is toxic at high levels, levels that typically are not found surrounding open-air lagoons, but which may be found at the top of unventilated areas such as closed manure pits. Moreover, persons exposed to toxic amounts may be unaware of the danger because methane is colorless, odorless, and tasteless. In August 2000, three farm workers in Canada died after they climbed into a liquid manure tank used to spread manure on a farm field; police believe that the cause of the deaths was inhalation of the methane gas. In high temperatures, the methane in the air can be highly combustible and thus extremely dangerous. The level of methane concentration along a waste lagoon's berm is greater than that at a surface coal mine. Methane is also a potent greenhouse gas implicated in global climate change. EPA estimated that nearly 13 percent of the total U.S. methane emissions was from livestock manure in 1998. Methane emissions from manure management activities increased 53 percent from 1990 to 1998 and EPA attributes the increase in methane emissions to the growing number of large hog and dairy operations and their use of liquid manure systems. EPA claims that liquid manure systems produce conditions that result in large quantities of methane emissions.[2]

Sleeping on It

Ben & Jerry's has decided to clean up its manure lagoons. Following the completion of the LCA, the company instituted a program to help farmers install technology to make cow bedding out of reprocessed manure. Cow bedding is what it sounds like it is—the material used to line the stalls where the cows sleep. Most cow bedding is made of sand but sand is very expensive and constantly has to be replaced—largely because (you guessed it) the sand fills up with manure. Processing the lagoon manure into bedding for the cows reduces the methane output of the manure by 50 percent.

As you can imagine, there are questions surrounding the notion of cows sleeping in manure, but agricultural scientists believe there is no reason manure cannot be reprocessed into clean bedding. The University of Minnesota looked into it and found that manure can be an acceptable substitution for sand. "Excellent cow preparation at milking time, sanitation of milking equipment, cow hygiene, adequate dry cow housing, and bedding/stall management appear to be critical in maintaining a low [sewage sludge compost] when using manure solids for bedding and making it work," wrote Marcia Endres, a dairy scientist for the University of Minnesota.[3]

Ben & Jerry's concluded that using manure for bedding can reduce the company's greenhouse gas emissions by 10,000 metric tons over the next decade. "The details of an LCA can be a bit messy," Ben & Jerry's said in a statement posted on the company's website, "But at Ben & Jerry's, we've always held fast that businesses have the responsibility to disclose their social and environmental efforts, as well as their shortcomings."[4]

Sustainability Assessments

A generation ago, it was hard to imagine an American corporation dedicating itself to a sustainable business model. Companies have to follow state and federal clean air and water laws, to be sure, but the interest Ben & Jerry's has shown in self examination and reducing its carbon footprint goes beyond what it must do to satisfy government regulations. Ben & Jerry's is not unique. Sustainability is becoming more and more a topic of discussion in corporate boardrooms. In fact, Ben & Jerry's is not alone in airing its sustainability record: 56 percent of the Standard & Poor's 500 Index companies provide annual corporate sustainability assessments.

The notion that manufacturers have as much a responsibility as the rest of us in practicing sustainability gained traction in 1999, when authors Paul Hawken, Amory Lovins, and L. Hunter Lovins published *Natural Capitalism: Creating the Next Industrial Revolution*. The book argued that it is not only the responsibility of corporations to adopt sustainable business models, but their profits would likely increase if they did. After all, who can argue with the notion that if you build your manufacturing plants closer to your suppliers or your markets, you would spend less money trucking raw materials or finished products.

It's the type of idea that American corporations are willing to consider. Toby Russell is CEO of Natural Capital Solutions, a nonprofit consulting agency established by Hunter Lovins to help businesses and governments implement sustainable models. According to Russell, many large American corporations now employ sustainability departments to show them how to do things more environmentally friendly and for less money as well.

"*Natural Capitalism* was published 20 years ago and there has been a lot of progress in the movement in all sorts of different areas," he says. "Since the book was published the term sustainability was only in existence a little bit.... The field of sustainability has grown massively. It is driven a lot by efficiency; the preferred principle of natural capitalism is to promote efficiency, to buy time, essentially. A lot of corporations have adopted sustainability and are really implementing efficiency while the communities are now embracing sustainability. Every major consulting firm in the country, if not the world, has a sustainability consulting arm now."[5]

Subtractive Manufacturing

Of course, real change cannot be expected to happen overnight. Indeed, it has taken twenty years or more just to get American corporations to begin thinking about sustainability. Essentially, to save the planet, they have to change the way they've been making and selling things since the earliest days of the Industrial Revolution more than 200 years ago.

Modern manufacturing is largely subtractive. In other words, to make an object, raw materials must be taken out of the earth—subtracted—and then repurposed. A company that makes metal picture frames, for example, buys rolls of sheet metal, stamping out the frames on a die press. The earth loses the ore that went into making the sheet metal and, chances are, after a roll of sheet metal has gone through a die press, a lot of it is left over—tossed away or, perhaps, recycled. Of course, after the frames are made they have to shipped to the wholesalers and retailers. The frames must be put into cardboard boxes—made out of trees, of course—then trucked to the Walmart for sale. Trucking the picture frames means that tractor-trailers have to burn fossil fuel—which is subtracted from the earth—while giving off greenhouse gases.

And unless the buyer owns a plug-in electric car (which itself doesn't give off greenhouse gases but is, nevertheless, manufactured through a subtractive process), the buyer is obviously burning fossil fuels to get to the Walmart and home again. Even the nail hammered into the wall to display the frame is made through a subtractive process. And the hammer used to bang the nail into the wall is made through a subtractive process. And the photograph displayed in the frame is processed and printed through a subtractive process. And the cardboard mat holding the photo in the frame is made through a subtractive process. And the wallpaper or latex paint covering the wall is made through a subtractive process. And the glue holding the wallpaper to the wall is made through a subtractive process. And the label on the paint can is made through a subtractive process. So is the paint can. And the drywall under the paint or wallpaper is made through a subtractive process. And the wooden two-by-four studs holding the drywall are made through a subtractive process. And the nails used to fasten the two-by-fours together are made through a subtractive process. And the bib overalls worn by the carpenter ...

You can see the challenge here. Measures must be found to make everything by using methods that are less subtractive. When the authors published *Natural Capitalism*, they calculated that 94 percent of the materials used to make the typical product does not actually go into the final product. That's a lot of subtraction.

Listening to the Termites

One way to make industry less subtractive is through a process known as biomimicry. Put simply, biomimicry is based on the notion that after millions of years, nature has already figured everything out. Here's an example. We think of termites as nasty little bugs that eat through our decks and cost a lot to exterminate. In Africa, though, termites are known as nature's most efficient HVAC designers. Researchers have studied termite mounds and have found the little guys build them with vertical shafts that vent hot air through the tops. As a result, the temperature inside a termite mound is some 20 degrees cooler than the outside environment. Explain biologist James L. Gould and Carol Grant Gould in their book, *Animal Architects: Building and the Evolution of Intelligence*:

Heat generated by the termites and their gardens in the core of the nest flows into the collecting pipes and rises in the chimneys at a rate of about five inches per minute. As this humid CO2-rich air flows up the chimneys it draws cooler air in through the cellar area under the nest, where it begins to flow up into the various chambers.... The buttresses are riddled with tiny holes too small even for the termites but large enough for the warm stale air to diffuse out while cooler fresh air percolates in.[6]

Architects in Harare, Zimbabwe, have taken the concept and applied it to the design of buildings in an office complex, thus greatly reducing the air-conditioning cost for those buildings. Says Russell, "When I think about design and technology I think of [the] concept of biomimicry. Rather than making the technology catch up with the challenges, we catch up with nature which has been addressing the challenges for the last millennial. Throughout history nature has created systems to be restorative and regenerative. How can we learn from those while we are looking to advance? How can we incorporate self-cleaning when we make paint products so they don't need to be replaced as often? Nature is phenomenal in everything it does.... There are a lot of practical applications that have happened in the last twenty years. If I am looking at what sort of technologies are out there that are addressing the issues we have in front of us, I would say most of the technologies that will be restorative we already have, we just haven't been looking for them."[7]

From Carpet Tiles to Burritos

You don't have to look too far to find corporations that are adopting sustainability as a business model. Maybe they aren't yet studying termites, but their efforts are noble. Interface, based in LaGrange, Georgia, makes carpet tiles mostly for commercial clients. The company made a commitment to sustainability in 1994, redesigning its products so they are more easily recycled. For example, the company found a substitute for glue that enables it to retrieve old carpet and grind it up much easier so that it can be recycled into new tiles. "People would use their carpet, and when they were finished with it, the broadloom carpet would go to the landfill. We said, 'Wait a minute. That's an awful lot of material.' It was literally millions of tons of carpet going to landfills every year," says Dianne Dillon Ridgley, who spent eighteen years on the Interface board before stepping down in 2014.[8]

Unilever, the British-Dutch consumer goods company (which, by the way, acquired Ben & Jerry's in 2000) has gotten behind a number of initiatives. Since 2008, the company has reduced its carbon emissions by a third by adopting cleaner technologies as well as efficiencies in transportation. The company also set up a "small actions, big differences fund" to finance cost-saving ideas proposed by its subsidiaries. Reported *The Economist*: "Many firms do such things. But to meet its broader goals Unilever has to change what goes on beyond its corporate walls. When it measured the greenhouse-gas emissions associated with its products, it found that significant emissions came in the supply chain—not from Unilever itself. So it had to get the support of its suppliers, who range from food giants such as Cargill to small farmers in India."[9]

Additive Manufacturing

A lot of this is possible because technology has improved, making it easier to be sustainable than it was a generation ago. Indeed, one of the fastest growing technologies is 3-D printing, where an object is designed on a computer screen and then literally "printed," layer by layer, on a device just a little larger than a desktop printer. (Those are the consumer models; industrial-sized 3-D printers are quite a bit larger.) 3-D printing is now used for everything from making personalized golf tees to prosthetic limbs to components for automobiles and aircraft. (The astronauts aboard the International Space Station have a 3-D printer.) In fact, in 2015 the Phoenix, Arizona, company Local Motors produced an electric car, the Strati, on a 3-D printer in 44 hours. Designers combined the thousands of parts found in the typical car into a handful of printable objects that were then easily assembled. Local Motors hopes to establish factories to produce the cars, with the first facility planned for suburban Washington.

3-D printing is not subtractive. In fact, 3-D printing is also known by the term additive manufacturing because whatever is fed into the 3-D printer—plastic, molten metals, even baking ingredients for 3-D printed cakes—is used. All of it. Instead of just 6 percent of the raw materials used in the manufacture of the object, 100 percent of what goes into the printer is used.

All of this is encouraging but Russell wonders whether the spirit is truly willing across the wider corporate world. It is true that young people—the millennials—seem most interested in adopting sustainable business practices, but most CEOs of major corporations aren't in their 20s and early 30s. It could be 25 years before the millennials gain the authority needed to change corporate thinking. "I don't think we have 25 years to wait and hope," he says. "There was a lot of thought given to changing the system in the 1960s, when there was the hippie movement, the Vietnam movement, and we thought let's just wait for all those people to get power and see what happens. The belief system in an individual changes with age so a lot of hope and belief that you are going to change everything kind of dies off as the day-to-day needs of your life and your family are addressed. So I would have a lot of skepticism in just hoping for the next generation to work it out. There are studies after studies that show the millennials and the generations X, Y, and Z care more about sustainability than the generations before them. They are value driven, they are only wanting to go into jobs and work for people who have similar values to their own, so there is hope there—don't get me wrong—but to sit here and hope and wish that the next generation will help is something that I would be reluctant to put all my eggs in that particular basket."[10]

As the future unfolds, and the corporate world learns to mimic nature, let's enjoy the Boom Chocolatta and give thought to the reprocessed manure where the cows are bedding down for the night. Or the office buildings in Zimbabwe, where architects get their ideas from termites. They are, perhaps, more comforting thoughts than the notion that we, as a society, toss out 94 percent of what we don't use.

NOTES

1. Quoted in *2014 Social & Environmental Assessment Report: A Life Cycle Analysis Study of Some of Our Flavors*, Ben & Jerry's, 2014, www.benjerry.com/values/issues-we-care-about/climate-justice/life-cycle-analysis. Accessed June 29, 2015.

2. Robbin Marks, *Cesspools Of Shame: How Factory Farm Lagoons and Sprayfields Threaten Environmental and Public Health*, Natural Resources Defense Council and the Clean Water Network, July 2001, pp. 19-20, https://www.nrdc.org/water/pollution/cesspools/cesspools.pdf. Accessed June 29, 2015.

3. Marcia Endres, "Manure Solids For Bedding . . . Does It Work?" University of Minnesota Extension, Nov. 12, 2011, www.extension.umn.edu/agriculture/dairy/manure/manure-solids-for-bedding-does-it-work. Accessed June 30, 2015.

4. Quoted in *2014 Social & Environmental Assessment Report: A Life Cycle Analysis Study of Some of Our Flavors*.

5. Interview with the author, May 21, 2015.

6. James L. Gould and Carol Grant Gould, *Animal Architects: Building and the Evolution Of Intelligence.* New York: Basic Books, 2007, p. 139.

7. Interview with the author, May 21, 2015.

8. Interview with the author, June 25, 2015.

9. Quoted in *The Economist,* "In Search of the Good Business: For the Second Time in Its 120-Year History, Unilever is Trying to Redefine What It Means to be a Virtuous Company," Aug. 9. 2014, www.economist.com/news/business/21611103-second-time-its-120-year-history-unilever-trying-redefine-what-it-means-be. Accessed June 30, 2015.

10. Interview with the author, May 21, 2015.

15 Environmental Dimensions of Population Stabilization

Lori M. Hunter

The ecological cost of consumption by the average U.S. citizen is 2.6 times greater than residents of the world's other nations and 4.4 times greater than those specifically in the least wealthy nations (Hoekstra and Wiedmann 2013; Global Footprint Network 2014). This "environmental footprint" includes consumptive use of natural resources such as land and water, as well as the use of the environment as a sink for emissions such as those related to production.

As U.S. population increases, so too does the nation's overall environmental footprint. Yet this is far more than a numbers game. Careful consideration of the environmental dimensions of population stabilization requires a critical look at *who* we are, not simply *how many* we are.

As measured by the environmental footprint, production and consumption combine with population to shape humans' environmental impact— this resembles the classic IPAT equation where environment impact (I) is the product of human population size (P), affluence (A), and technology (T) (Ehrlich and Holdren 1971).

Although IPAT outlines three important factors shaping humans' environmental impact, media coverage and policy reports on the environmental aspects of population have tended to overly emphasize the equation's "P" vis-à-vis the importance of production or consumption patterns as reflected within IPAT's "A" and "T". Such neo-Mathusian outlooks set their sights squarely on demographic pressures and harken to the influential 1798 treatise of Thomas Robert Malthus, who argued that unchecked population growth would lead to poverty, famine, and war.

But when we think beyond *how many* we are, to ask *who* we are, the answer requires attention to IPAT's inclusion of affluence and technology. Simply stated, we are a nation of consumers, and it is excessive consumption and the technological underpinnings of our lifestyles that predominantly drive our large environmental footprint.

In our culture of consumption, meaning and purpose are derived from purchasing products and services (Ritzer 2001). American children are socialized into this culture of commodities (Schor 2004) where individual identities are bound up in makes and models of cars, brands of clothes (McCracken 2005). Consumerism in America has even been equated with freedom and power (Cohen 2005).

The Treadmill of Production and Consumption

Scholars of political economy have characterized our economic system as a fast-moving treadmill of production and consumption (Schnaiberg 1980)—a treadmill that seems capable only of speeding up, not slowing down. Individual changes in consumption can offer some improvement in our overall environmental footprint (Dietz 2014). Yet our politics, economic system, and broader culture remain tightly bound to materially significant consumption. Corporate marketing and government interventions fuel market expansion, economic growth and therefore jobs. Obviously these employment opportunities are critical to well-being, yet the consumption associated with that well-being further fuels the treadmill and its environmental consequences (Schnaiberg 1980). A vicious cycle.

An intriguing paper published in the academic journal *Sustainable Development* tells the tale of a group of MBA students from Sweden's Stockholm School of Economics during a workshop in Shanghai, China. After a series of visits focused on globalization and sustainability to Brazil, Russia and India, the students were well-versed on the importance of buying authentic Chinese handicrafts, silk, and tailored goods to remember their journey to Shanghai. They had learned first-hand that "fake branded goods" often represented poor labor practices, hazardous work places, and unsustainable use of natural resources. Yet two days later, the visitors proudly displayed their "Gucci, Prada, Armani, and Louis Vuitton ... thrilled [and] heavily engaged in triumphal conversations around the bargains they had made." The study's authors, Lars Strannegård and Peter Dobers, argue that "Identities are fragile, temporal and central to our understanding of the sustainability challenge" (Strannegård and Dobers 2010). They contend that every single day is filled with identity-creating interactions and, particularly in urban environments, these interactions are highly commercialized.

Population and the Environmental Cost of Consumption as Identity

Of course, population size and growth also fuel the production and consumption treadmill—both within national borders and on a global scale. Simplistically, more consumers create more economic demand. And today's marketplace finds an increasing number of consumers making materially-significant purchasing decisions that are associated with higher social status.

As an example, with increasing affluence comes increasing meat consumption—a food product representing social status but with large environmental cost. Meat production yields greenhouse gas emissions due to feed production, energy use in animal houses, and flatulence, which emits methane (Steinfeld et al. 2006). Developing nations have seen a threefold increase in the available food consumption of meat since 1963, with much of this occurring in Asia, and China specifically (Kearney 2010).

A Different Economy-Environment Future

Overall, the past century has witnessed steady increases in the environmental price paid to sustain humans. Our global "environmental footprint" has steadily marched uphill for decades.

A different environmental future would be one in which economic gains could be, in part, decoupled from the consumptive underpinnings of current environmental "footprints." Within the United States, such decoupling must occur at national, regional and household levels.

At the national and regional levels, future economic gains should aim to lessen their environmental cost. In their influential 1999 book, *Natural Capitalism: Creating the Next Industrial Revolution*, Paul Hawken, Amory Lovins, and Hunter Lovins outlined the concept of "natural capitalism." A fundamental assumption of natural capitalism is appropriate valuation of the natural resources that underpin economic systems. Such valuation stems from an emphasis on human and ecological well-being and the creation of sustainable socio-environmental systems.

The concept of natural capitalism has been called "palpable and seductive" yet simultaneously critiqued as representing an impossibility since it operates within the very paradigm socio-environmental capitalism—it desires to reconfigure (Kendall 2008). Even so, the concept and follow-up writings have offered much food for thought.

To lower population's environmental footprint, shifts regarding consumption must occur at the household scale as well. Consumers must engage a new definition of quality of life, one less bound up in makes, models and brands (Schor 2013). Research on today's "ethical consumers" (Shaw et al. 2004) and "conscious consumers" is demonstrating that these shifts are more common today among today's wealthier groups (Carfagna et al. 2014). Basically, the options of purchasing local and/or organic foods, hybrid-fuel cars, and convenient downtown residences is not evenly distributed across social classes. Even so, the introduction of organic foods and other eco-friendly options at big-box stores signals some broadening of consumer options. Research does suggest that environmental concern tends to originate among those with higher socioeconomic status and diffuses across time to diverse social classes (Pampel and Hunter 2012).

Some characterize the movement away from the treadmill of consumption and production as the growth of a "Culture of the Slow—deceleration in an accelerated world" (Osbaldiston 2013). Proponents of this transition desire downshifting, movement away from consumer modernity and reconnection to local community (Schor 2013).

A Different Population-Environment Future

As to population, a different environmental future would be one in which global population stabilization were prioritized.

Although our culture of materialism is a key force shaping the environmental footprint of U.S. residents, as we consider environmental futures, population size and growth cannot be ignored. To bridge these two issues, it's useful to engage the concept of "sustainability wedges" as used by the climate research and policy communities. Figure 1 illustrates the concept, with the projected increase in fossil fuel emissions broken into "wedges," each

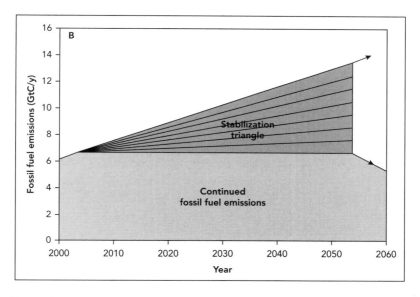

Figure 1

representing particular socioeconomic changes with potential to reduce the longer-term emissions trajectory. Wedges include improvements in efficiency and conservation such as increased fuel economy, reduced reliance on cars, and building and power plant efficiency upgrades. If such activities were embedded in a broader scale reduction in the U.S.' carbon intensity—carbon emissions per GDP—this would obviously represent a substantial emissions reduction wedge (Figure and cites are from Pacala and Socolow 2004).

Can population stabilization be considered a wedge? Researchers from the National Center for Atmospheric Research (NCAR) have decomposed projections of future greenhouse gas emissions to better understand climate change's demographic dimensions. Their estimates suggest that lower population growth at the global scale may reduce emissions by 1.0 – 1.5 "wedges." This represents 16–29% of the emission reductions required to meet long-term policy goals such as preventing a doubling of atmospheric CO_2 concentrations (O'Neill et. al. 2010).

The NCAR researchers note the policies that fulfill unmet need for family planning may offer environmental benefit. Even in the U.S., over 6% of women who want to stop or delay childbearing are not using any method of contraception (Alkema et. al. 2013). Although this "unmet need" for family planning is far lower in the U.S. than other nations, it can likely be readily met through expansion of existing programs.

While stabilizing U.S. population represents only one wedge, it's a wedge nonetheless. Population stabilization holds potential to yield environmental gains through reduction in future consumption. Yet the ecological footprint of the U.S. is driven not only—or even primarily—by how many we are, but rather, who we are.

Overall, key to future environmental well-being is the decoupling of aggregate economic growth and household economic status from environmental cost. Instead, economic growth and economic status can be coupled with advancements in environmental efficiencies. In general, concern for the global environment must centrally engage cultures of consumption alongside demographic targets. As argued by the UK Royal Society in their report, *People and the Planet*, "population and the environment should not be considered as two separate issues." (2012: p. 9) Those concerned with global environment change must engage both consumption and demographic issues for the sake of both ecological and human well-being.

REFERENCES

Alkema, L., Kantorova, V., Menozzi, C., & Biddlecom, A. (2013). National, regional, and global rates and trends in contraceptive prevalence and unmet need for family planning between 1990 and 2015: a systematic and comprehensive analysis. *The Lancet*, *381*(9878), 1642–1652.

Carfagna, L. B., Dubois, E. A., Fitzmaurice, C., Ouimette, M. Y., Schor, J. B., Willis, M., & Laidley, T. (2014). An emerging eco-habitus: The reconfiguration of high cultural capital practices among ethical consumers. *Journal of Consumer Culture*, 1469540514526227.

Cohen, L. (2004). *A consumers' republic: The politics of mass consumption in postwar America*. Random House LLC.

Dietz, T. (2014). Understanding environmentally significant consumption. *Proceedings of the National Academy of Sciences*, *111*(14), 5067–5068.

Ehrlich, P. and J. Holdren. (1971). Impact of population growth. *Science* 171: 1212–1217.

Global Footprint Network (2014). Author calculations based on data from http://www.footprintnetwork.org/ (accessed November 2014).

Hoekstra, A. and Wiedmann, T. (2013). Humanity's unsustainable environmental footprint. *Science* 344 (6188), 1114-1117.

Kearney, J. (2010). Food consumption trends and drivers. *Philosophical transactions of the royal society B: biological sciences*, *365*(1554), 2793–2807.

Kendall, B. E. (2008). Personae and natural capitalism: Negotiating politics and constituencies in a rhetoric of sustainability. *Environmental Communication* 2(1), 59–77.

McCracken, G. D. (2005). *Culture and consumption II: Markets, meaning, and brand management*

Nolan, J. M. (2013). Creating a culture of conservation: Willingness to confront environmental transgressors. *Ecopsychology, 5*(1), 3–8.

O'Neill, B. C., Dalton, M., Fuchs, R., Jiang, L., Pachauri, S., & Zigova, K. (2010). Global demographic trends and future carbon emissions. *Proceedings of the National Academy of Sciences, 107*(41), 17521–17526.

Osbaldiston, N. (Ed.). (2013). *Culture of the slow: Social deceleration in an accelerated world*. Palgrave Macmillan.

Pacala, S., & Socolow, R. (2004). Stabilization wedges: solving the climate problem for the next 50 years with current technologies. *Science, 305*(5686), 968–972.

Pampel, F.D. and Hunter, L. "Cohort Change, Diffusion, and Support for Environmental Spending." *American Journal of Sociology* 118(2):420-448.

Ritzer, G. (2001). *Explorations in the sociology of consumption: fast food, credit cards and casinos*. Sage.

Royal Society. (2012). *People and the planet*. The Royal Society Science Policy Centre report 01/12 April 2012 DES2470, London UK.

Schnaiberg, A. (1980). *Environment: from surplus to scarcity*. Oxford University Press.

Schor, J. (2004). *Born to buy: The commercialized child and the new consumer culture*. Simon and Schuster.

Schor, J. B. (2013). From Fast Fashion to Connected Consumption: Slowing Down the Spending Treadmill. *Culture of the Slow: Social Deceleration in an Accelerated World*, 34.

Shaw, D., & Newholm, T. (2002). Voluntary simplicity and the ethics of consumption. *Psychology & Marketing, 19*(2), 167–185.

Strannegård, L. and P. Dobers. (2010). Unstable identities: stable unsustainability. *Sustainable Development*, 18: 119–122. doi: 10.1002/sd.459/

Steinfeld, H., Gerber, P., Wassenaar, T., Castel, V., Rosales, M., de Haan, C., 2006. Livestock's Long Shadow. Environmental Issues and Options. FAO, Rome, Italy.

16

All Wrapped Up In Polyisocyanurate: Living the Net Zero Life

Hal Marcovitz

If you were among the 51 million people who visited the New York World's Fair in 1964 and 1965, chances are you were awed by the exhibit titled *Futurama*. As the name suggests, *Futurama* purported to provide a peek into the future—a looksee at the world fifty years hence, where high-speed buses and trains ferried commuters to their jobs in skyscrapers, where people negotiated the clean urban streets on moving sidewalks, and where helicopters based at mid-city airports ferried executives and tourists to far-flung destinations. Upon departing the *Futurama* exhibit, visitors were handed lapel buttons that said, "I have seen the future."

Those of us who have seen the future may beg to disagree. *Futurama* depicted none of the problems that have plagued society well into the 21st century: urban decay, deteriorating infrastructure, loss of jobs due to outsourcing of manufacturing to Asia, and so on. Moreover, all those people-movers, skyscrapers, and mid-city airports depicted fifty years ago were certainly well-intentioned, but the sponsors of *Futurama* declined to say how it would all be powered. Electricity was certainly a logical guess, but where would the electricity come from? The answer today is the same answer as it was fifty years ago: nuclear power plants, certainly, but also coal-fired plants. And in the cities and suburbs, homes and businesses are heated by oil burners and gas furnaces.

Futurama was, by the way, sponsored by General Motors—then, and now, one of the world's leading manufacturers of internal combustion engines. It is likely that nobody at General Motors would have dared suggest in 1964 that oil would one day be in short supply, or that carbon pollution would lead to climate change, so that to truly depict the world of tomorrow the *Futurama* exhibit would do well to feature cars powered by something other than gasoline.

Solar Panels Everywhere

American cities stopped hosting world fairs decades ago, sparing countless millions the opportunities to glimpse into a utopian and largely fictitious future that was afforded to the 1964–65 fairgoers. But that doesn't mean some people have given up envisioning the future, particularly when it comes to the knotty problem of how to power all those people-movers, skyscrapers, and the places where families will be living fifty years or so from now. Sachu Constantine has given the future a lot of thought, and he sees a vastly different world than *Futurama* predicted, particularly when it comes to energy. Constantine is director of policy for the California-based Center for Sustainable Energy, which provides advocacy and technical assistance to homeowners, industries, institutions, and others seeking to transition to renewable energy.

"Let's go to New York City," Constantine says, jumping ahead to the year 2065. "You can stand in a high-rise building and look out over the rooftops of the city and you should see almost nothing but solar panels."[1] As that comment suggests, Constantine does not believe fossil fuels would be widely available or affordable fifty years from now, nor does he think the planet can endure fifty more years of carbon emissions.

Moreover, in the future, he believes there would be more than just solar panels on everybody's rooftops. He suggests all homes will employ something similar to the Nest thermostat, which is a project undertaken by Google to take programmable thermostats a step further.

Programmable thermostats are not new; for many years homeowners have been able to program their thermostats to reduce the heat when they are away from home or at night when they are asleep. Nest can do all that, too, but the thermostat responds to peak demand periods. On very hot days, for example, power plants have to produce more electricity because a lot of people turn up the air-conditioning. During such peak demand periods, the price for electricity invariably rises. Nest responds to these peak demand periods by reducing the electricity supplied to nonessential gadgets in the home. Nest may, for example, delay a dishwashing cycle until demand—and therefore the price of the electricity—is reduced. If somebody loads the dishwasher and turns it on after supper, Nest would not permit the washer to kick on until late at night when demand is reduced.

"The Nest thermostat is being used by people to control their home's temperature remotely and maximize efficiency. But that is 10 percent of the capacity of that device. It can do so much more," says Constantine. "We can envision in the very near future a home with a whole network of devices...[with Nest] controlling your heating, your hot water, your lighting, everything in your home."[2]

Innovative Financing

Of course, homeowners have been putting solar panels on their roofs since, well, since before people attended the 1964 World's Fair. Still, relatively few American homes—an estimated 400,000—receive energy from solar cells. And, certainly, installing solar is still not cheap. Although the federal government has provided a 30 percent tax credit for homeowners to convert to solar, unless extended by Congress the tax credit is set to expire in 2016. Some states provide their own incentives, such as outright grants to aid homeowners to convert to solar and other renewables, but even so, installation of solar panels can still cost homeowners tens of thousands of dollars.

Seems like a lot of money, but Constantine says consider the alternative: In 2065, when heating oil is either unavailable or prohibitively expensive or banned under law by a government that finally accepts the dangers of climate change, solar may be the only viable energy source. In fact, Constantine argues, solar is already cheaper than oil. The only difference is a homeowner has to buy a solar array and pay tens of thousands of dollars in upfront costs. The oil consumer, over a lifetime of use, will probably pay more. The key difference is the oil user pays an oil company to fill up a tank several times a year, meaning the cost is incurred little by little.

Constantine notes, "If you were to compare the cost of your solar system to the cost of [oil] over that same timeframe, they are already pretty close to equal. In many cases you should be getting a return on your investment. The problem is not so much the cost anymore, although it is still expensive, but it will come down. But everything is becoming more expensive, so the gap between the cost of solar and the cost of conventional brown power is getting smaller and I would posit that in many cases like California or Hawaii and other places it is already there."

He continues, "The problem is not so much the cost, the problem is the timing. I don't have $30,000 right now, that's why I pay my bill on a monthly basis. Over the next 20 years I will spend $30,000. The innovation needs to happen in financing, not in solar technology. I'm not saying we should not have more innovation, but we should be focusing our efforts on financing and getting a bank to recognize that they can give you a $30,000 loan at essentially a revolving line of credit rate, say 2 percent or 3 percent like you would get on a really good home mortgage loan."[3]

Solar Is Stationary

As Constantine suggests, banks and governments need to come up with creative ways to help homeowners convert their homes to solar, but he also acknowledges that solar technology should not stand still. And, to be sure, there are constant improvements in the materials used to construct photo-voltaic solar cells, which helps make them more efficient.

The photovoltaic process dates back to 1839 when a French scientist, Edmund Bequerel, found that certain materials produce electric current when exposed to sunlight. Albert Einstein went on to win the Nobel Prize after describing the photoelectric effect, essentially saying that metals emit electrons when exposed to sunlight. Photovoltaic cells capture those electrons, turning them into electricity and employing them as an electrical circuit, which transfers the electricity into the house.

But there is a problem with photovoltaic cells that limits their overall effectiveness—and that problem has to do with the fact that they are screwed onto rooftops. In other words, they are stationary. As such, solar panels fixed to rooftops make very little electricity in the morning when the sun is low in the sky because little sunlight strikes the cells. At midday, when the sun is high in the sky, the cells make a lot of electricity. But in late afternoon, the productivity of the cells again goes down because the sun is again low in the sky. Certainly, a house with an adequate array fixed to its roof should made enough energy to power the house and even have some left over to feed back into the grid.

Still, the potential of photovoltaic cells is limited because they are stationary. Every afternoon, as the Earth spins away from the sun, the cells make less and less energy. But that problem may be on its way to being resolved. In 2009, David Blittersdorf thought about how the Earth spins away from the sun, and wondered whether there was a way to continually point the panels toward the sun. An engineer, Blittersdorf was able to incorporate global positioning system technology as a component in making solar energy by devising a solar array that continually follows the sun, no matter where it is in the sky, no matter the season.

As everybody knows from their fifth-grade science textbooks, the sun is never in the same place in the sky one day to the next. In winter, when the Earth is tilted away from the sun, the sun is low in the sky. In summer, when the Earth is tilted toward the sun, the sun is high in the sky. This change occurs daily. That is why even on the sunniest day in January, a rooftop solar array is likely to make no more than half the energy it would make on a sunny day in June.

Blittersdorf solved that problem by placing a solar array on a pier and employing GPS technology to continually track the sun on its path across the sky. Pier-mounted spinning solar arrays are not new—they have been used for years. The difference is, though, that the old-style pier-mounted array merely turned at the same rate as the Earth turned, meaning the panel was always pointed toward the sun. Well, not quite pointed toward the sun. The old pier-mounted arrays had no way of adjusting their angles according to the season. In essence, the old pier-mounted arrays merely pointed to where the sun should be, under the assumption that the sun would be in the same place in the sky every day, no matter the season. Which is, of course, not the case.

But Blittersdorf's arrays improved on that idea and now they are able to pick up the maximum solar energy possible. Blittersdorf estimates the new pier-mounted arrays draw up 40 to 45 percent more sunlight than rooftop-mounted arrays.

Blittersdorf is a founder of AllEarth Renewables, a Vermont-based company that manufactures the GPS-directed arrays. There are, of course, some drawbacks to GPS-directed arrays, the main one being that a pier-mounted array requires a backyard—one that is unobstructed by trees or the shadows cast from a neighbor's home—most of its clients are therefore commercial and industrial users. Still, the company does find residential customers for its

GPS-directed arrays, and by 2015 AllEarth Renewables had manufactured pier-mounted tracking arrays for customers in more than half the states.

A Bleak Tomorrow

Does Blittersdorf envision a future where everybody's backyard features a GPS-controlled solar array mounted on a pier? Yes and no. Ground-based renewables, such as solar farms or wind farms, will certainly be a big part of the future, he says. But like Constantine, he believes rooftop solar arrays are still the most viable option for most homeowners. And, like Constantine, he believes that in fifty years one could stand atop a hill overlooking a city and see roof-mounted solar panels from city limit to city limit. He says, "The numbers show that we still have to do probably every available rooftop. It's not an either or. We have to do every available roof and then we have to do a tremendous amount of ground-available solar and wind."[4]

Vermont is, of course, a small state with a population of about 640,000. Even so, Vermont's political leaders have recognized that the state's current level of energy consumption is not sustainable. And that is why Vermont lawmakers have set a goal of making 90 percent of the state's energy through renewables by 2050. Says Blittersdorf, "We are not going to do it at the federal level, we are totally screwed up there. But we are trying to do it at the state level. Vermont has a goal: 90 percent of its total energy by 2050 will be renewable. We have 35 years to change from 88 percent fossil fuel to 90 percent renewables. We have a fundamental huge problem. We are at 12 percent renewables in total energy. When I talk total energy I mean all energy, not just electricity. That's replacing all the liquid fuels, changing our transportation and heat over to electrifying.

"In Vermont, half the people heat their homes with oil which is going to change; we have to get them off oil. And so heat pumps and electricity that comes from renewables—wind or solar or hydro—is key. And to make all this work we do need tremendous amounts of installation. All the homes need solar on their roofs. We need wind farms in the hills, we need solar farms and fields. We have a huge amount to do."[5]

As for transportation, Blittersdorf is a big fan of railroads and other large-scale people-movers, such as buses. That is where he would like to see a lot of public and private resources directed: improving the rail system as well as other modes of mass transit. "I'm a big fan of railroads and mass transit buses, not cars. Even in rural Vermont one of the myths is we can't get out of the cars because we're a rural state but when we have people driving 60 to 100 miles to an IBM plant in Burlington that is crazy. It is the wrong thing to do...I like to joke that I'd like to start grinding up SUVs and turning them into wind turbines because someday we are going to do that. We are going to need the materials. The world has finite materials, whether it's iron or copper or whatever. We are not unlimited so that is why we cannot overpromise that renewables will be this infinite source of energy because you have to build all the collection devices that come from finite raw materials."[6]

Net Zero

East of Vermont, in the Portland, Maine suburb of Falmouth, Marian Starkey and her husband, Alex, have decided not to wait for the future. On January 1, 2015, they moved into a newly built net zero energy home. A home that achieves net zero is one that makes its own energy—in the case of the Starkeys' home, through solar panels—and, therefore, the average annual expenditure for energy is zero. In the spring, summer, and early fall, the homes make more than enough photovoltaic energy on their own to power their electric heat pumps, water heaters, refrigerators, lights, and even their plug-in cars. The extra energy is fed into the grid and credited to the homeowners, which offsets the cost of the electricity they draw from the grid in the winter when the solar panels on the roof don't capture enough sunlight to power the home on their own.

Before moving into their net zero home, the Starkeys lived in a 100-year-old home with tin ceilings and plaster walls and a lot of charm, but it was also drafty and heated by a gas furnace. Despite spending as much as $500 a month on gas heat during the winter months, the temperature inside the home never seemed to rise above 65 degrees during the day and 62 degrees at night. "I loved the house but we were just sick of that," says Marian Starkey. "We live in Maine and it's cold here most of the year."[7]

The architect for the Starkeys' net zero home is BrightBuilt Home of Portland, Maine. The Starkeys' home is new, which made installing two inches of rigid foam insulation around the entire house envelope, banks of south-facing triple glazed casement windows, and other high-performance features a simpler task than retrofitting an existing home would have been. Moreover, the home is modular—built in a factory and assembled onsite—which made the project more affordable than it would have been if the home had been stick-built.

Air-Tight Homes

Parlin Meyer is the director of BrightBuilt Home and also the firm's architect. Her company has shown that using the modular concept for construction, a net zero home can cost virtually the same price as a stick-built home that does not include solar and the other energy-saving features. Because of the solar panels, insulation, and other features, Meyer says, "There is a slight difference in cost upfront.... However, on a monthly basis the operational costs are significantly less for the high-performance home. And when you add to that the fact that you are striving for net zero and you are producing all of your own electricity on-site you are effectively much more in the black then you would be in a comparable code-built home that is running on traditional fuel and electrical resources."[8]

The modular net zero homes include solar panels on their roofs but they also include much more. The wall cavities are slightly larger than you would find in conventional construction, and they are filled with densely-packed cellulose insulation. Once the house is delivered to the site it is literally wrapped in sheets of polyisocyanurate foam applied under the siding. (Polyisocyanurate is rigid insulation, typically used in cold climates.) Doors and windows are selected for their abilities to seal tightly against the weather. The whole house is so well-sealed, in fact, that an air exchanger system has to be installed in order for fresh air to enter the house. But even the air exchanger adds to the net zero effect because as warm, stale air is expelled from the house the exchanger transfers its heat to the fresh, cool air entering the house.

Says Meyer, "It's not that the home is hermetically-sealed. A lot of people hear 'air-tight' and it sounds disconcerting. It means in lieu of allowing the house to breathe in, at least the way you see in old farm houses—and in my house that includes generations of mouse droppings—the exchange of air is coming through known places you can manage but it is also filtering that air and taking advantage of the outgoing warm air that you are extracting from the house to pre-heat the incoming air. It is an active thermal exchange as well as the filtration of fresh air."[9]

A city where the roof of every home and business is covered in solar panels. Solar panels mounted on piers that use GPS technology to track the sun. Modular-built homes that make all their energy and are so well-insulated that air exchangers need to be installed—and even the air exchangers help heat the home. This is the real world of tomorrow. Of course, the New York World's Fair's *Futurama* exhibit predicted none of this. But the *Futurama* exhibit also failed to predict peak oil, carbon pollution, global warming, and a lot of other 21st century ills. But thinking back, those moving sidewalks must have looked pretty neat.

NOTES

1. Interview with the author, March 27, 2015.
2. Ibid.
3. Ibid.
4. Interview with the author, March 24, 2015.
5. Ibid.
6. Ibid.
7. Interview with the author, March 23, 2015.
8. Interview with the author, March 31, 2015.
9. Ibid.

Moving to a Steady State Economy*

Herman Daly

Sustainable development, I argue, necessarily means a radical shift from a growth economy and all it entails to a steady-state economy, certainly in the North, and eventually in the South as well. My first task has to be to elaborate the case for that theoretical and practical shift in worldview. What are the main theoretical and moral anomalies of the growth economy, and how are they resolved by the steady state? And what are the practical failures of the growth economy, viewed as forced first steps toward a steady state?

It is necessary to define what is meant by the terms "steady-state economy" (SSE) and "growth economy." Growth, as here used, refers to an increase in the physical scale of the matter/energy throughput that sustains the economic activities of production and consumption of commodities. In an SSE the aggregate throughput is constant, though its allocation among competing uses is free to vary in response to the market. Since there is of course no production and consumption of matter/energy itself in a physical sense, the throughput is really a process in which low-entropy raw materials are transformed into commodities and then, eventually, into high-entropy wastes. Throughput begins with depletion and ends with pollution. Growth is quantitative increase in the physical scale of throughput. Qualitative improvement in the use made of a given scale of throughput, resulting either from improved technical knowledge or from a

* This chapter is an excerpt from Herman E. Daly, *Beyond Growth: The Economics of Sustainable Development* (Boston: Beacon Press, 1996: pp. 31–44.)

deeper understanding of purpose, is called "development." An SSE therefore can develop, but cannot grow, just as the planet earth, of which it is a subsystem, can develop without growing.

The steady state is by no means static. There is continuous renewal by death and birth, depreciation and production, as well as qualitative improvement in the stocks of both people and artifacts. By this definition, strictly speaking, even the stocks of artifacts or people may occasionally grow temporarily as a result of technical progress that increases the durability and repairability (longevity) of artifacts. The same maintenance flow can support a larger stock if the stock becomes longer-lived. The stock may also decrease, however, if resource quality declines at a faster rate than increases in durability-enhancing technology.

The other crucial feature in the definition of an SSE is that the constant level of throughput must be ecologically sustainable for a long future for a population living at a standard or per capita resource use that is sufficient for a good life. Note that an SSE is not defined in terms of gross national product. It is not to be thought of as "zero growth in GNP."

Ecological sustainability of the throughput is not guaranteed by market forces. The market cannot by itself register the cost of its own increasing scale relative to the ecosystem. Market prices measure the scarcity of individual resources relative to each other. Prices do not measure the absolute scarcity of resources in general, of environmental low entropy. The best we can hope for from a perfect market is a Pareto-optimal allocation of resources (i.e., a situation in which no one can be made better off without making someone else worse off). Such an allocation can be achieved at any scale of resource throughput, including unsustainable scales, just as it can be achieved with any distribution of income, including unjust ones. The latter proposition is well known, the former less so, but equally true. Ecological criteria of sustainability, like ethical criteria of justice, are not served by markets. Markets singlemindedly aim to serve allocative efficiency. Optimal *allocation* is one thing; optimal *scale* is something else.

Economists are always preoccupied with maximizing something: profits, rent, present value, consumers' surplus, and so on. What is maximized in the SSE? Basically the maximand is life, measured in cumulative person-years ever to be lived at a standard of resource use sufficient for a good life. This certainly does not imply maximizing population growth, as advocated by Julian Simon (1981), because too many people simultaneously alive, especially high-consuming people, will be forced to consume ecological "capital" and thereby lower the carrying capacity of the environment and the cumulative total of future lives. Although the maximand is human lives, the SSE would go a long way toward maximizing cumulative life for all species by imposing the constraint of a constant throughput at a sustainable level, thereby halting the growing takeover of habitats of other species, as well as slowing the rate of drawdown of geological capital otherwise available to future generations.

I do not wish to put too fine a point on the notion that the steady state maximizes cumulative life over time for all species, but it certainly would do better in this regard than the present value-maximizing growth economy, which drives to extinction any valuable species whose biological growth rate is less than the expected rate of interest, as long as capture costs are not too high (Clark 1976).

Of course many deep issues are raised in this definition of the SSE that, in the interests of brevity, are only touched on here. The meanings of "sufficient for a good life" and "sustainable for a long future" have to be left vague. But any economic system must give implicit answers to these dialectical questions, even when it refuses to face them explicitly. For example, the growth economy implicitly says that there is no such thing as sufficiency because more is always better, and that a twenty-year future is quite long enough if the discount rate is 10%. Many would prefer explicit vagueness to such implicit precision.

Moving from Growthmania to the Steady State in Thought: Theoretical and Moral Anomalies of the Growth Paradigm That Are Resolved by the Steady State

The growth economy runs into two kinds of fundamental limits: the biophysical and the ethicosocial. Although they are by no means totally independent, it is worthwhile to distinguish between them.

Biophysical Limits to Growth The biophysical limits to growth arise from three interrelated conditions: finitude, entropy, and ecological interdependence. The economy, in its physical dimensions, is an open subsystem of our finite and closed ecosystem, which is both the supplier of its low-entropy raw materials and the recipient of its high-entropy wastes. The growth of the economic subsystem is limited by the fixed size of the host ecosystem, by its dependence on the ecosystem as a source of low-entropy inputs and as a sink for high-entropy wastes, and by the complex ecological connections that are more easily disrupted as the scale of the economic subsystem (the throughput) grows relative to the total ecosystem. Moreover, these three basic limits interact. Finitude would not be so limiting if everything could be recycled, but entropy prevents complete recycling. Entropy would not be so limiting if environmental sources and sinks were infinite, but both are finite. That both are finite, plus the entropy law, means that the ordered structures of the economic subsystem are maintained at the expense of creating a more-than-offsetting amount of disorder in the rest of the system. If it is largely the sun that pays the disorder costs, the entropic costs of throughput, as it is with traditional peasant economies, then we need not worry. But if these entropic costs (depletion and pollution) are mainly inflicted on the terrestrial environment, as in a modern industrial economy, then they interfere with complex ecological life-support services rendered to the economy by nature. The loss of these services should surely be counted as a cost of growth, to be weighed against benefits at the margin. But our national accounts emphatically do not do this.

Standard growth economics ignores finitude, entropy, and ecological interdependence because the concept of throughput is absent from its preanalytic vision, which is that of an isolated circular flow of exchange value (see figure 2, page 47), as can be verified by examining the first few chapters of any basic textbook (Daly 1985; Georgescu-Roegen 1971). The physical dimension of commodities and factors is at best totally abstracted from (left out altogether) and at worst assumed to flow in a circle, just like exchange value. It is as if one were to study physiology solely in terms of the circulatory system without ever mentioning the digestive tract. The dependence of the organism on its environment would not be evident. The absence of the concept of throughput in the economists' vision means that the economy carries on no exchange with its environment. It is, by implication, a self-sustaining isolated system, a giant perpetual motion machine. The focus on exchange value in the macroeconomic circular flow also abstracts from use value and any idea of purpose other than maximization of the circular flow of exchange value.

But everyone, including economists, knows perfectly well that the economy takes in raw material from the environment and gives back waste. So why is this undisputed fact ignored in the circular flow paradigm? Economists are interested in scarcity. What is not scarce is abstracted from. Environmental sources and sinks were considered infinite relative to the demands of the economy, which was more or less the case during the formative years of economic theory. Therefore it was not an unreasonable abstraction. But it is highly unreasonable to continue omitting the concept of throughput after the scale of the economy has grown to the point where sources and sinks for the throughput are obviously scarce, even if this new absolute scarcity does not register in relative prices. The current practice of ad hoc introduction of "externalities" to take account of the effects of the growing scale of throughput that do not fit the circular flow model is akin to the use of "epicycles" to explain the departures of astronomical observations from the theoretical circular motion of heavenly bodies.

Nevertheless, many economists hang on to the infinite-resources assumption in one way or another, because otherwise they would have to admit that economic growth faces limits, and that is "unthinkable." The usual ploy is to appeal to the infinite possibilities of technology and resource substitution (ingenuity) as a dynamic force that can continuously outrun depletion and pollution. This counterargument is flawed in many respects. First, technology and infinite substitution mean only that one form of low-entropy matter/energy is substituted for another, within a finite and diminishing set of low-entropy sources. Such substitution is often very advantageous, but we never substitute high-entropy wastes for low-entropy resources in net terms. Second, the claim is frequently made that reproducible capital is a near-perfect substitute for resources. But this assumes that capital can be produced independently of resources, which is absurd. Furthermore, it flies in the teeth of the obvious complementarity of capital and resources in production. The capital stock is an agent for transforming the resource flow from raw material into a product (Georgescu-Roegen 1971). More capital does not substitute for less resources, except on a very restricted margin. You cannot make the same house by substituting more saws for less wood.

The growth advocates are left with one basic argument: resource and environmental limits have not halted growth in the past and therefore will not do so in the future. But such logic proves too much, namely, that nothing new can ever happen. A famous general survived a hundred battles without a scratch, and that was still true when he was blown up.

Earl Cook offered some insightful criticism of this faith in limitless ingenuity in one of his last articles (Cook 1982). The appeal of the limitless-ingenuity argument, he contended, lies not in the scientific grounding of its premises nor in the cogency of its logic but rather in the fact that

> the concept of limits to growth threatens vested interests and power structures; even worse, it threatens value structures in which lives have been invested.... Abandonment of belief in perpetual motion was a major step toward recognition of the true human condition. It is significant that "mainstream" economists never abandoned that belief and do not accept the relevance to the economic process of the Second Law of Thermodynamics; their position as high priests of the market economy would become untenable did they do so. [Cook 1982, p. 198]

Indeed it would. Therefore, much ingenuity is devoted to "proving" that ingenuity is unlimited. Julian Simon, George Gilder, Herman Kahn, and Ronald Reagan trumpeted this theme above all others. Every technical accomplishment, no matter how ultimately insignificant, is celebrated as one more victory in an infinite series of future victories of technology over nature. The Greeks called this hubris. The Hebrews were warned to "beware of saying in your heart, 'My own strength and the might of my own hand won this power for me'" (Deut. 8:17). But such wisdom is drowned out in the drumbeat of the see-no-evil "optimism" of growthmania. All the more necessary is it then to repeat Earl Cook's trenchant remark that "without the enormous amount of work done by nature in concentrating flows of energy and stocks of resources, human ingenuity would be onanistic. What does it matter that human ingenuity may be limitless, when matter and energy are governed by other rules than is information?" (Cook 1982, p. 194).

Ethicosocial Limits Even when growth is, with enough ingenuity, still possible, ethicosocial limits may render it undesirable. Four ethicosocial propositions limiting the desirability of growth are briefly considered below.

1. *The desirability of growth financed by the drawdown of geological capital is limited by the cost imposed on future generations.* In standard economics the balancing of future against present costs and benefits is done by discounting. A time discount rate is a numerical way of expressing the value judgment that beyond a

certain point the future is not worth anything to presently living people. The higher the discount rate, the sooner that point is reached. The value of the future to future people does not count in the standard approach.

Perhaps a more discriminating, though less numerical, principle for balancing the present and the future would be that the basic needs of the present should always take precedence over the basic needs of the future but that the basic needs of the future should take precedence over the extravagant luxury of the present.

2. *The desirability of growth financed by takeover of habitat is limited by the extinction or reduction in number of sentient subhuman species whose habitat disappears.* Economic growth requires space for growing stocks of artifacts and people and for expanding sources of raw material and sinks for waste material. Other species also require space, their "place in the sun." The instrumental value of other species to us, the life-support services they provide, was touched on in the discussion of biophysical limits above. Another limit derives from the intrinsic value of other species, that is, counting them as sentient, though probably not self-conscious, beings which experience pleasure and pain and whose experienced "utility" should be counted positively in welfare economics, even though it does not give rise to maximizing market behavior.

The intrinsic value of subhuman species should exert some limit on habitat takeover in addition to the limit arising from instrumental value. But it is extremely difficult to say how much (Birch and Cobb 1981). Clarification of this limit is a major philosophical task, but if we wait for a definitive answer before imposing any limits on takeover, then the question will be rendered moot by extinctions which are now occurring at an extremely rapid rate relative to past ages (Ehrlich and Ehrlich 1981).

3. *The desirability of aggregate growth is limited by its self-canceling effects on welfare.* Keynes (1930) argued that absolute wants (those we feel independently of the condition of others) are not insatiable. Relative wants (those we feel only because their satisfaction makes us feel superior to others) are indeed insatiable, for, as Keynes put it, "The higher the general level, the higher still are they." Or, as J. S. Mill expressed it, "Men do not desire to be rich, but to be richer than other men." At the current margin of production in rich countries it is very likely that welfare increments (increments in well-being) are largely a function of changes in relative income (insofar as they depend on income at all). Since the struggle for relative shares is a zero-sum game,

it is clear that aggregate growth cannot increase aggregate welfare. To the extent that welfare depends on relative position, growth is unable to increase welfare in the aggregate. It is subject to the same kind of self-canceling trap that we find in the arms race.

Because of this self-canceling effect of relative position, aggregate growth is less productive of human welfare than we heretofore thought. Consequently, other competing goals should rise relative to growth in the scale of social priorities (Abramowitz 1979). Future generations, subhuman species, commnity, and whatever else has been sacrificed in the name of growth should henceforth be sacrificed less simply because growth is less productive of general happiness than used to be the case when marginal income was dedicated mainly to the satisfaction of absolute rather than relative wants.

4. *The desirability of aggregate growth is limited by the corrosive effects on moral standards resulting from the very attitudes that foster growth, such as glorification of self-interest and a scientistic-technocratic worldview.* On the demand side of commodity markets, growth is stimulated by greed and acquisitiveness, intensified beyond the "natural" endowment from original sin by the multibillion-dollar advertising industry. On the supply side, technocratic scientism proclaims the possibility of limitless expansion and preaches a reductionistic, mechanistic philosophy which, in spite of its success as a research program, has serious shortcomings as a worldview. As a research program it very effectively furthers power and control, but as a worldview it leaves no room for purpose, much less for any distinction between good and bad purposes. "Anything goes" is a convenient moral slogan for the growth economy because it implies that anything also sells. To the extent that growth has a well-defined purpose, then it is limited by the satisfaction of that purpose. Expanding power and shrinking purpose lead to uncontrolled growth for its own sake, which is wrecking the moral and social order just as surely as it is wrecking the ecological order (Hirsch 1976).

The situation of economic thought today can be summarized by a somewhat farfetched but apt analogy. Neoclassical economics, like classical physics, is relevant to a special case that assumes that we are far from limits—far from the limiting speed of light or the limiting smallness of an elementary particle in physics—and far from the biophysical limits of the earth's carrying capacity and the ethicosocial limits of satiety in economics. Just as in physics, so in economics: the classical theories do not work well in regions close to limits. A more general theory is needed to embrace both normal and limiting cases. In economics this need becomes greater with time because the ethic of growth itself guarantees that the close-to-the-limits case becomes more and more the norm. The nearer the economy is to limits, the less can we accept the practical judgment most economists make, namely, that "a change in economic welfare implies a change in total welfare in the same direction if not in the same degree" (Abramowitz 1979). Rather, we must learn to define and explicitly count the other component of total welfare that growth inhibits and erodes when it presses against limits.

Moving from Growthmania to the Steady State in Practice: Failures of Growth as Forced First Steps Toward a Steady-State Economy

No doubt the biggest growth failure is the continuing arms race, where growth has led to less security rather than more and has raised the stakes from loss of individual lives to loss of life itself in wholesale ecocide. Excessive population growth, toxic wastes, acid rain, climate modification, devastation of rain forests, and the loss of ecosystem services resulting from these aggressions against the environment represent case studies in growth failure. Seeing them as first steps toward a steady-state economy requires the conscious willing of a hopeful attitude.

All the growth failures mentioned above are failures of the growth economy to respect the biophysical limits of its host. I would like also to consider some symptoms of growthmania within the economy itself. Three examples will be considered: money fetishism and the paper economy, faulty national accounts and the treachery of quantified success indexes, and the ambivalent "information economy."

Money Fetishism and the Paper Economy Money fetishism is a particular case of what Alfred North Whitehead called "the fallacy of misplaced concreteness," which consists in reasoning at one level of abstraction but applying the conclusions of that reasoning to a different level of abstraction. It argues that, since abstract exchange value flows in a circle, so do the physical commodities constituting real GNP. Or, since money in the bank can grow forever at compound interest, so can real wealth, and so can welfare. Whatever is true for the abstract symbol of wealth is assumed to hold for concrete wealth itself.

Money fetishism is alive and well in a world in which banks in wealthy countries make loans to poor countries and then, when the debtor countries cannot make the repayment, simply make new loans to enable the payment of interest on old loans, thereby avoiding taking a loss on a bad debt. Using new loans to pay interest on old loans is worse than a Ponzi scheme, but the exponential snowballing of debt is expected to be offset by a snowballing of real growth in debtor countries. The international debt impasse is a clear symptom of the basic disease of growthmania. Too many accumulations of money are seeking ways to grow exponentially in a world in which the physical scale of the economy is already so large relative to the ecosystem that there is not much room left for growth of anything that has a physical dimension.

Marx, and Aristotle before him, pointed out that the danger of money fetishism arises as a society progressively shifts its focus from use value to exchange value, under the pressure of increasingly complex division of labor and exchange. The sequence is sketched below in four steps, using Marx's shorthand notation for labels.

1. *C-C'*. One commodity (C) is directly traded for a different commodity (C'). The exchange values of the two commodities are by definition equal, but each trader gains an increased use value. This is simple *barter*. No money exists, so there can be no money fetishism.

2. *C-M-C'*. *Simple commodity circulation* begins and ends with a use value embodied in a commodity. Money (M) is merely a convenient medium of exchange. The object of exchange remains the acquisition of an increased use value. C represents a greater use value to the trader, but C' is still a use value, limited by its specific use or purpose. One has, say, a greater need for a hammer than a knife but has no need for two hammers, much less for fifty. The incentive to accumulate use values is very limited.

3. *M-C-M'*. As simple commodity circulation gave way to *capitalist circulation*, the sequence shifted. It now begins with money capital and ends with money capital. The commodity or use value is now an intermediary step in bringing about the expansion of exchange value by some amount of profit, $\Delta M = M'-M$. Exchange value has no specific use or physical dimension to impose concrete limits. One dollar of exchange value is not as good as two, and fifty dollars is better yet, and a million is much better, etc. Unlike concrete use

values, which spoil or deteriorate when hoarded, abstract exchange value can accumulate indefinitely without spoilage or storage costs. In fact, exchange value can grow by itself at compound interest. But as Frederick Soddy (Daly 1980) pointed out, "You cannot permanently pit an absurd human convention [compound interest] against a law of nature [entropic decay]."[1] "Permanently," however, is not the same as "in the meantime," during which we have, at the micro level, bypassed the absurdity of accumulating use values by accumulating exchange value and holding it as a lien against future use values. But unless future use value, or real wealth, has grown as fast as accumulations of exchange value have grown, then at the end of some time period there will be a devaluation of exchange value by inflation or some other form of debt repudiation. At the macro level limits will reassert themselves, even when ignored at the micro level, where the quest for exchange value accumulation has become the driving force.

4. M-M'. We can extend Marx's stages one more step to the *paper economy*, in which, for many transactions, concrete commodities "disappear" even as an intermediary step in the expansion of exchange value. Manipulations of symbols according to arbitrary and changing tax rules, accounting conventions, depreciation, mergers, public relations imagery, advertising, litigation, and so on, all result in a positive ΔM for some, but no increase in social wealth, and hence an equal negative ΔM for others. Such "paper entrepreneurialism" and "rent-seeking" activities seem to be absorbing more and more business talent. Echoes of Frederick Soddy are audible in the statement of Robert Reich (1983, p. 153) that "the set of symbols developed to represent real assets has lost the link with any actual productive activity. Finance has progressively evolved into a sector all its own, only loosely connected to industry." Unlike Soddy, however, Reich does not appreciate the role played by biophysical limits in redirecting efforts from manipulating resistant matter and energy toward manipulating pliant symbols. He thinks that, as more flexible and information-intensive production processes replace traditional mass production, somehow financial symbols and physical realities will again become congruent. But it may be that as physical resources become harder to acquire, as evidenced by falling energy rates of return on investment (Cleveland et al. 1984), the incentive to bypass the

---

[1] Frederick Soddy's ideas on finance and banking are further discussed in Part 6 of Herman Daly, *Beyond Growth: The Economics of Sustainable Development.*

physical world by moving from *M-C-M'* to *M-M'* becomes ever greater. We may then keep growing on paper, but not in reality. This illusion is fostered by our national accounting conventions. It could be that we are moving toward a nongrowing economy a bit faster than we think. If the cost of toxic waste dumps were subtracted from the value product of the chemical industry, we might discover that we have already attained zero growth in value from that sector of the economy.

Faulty National Accounting and the Treachery of Quantified Success Indicators Our national accounts are designed in such a way that they cannot reflect the costs of growth, except by perversely counting the resulting defensive expenditures as further growth. It is by now a commonplace to point out that GNP does not reveal whether we are living off income or capital, off interest or principal. Depletion of fossil fuels, minerals, forests, and soils is capital consumption, yet such unsustainable consumption is treated no differently from sustainable yield production (true income) in GNP. But not only do we decumulate positive capital (wealth), we also accumulate negative capital (illth) in the form of toxic-waste deposits and nuclear dumps. To speak so insouciantly of "economic growth" whenever produced goods accumulate, when at the same time natural wealth is being diminished and man-made illth is increasing represents, to say the least, an enormous prejudgment about the relative size of these changes (Hueting 1980). Only on the assumption that environmental sources and sinks are infinite does such a procedure make sense.

Another problem with national accounts is that they do not reflect the "informal" or "underground" economy. Estimates of the size of the underground economy in the United States range from around 4% to around 30% of GNP, depending on the technique of estimation (Tanzi 1983). The underground economy has apparently grown in recent times, probably as a result of higher taxes, growing unemployment, and frustration with the increasing complexity and arbitrariness of the paper economy. Like household production, of which they are extensions, none of these informal productive activities are registered in GNP. Their growth represents an adaptation to the failure of traditional economic growth to provide employment and security. As an adaptation to growth failure in the GNP sector, the underground economy may represent a forced first step toward an SSE.

But not everything about the underground economy is good. Many of its activities (drugs, prostitution) are illegal, and much of its basic motivation is tax evasion, although in today's world there may well be some noble reasons for not paying taxes.

The act of measurement always involves some interaction and interference with the reality being measured. This generalized Heisenberg principle is especially relevant in economics, where the measurement of a success index on which rewards are based, or taxes calculated, nearly always has perverse repercussions on the reality being measured. Consider, for example, the case of management by quantified objectives applied to a tuberculosis hospital, as related to me by a physician. It is well known that TB patients cough less as they get better. So the number of coughs per day was taken as a quantitative measure of the patient's improvement. Small microphones were attached to the patients' beds, and their coughs were duly recorded and tabulated. The staff quickly perceived that they were being evaluated in inverse proportion to the number of times their patients coughed. Coughing steadily declined as doses of codeine were more frequently prescribed. Relaxed patients cough less. Unfortunately the patients got worse, precisely because they were not coughing up and spitting out the congestion. The cough index was abandoned.

The cough index totally subverted the activity it was designed to measure because people served the abstract quantitative index instead of the concrete qualitative goal of health. Perversities induced by quantitative goal setting are pervasive in the literature on Soviet planning: set the production quota for cloth in linear feet, and the bolt gets narrower; set it in square feet, and the cloth gets thinner; set it by weight, and it gets too thick. But one need not go as far away as the Soviet Union to find examples. The phenomenon is ubiquitous. In universities a professor is rewarded according to number of publications. Consequently the length of articles is becoming shorter as we approach the minimum publishable unit of research. At the same time the frequency of coauthors has increased. More and more people are collaborating on shorter and shorter papers. What is being maximized is not discovery and dissemination of coherent knowledge but the number of publications on which one's name appears.

The purpose of these examples of the treachery of quantified success indexes is to suggest that, like them, GNP is not only a passive mismeasure but also an actively distorting influence on the very reality that it aims only to reflect. GNP is an index of throughput, not welfare. Throughput is positively correlated with welfare in a world of infinite sources and sinks, but in a finite world with fully employed carrying capacity, throughput is a *cost*. To design national policies to maximize GNP is just not smart. It is practically equivalent to maximizing depletion and pollution.

The usual reply to these well-known criticisms of GNP is, "So it's not perfect, but it's all we have. What would you put in its place?" It is assumed that we *must* have some numerical index. But why? Might we not be better off without the GNP statistic, even with nothing to "put in its place"? Were not the TB patients better off without the cough index, when physicians and administrators had to rely on "soft" qualitative judgment? The world before 1940 got along well enough without calculating GNP. Perhaps we could come up with a better system of national accounts, but abandoning GNP need not be postponed until then. Politically we are not likely to abandon the GNP statistic any time soon. But in the meantime we can start thinking of it as "gross national cost."

The Ambivalent "Information Economy" The much-touted "information economy" is often presented as a strategy for escaping biophysical limits. Its modern devotees proclaim that "whereas matter and energy decay according to the laws of entropy ... information is ... immortal." And, further, "The universe itself is made of information—matter and energy are only simple forms of it" (Turner 1984). Such half-truths forget that information does not exist apart from physical brains, books, and computers, and, further, that brains require the support of bodies, books require library buildings, computers run on electricity, etc. At worst the information economy is seen as a computer-based explosion of the symbol manipulations of the paper economy. More occult powers are attributed to information and its handler, the computer, by the silicon gnostics of today than any primitive shaman ever dared claim for his favorite talisman. And this in spite of the enormous legitimate importance of the computer, which needs no exaggeration.

Other notions of the information economy are by no means nonsensical. When the term refers to qualitative improvements in products to make them more serviceable, longer-lasting, more repairable, and better-looking (Hawken 1983), then we have what was earlier referred to as "development."

To think of qualitative improvement as the embodiment of more information in a product is not unreasonable.

But the best question to ask about the information economy is that posed by T. S. Eliot in "Choruses from 'The Rock'":

Where is the wisdom we have lost in knowledge?
Where is the knowledge we have lost in information?

Why stop with an information economy? Why not a knowledge economy? Why not a wisdom economy?

Knowledge is structured, organized information rendered intelligible and understandable. It is hard to imagine embodying a bit of isolated information (in the sense of communications theory) in a product. What is required for qualitative improvement of products is knowledge—an understanding of the purpose of the item, the nature of the materials, and the alternative designs that are permitted within the restrictions of purpose and nature of the materials. Probably many writers on the subject use the term "information" synonymously with "knowledge," and what they have in mind is really already a "knowledge economy." The important step is to go to a "wisdom economy."

Wisdom involves a knowledge of techniques plus an understanding of purposes and their relative importance, along with an appreciation of the limits to which technique and purpose are subject. To distinguish a real limit from a temporary bottleneck, and a fundamental purpose from a velleity, requires wise judgment. Growthmania cannot be checked without wise judgment. Since events are forcing us to think in terms of an information economy, it is perhaps not too much to hope that we will follow that thrust all the way to a wisdom economy, one design feature of which, I submit, will be that of a dynamic steady state.

The main characteristics of such a wisdom economy were adumbrated by Earl Cook (1982) in his list of nine "Beliefs of a Neomalthusian," and I will conclude by listing them:

1. "Materials and energy balances constrain production.
2. "Affluence has been a much more fecund mother of invention than has necessity." That is, science and technology require an economic surplus

to support them, and a few extra but poor geniuses provided by rapid population growth will not help.

3. "Real wealth is by technology out of nature," or, as William Petty would have said, technology may be the father of wealth, but nature is the mother.

4. "The appropriate human objective is the maximization of psychic income by conversion of natural resources to useful commodities and by the use of those commodities as efficiently as possible," and "the appropriate measure of efficiency in the conversion of resources to psychic income is the human life-hour, with the calculus extended to the yet unborn."

5. "Physical laws are not subject to repeal by men," and of all the laws of economics, the law of diminishing returns is closest to a physical law.

6. "The industrial revolution can be defined as that period of human history when basic resources, especially nonhuman energy, grew cheaper and more abundant."

7. "The industrial revolution so defined is ending."

8. "There are compelling reasons to expect natural resources to become more expensive."

9. "Resource problems vary so much from country to country that careless geographic and commodity aggregation may confuse rather than clarify." That is, "it serves no useful purpose to combine the biomass of Amazonia with that of the Sahel to calculate a per capita availability of firewood."

Earl Cook would have been the last person to offer these nine points as a complete blueprint for a wisdom economy. But I think that he got us off to a good start.

REFERENCES

Abramowitz, M. 1979. "Economic Growth and its Discontents." *Economics and Human Welfare*, M. Boskin, ed. New York: Academic Press.

Birch, C. and John Cobb. 1981. *The Liberation of Life*. Cambridge: Cambridge University Press.

Clark, C. W. 1976. *Mathematical Bioeconomics*. New York: Wiley.

Cleveland et al. 1984. "Energy and the U.S. Economy: A Biophysical Perspective." *Science 225*.

Cook, E. 1982. "The Consumer as Creator: A Criticism of Faith in Limitless Ingenuity." *Energy Exploration and Exploitation* I(3): 194.

Daly, Herman E. 1980. "The Economic Thought of Frederick Soddy." *History of Political Economy* 12(4).

Daly, Herman E. 1985. "The Circular Flow of Exchange Value and the Linear Throughput of Matter-Energy: A Case of Misplaced Concreteness." *Review of Social Economy* 43(3): 279-97.

Ehrlich, P. and A. Ehrlich. 1981. *Extinction.* New York: Random House.

Georgescu-Roegen, Nicholas. 1971. *The Entropy Law and the Economic Process.* Cambridge, MA: Harvard University Press.

Hawken, P. 1983. *The Next Economy.* New York: Ballantine.

Hirsch, F. 1976. *Social Limits to Growth.* Cambridge, MA: Harvard University Press.

Hueting, Roefie. 1980. *New Scarcity and Economic Growth.* Amsterdam: North Holland Publishing Co.

Keynes, J. M. 1930. "The Economic Possibilities for Our Grandchildren." *Essays in Persuasion.* New York: Norton.

Reich, R. B. 1983. *The Next American Frontier.* New York: Penguin.

Simon, J. 1981. *The Ultimate Resource.* Princeton, NJ: Princeton University Press.

Tanzi, V., ed. 1983. *The Underground Economy in the United States and Abroad.* Lexington, KY: Heath.

Turner, F. 1984. "Escape from Modernism." *Harper's.* November.

18 Shrink and Prosper*

Alan Weisman

Contraction

"I will do my best," promises the little white bear. "I will carry you," it continues in the politest Japanese, "as though you were a princess."

The bear's sex is unclear, its voice falling in the range that overlaps tenor and contralto. From its gracefully tapered waist, suggestive of a female nurse, it bends forward over a man—far from a princess—who lies on a hospital bed in a large windowless room. The bright green floor is polished so highly that it reflects the bear's round ears, big black eyes, crinkly smile, and smooth white skin.

It extends two slim paws. One forearm slides under the patient's knees, while the other reaches under his back. Behind it, Susumu Sato, a young engineer with an unruly crew cut and black-rimmed glasses, reaches to touch a spot on the polar bear's left triceps, and it moves closer. Three men who are watching audibly inhale. Gently, the bear lifts and straightens until the patient is suspended over the floor, cradled in its arms.

"Is it all right?" asks Sato. A silver ballpoint protrudes from a penholder on his left sleeve.

"Quite comfortable," the man replies. To be snug against the bear's well-padded chest is, in fact, oddly comforting.

The bear's name is Riba II, meaning Robot for Interactive Body Assistance, Second Edition. According to its inventors, it is the world's first robot that can

---

* This chapter is an excerpt from Alan Weisman, *Countdown: Our Last, Best Hope for a Future on Earth?* New York: Little, Brown and Company, 2013: pp. 297–329.

lift a human in its arms. Now it pivots on rollers concealed in its wheeled base—no rear paws—and glides soundlessly over the shiny green floor to a waiting wheelchair. On its shoulders are tiny blinking green lights. "They're just decorative," says chief engineer Shijie Guo, who follows anxiously behind, his hair falling onto his forehead. Now comes the hard part, but RIBA II is the least nervous creature in the room—and it actually does seem like a creature, and not just in the Shinto sense that everything contains a spirit. Almost tenderly, the bear sets its human cargo onto the chair. Its right arm carefully lowers his legs, then slides away. Sato presses a rubber sensor on its left forearm. The bear straightens up.

"I'm finished," it announces.

Everybody in the room exhales and claps. They are in the Nagoya Science Park, where RIBA II was built jointly by RIKEN, Japan's oldest scientific research and development firm, and Tokai Rubber Industries. Since 1929, Tokai Rubber has mainly made automotive parts, such as hoses and wiper blades. But Japan is the first country to be facing the inevitable fate of other developed nations, and its industries are shifting accordingly. Already, more

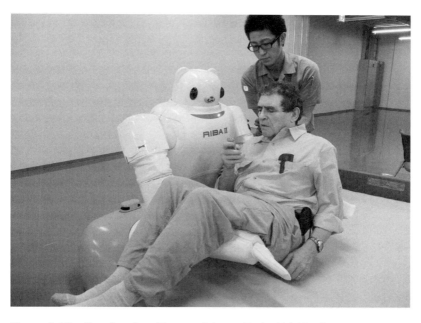

Figure 1 Riba II and author, Nagoya Science Park, Aichi Prefecture, Japan

CREDIT: photograph by Tunko Takahashi

than 60 percent of the world's industrial assembly robots are from Japan, and the reason is no accident.

What the Ayatollah Khamenei fears for Iran is already happening in Japan: a country with below-replacement growth is now reaching the end of the momentum that kept its numbers rising for two generations after its fertility plummeted. In Japan's case, however, there was no intentional program to curb runaway population growth. Like Iran, it had just suffered through a terrible war, albeit one of its own making.

In 1931, Japan, a mountainous country with only 15 percent of its land suitable for agriculture, found itself in an unprecedented situation: Its population had grown to 65 million, far more than it could feed. It was already importing soybeans from Manchuria, the Chinese region bordering Korea, which also had iron and coal that resource-poor Japan needed. With China weakened by internal strife during the early Mao years, the temptation to invade was irresistible.

As Germany would soon similarly conclude about its neighbor Poland, Japan saw thinly settled Manchuria as a place to move surplus population. But one invasion led to another, and by 1937, Japanese expansionism had pushed deeper into China. In 1941, bent on controlling the entire Asian Pacific, it attacked the United States at Pearl Harbor.

Four years later, Japan's dreams of empire were dead. Its defeated soldiers returned to their wives, and predictably, a baby boom followed. Unlike the victorious United States, whose armaments industry had pulled it out of the Depression, Japan's economy was wrecked. Nevertheless, over the next five years its wartime population of 72 million spurted to 83 million.

The country that couldn't feed itself two decades earlier now had millions on the verge of starvation. By the late 1940s, hundreds of thousands of Japanese mothers desperate to feed their children were seeking illegal abortions, with the usual percentage of unfortunate outcomes. Until then, legal abortions involved a complicated process to verify an emergency. Now, faced with a nationwide emergency, in 1948 Japan passed the Eugenic Protection Law, legalizing contraception, abortion, and sterilization for health reasons.

A year later, with the crisis unabated, the law was extended to permit abortions and family planning for economic reasons. Thus, Japan cut off its postwar baby boom. Birth rates soon hovered near replacement. The country's economy struggled back. In the 1950s, the phrase "Made in Japan" was mocked by the victors across the Pacific as synonymous with cheap, but the victors kept buying. Gradually, Japan's humble industries evolved into electronics and automobile manufacturing that earned billions and restored its respect. Wealth financed education, including for women, and fertility rates dropped further, to under 1.4 children per female.

Which is why RIKEN and Tokai Rubber are making robots—specifically, a nice white teddy bear robot that can carefully cradle elderly people in its padded arms, soothe them with courtesy and a secure embrace, and move them from bed to chair and ultimately to the most critical challenge: the bathroom.

"We have to do this," says chief engineer Guo, "because there is a double problem to solve: Soon Japan will have many more old people who have trouble moving by themselves, and many fewer young people available to help them. There is already a shortage of geriatric nurses. It is hard to lift people forty times a day while working two shifts in twenty-four hours. Half of elderly caregivers complain of back pain. We'll need robots for all the jobs people don't want to do, because there will not be enough workers."

So far, Riba II takes a minute and a half to pick people up from bed and deposit them in the wheelchair. "A human usually takes ten seconds. We have to get under a minute to be acceptable." After lifting, nurses say that dealing with adult diapers is their hardest task. Guo took a class in how to clean up geriatric patients. "It's a tough one," he admits. Then there's communication: much R&D has gone into what the robot should say to people. "It has to talk, to make the patient feel safe. This one can identify voices, but only recognizes some simple words. But we plan for it to greet people, to do therapeutic massage, even to sing to lonely old people."

Whether technology can meet such human psychological needs remains to be seen, but something has to deal with the larger demographic dilemma that Riba II was invented to help solve. Western Europe is watching closely to see what will happen here, because Japan is the first to reach the end of its demographic transition—when high mortality and high birthrates both turn to low. Japan's first shrunken generation—born in the late forties and early fifties, when Japanese severely curtailed their reproduction—is now entering retirement, and members of the generation before them are entering their final years.

With nearly the world's highest life expectancy—until the March 2011 earthquake and tsunami that hit Fukushima and surrounding prefectures killed twenty thousand people in one day, it was the highest—its elderly population will continue to boom. (Japan's 79.4 years for men and 85.9 years for women is only slightly behind Hong Kong.) The U.S. Census Bureau projects that by 2040 there will one Japanese centenarian for every new Japanese baby. But long before that, as the large generation that preceded the demographic downsizing passes on, Japan's numbers will suddenly plunge.

This demographic destiny cannot be reversed, and has already begun. In 2006, for the first time since World War II, Japan recorded more deaths than births. Its population peaked at just over 128 million. Since then, it has fallen each year; by 2012, it was at 126.5 million and dropping. Before 2060, even if life expectancy continues to rise, Japan will be back to around 86 million, which was its population in 1950.

There is a quick fix to looming labor problems like Japan's, one that another country whose population is already declining—Cuba—is contemplating. Cuba's 11 million are diminishing due both to emigration and to low fertility rates resulting from a high percentage of female university graduates, plus decades of economic difficulty, universal health coverage, and legal abortion to back up family planning. To shore up its contracting labor force, Cuba is considering wooing immigrants from nations with even less favorable economics, such as Haiti.

Likewise, immigrants should fill Europe's labor breach in coming decades. Despite below-replacement birthrates, in 2012 Germany's population actually grew by nine hundred thousand, mainly due to immigration from eastern Europe made possible by EU membership. But Germany's first wave of immigrant labor—thousands of Turks, imported after the Berlin Wall cut off the supply of East German migrants—has been less easy to absorb. Today, there are 4 million Turks in Germany, a source of unresolved cultural tension and tightened immigration policies. In 2010, German chancellor Angela Merkel told a meeting of Christian Democratic Union Party youth, "At the start of the '60s we invited the guestworkers to Germany. We kidded ourselves for a while that they wouldn't stay, that one day they'd go home. That isn't what happened. And of course the tendency was to say: let's be multikulti and live next to each other and enjoy being together, [but] this concept has failed, failed utterly."[1]

The Cold War that cleaved Germany shortened its postwar baby boom, and the advent of birth control pills nearly halved birthrates on both sides of the Iron Curtain. Reunification of East and West Germany in 1990 only seemed to further depress fertility. Even tempting couples with €2,000 a year for having a second child hasn't made a difference. German working mothers complain that with inadequate day care, school days that end as early as 1:00 p.m. make it even more complicated to have children. The result is rock-bottom birthrates, and a population aging as fast as Japan's.

Should the rise of xenophobic political parties continue, European immigration rates could lower. But immigration so far has never been an option for Japan, which deeply values its largely homogeneous population: fewer than 2 percent of Japanese residents are foreign-born. One rationale offered for robot nurses is that they aren't burdened with cultural differences or unpleasant wartime histories that elderly Japanese might associate with East Asian health-care workers. Although some Japanese accuse their country of racism, most agree that shared cultural values are why Japanese society functions so smoothly, why its cities are so orderly, and why crime in Japan is so low.

And now it will have a low population to match, making it a laboratory for the question we all will face if we decide—or if nature decides for us— that to reduce human impact for our safety and survival, we must reduce the number of people on the planet. If we were any other species, as long as our numbers didn't drop low enough to endanger our gene pool, bringing our population into a more compatible balance with the rest of nature would be sufficient. But we are more complicated than that. We gather into societies, some as small as our own families, some as large as nations or multinational corporations, that thrive by trading with each other. Unlike nesting birds or pods of dolphins, however, we are not content with merely thriving. We always want more.

The measure of nearly every economy that humans have designed has been defined by whether or not it grows. The exceptions—potlatch societies of the Pacific Northwest; co-op communities—may have much to teach us, but they are so rare as to prove the rule. The business news judges how healthy the economy is by whether housing starts rose or fell this month. Never mind that each new house pushes sprawl ever farther, chews up landscape, and requires more resources to provide plumbing, sewers, electricity, and roads. That house represents profit for developers and real estate brokers, and jobs for carpenters, masons, plumbers, electricians, painters, carpet layers, landscapers, paving crews, and furnishers. Maintenance during its lifespan will create even more jobs. And the economy will grow on.

So what happens if there are fewer of us, needing fewer homes and fewer things? What happens during the transition to a smaller society, with fewer consumers every year—and fewer laborers paying into welfare coffers to support a surplus of unproductive, needy elderly people?

And what happens if we actually reach some optimum number of humans who can harvest and recycle resources at a replenishable pace, so that we achieve equilibrium with the planet that supports us? To maintain such an ideal level would mean never growing beyond it.

Can we do that? Can we have prosperity without growth?

Japan has no choice but to become the first modern society to try.

"Paradoxically," says Akihiko Matsutani, "our shrinking situation could end up being beneficial. We have to change our business model. That usually takes a long time, but we can't wait. This is the moment we have to change."

Matsutani, professor emeritus at one of Japan's premier economics schools, the National Graduate Institute for Policy Studies, has been saying things like this for years. Until recently, he's gotten scant attention: No one has wanted to hear that Japan's economy was demographically doomed to downsize. But now, events 180 miles north of his Tokyo institute have abruptly forced the entire nation to reconsider living beyond its means.

The moment Matsutani refers to is the aftermath of a 9.0-magnitude earthquake on March 11, 2011, off the Tohoku Peninsula in northeastern Japan, which pushed a tidal wave over the sea barriers at the Fukushima Daiichi Nuclear Power Plant. Three reactors exploded and melted down, and everyone living in a fifty-mile radius of the damaged facility had to evacuate.

That fifty-mile radius included some of Japan's richest farmland: until the disaster, Fukushima was known as the Kingdom of Fruits. A bunch of Fukushima grapes would sell for ¥2,500—over US$30—that is, until they vanished from the market because no one would buy them. The same for its sweet akatsuki peaches and its apples, cucumbers, and turnips.

The tragedy also caused Japanese to ask if it was wise to build nuclear plants near seismic faults and coastlines—a description that applied to most of the fifty-four atomic reactors that provided nearly one-third of Japan's electricity. In the building where Matsutani has his office, months later elevators were still off because of post-Fukushima energy restrictions, as were the air-conditioning and the electric toilet seats with their heated bidets, so beloved in Japan.

Akihiko Matsutani is shocked by the terrible losses his country has sustained, but not surprised. "People who keep saying that Japan should be like France, which gets most of its power from nuclear energy, forget that France isn't in an earthquake zone. But now that this accident has happened, we have an opportunity to do something positive." That something is learning to live within its limits, which both Fukushima and the shrinking Japanese population are forcing them to do. "This will actually be good for Japan," he insists.

Matsutani is the author of a book whose title makes progrowth economists shudder: Shrinking-Population Economics: Lessons from Japan, a copy of which sits on his uncluttered desk. On a blank piece of paper he sketches the iconic symbol of demography: a pyramid, which he divides into three sections. "In most countries, the tip of the pyramid represents the elderly. The middle"—he shades this portion with his pen —"is the active portion of the population, the labor force. The base, the biggest portion, is the young people. Babies, children, students."

Then he flips the drawing upside down. "This is Japan. Fewer children. Lots of elderly." He points to the shaded middle zone. "As more of these move up, we'll have fewer workers to replace them."

Recently, a research group at Tohoku University warned that in a thousand years, Japan's childbearing will cease—statistically anyway. They posted a simulated "Child Population Web Clock" showing that every one hundred seconds, the number of Japanese children drops by one—they're not dying, but growing up, and fewer babies are replacing them. At that rate, they conclude, "Japan would have only one child in May 3011. By the next year, therefore, there would be no children in Japan."

These kinds of horror stories about Japan's subreplacement fertility are nonsense, says Matsutani. Japan is certainly top-heavy with old people, and becoming more so. But once the age bubble bursts with the old, high-fertility generations dying off, subsequent generations will even out, and the pyramid will become a cube as the number of children will be closer to the numbers who are passing on. People won't stop having babies, and if fertility readjusts toward two children per couple—a reasonable outcome in a less-crowded world—population would stabilize.

However, he warns, reshaping demographic geometry from triangular to rectangular in a country with such long life spans takes at least a century. Either way, stable or shrinking, the population would not be growing, which raises a big question:

What happens to the economy?

Traditional economics preaches perpetual growth as a self-evident truth, even though nothing, save God or the universe, can possibly be perpetual—and there's some doubt about the universe. But assuming an ever-expanding economy were possible, there are only two ways to achieve it: keep inventing more new products (or new versions of old ones) and keep finding new consumers.

Being endlessly creative is hard. Being endlessly competitive to win all the customers works only as long as there are still more customers left—unless, of course, a growing population keeps giving birth to more new consumers. This is one of two reasons why most economists traditionally favor population growth. The other is bigger labor pools: the more workers competing for jobs, the less companies have to pay them.

Unfortunately for those economists—and for us, as long as the system works their way—on a finite planet, an economy dependent on constant growth is no more perpetual than a chain letter or pyramid scheme, which always needs more people buying in. Eventually, there aren't any more, and everything collapses. Or the raw stuff to make whatever's being sold grows scarce, and the substitutes aren't as good, or they run out, too.

* * *

Akihiko Matsutani is convinced that his shrinking country can and will have a viable economy, because Japan has no other choice. But it isn't as simple as fewer people needing fewer things. Although Matsutani agrees that a smaller population means less pressure on resources and land, he cautions that the transition to fewer people will place different strains on the environment.

"Suppose you have a sewage treatment plant for a million people," he says. It's an example he knows well; along with his economics degrees, he has a doctorate in civil engineering. "Then suppose the population drops to nine hundred thousand. You can't just remove 10 percent of the pipes. Even if population drops by half, you still have to maintain 100 percent of the infrastructure. That won't be easy when we have fewer laborers."

An economical alternative might be to abandon huge treatment facilities in favor of individual purification tanks for each house. "Centralized sewage treatment is probably better for the environment, but it will be impossible to maintain. So we may have to revise our standards, and accept a dirtier environment."

But he's encouraged that personal lifestyles need not suffer in a Japan with fewer people. A leaner economy, he says, will bring its own advantages.

"In the beginning, companies will try to save by cutting wages or workers, but they'll soon realize that laborers will have become more valuable, and they'll want to keep the ones they have. So lowering wages won't work. What will work instead is higher pay, but fewer hours. Right now, we work long hours for lower pay. Laborers will be pleased to have more leisure time. Since World War II ended, we've been obsessed with gross domestic product. But GDP has no direct bearing on living standards in a shrinking population economy."

The hope he sees is the chance to define prosperity by people's quality of life rather than what money can buy. In this paradoxical nation, where the world's most populous metropolitan area—Greater Tokyo, with 35 million people—coexists with the fastest-shrinking population, he sees a perfect opportunity for the country to decentralize.

"We'll have to think in terms of smaller systems, not a big government taking care of everything with big infrastructure. Smaller cities will make more sense. When population grows, prosperity means going to Disneyland once a month, and buying too much and throwing away too much. When population shrinks, prosperity is going on picnics, or taking your children camping. You don't throw things away—your values change from constant new things to things that last."

What will inspire investors in a shrinking world? Before he started teaching, Matsutani spent twenty-seven years in Japan's Finance Ministry. "Just like sewers, finance will get worse until we learn to adjust to a smaller scale. We will go to perpetual bonds—in a sense, we're already doing it. Japan's debt is trillions of yen. It's impossible to repay, so we just pay the interest. Perpetual bonds would work like that. We won't be as wealthy as when population was growing, but that doesn't mean we can't have profit. Total productivity will be less with fewer workers, but per-capita productivity won't change. The number of workers drops 10 percent, so do sales, and so do profits. But per person, it all remains the same."

In fact, something that traditional economists have ignored—especially those in Europe wringing their hands over declining populations—is that both Japan's and Germany's economies began recovering from a decade of slump and recession in the early years of the new millennium, at the same time their populations began to contract. By 2010, Germany had record economic growth, more than twice the rest of the European Union.

In Russia, precipitously dropping numbers predating even Japan's have panicked economic advisors to the Kremlin. Russia's birthrate began its descent with the 1991 collapse of communism and the loss of the Soviet Union's cradle-to-grave assurances of work, education, and shelter. Add to that Russia's high divorce rate, and since the USSR dissolved, Russia's population has dropped by 5 million. But even more significant than low fertility is the grim state of Russian health. Russia's incidence of syphilis is several hundred times higher than in western Europe. Its HIV rates are the world's fastest growing; by 2020, up to 10 percent of the population could be infected. Cardiovascular deaths are at epidemic levels, and the incidence of mortal violence and accidents is a dozen times higher than Britain's. Both heart disease and fatal injuries are linked to the Russian addiction to vodka, a national rate of alcoholism unmatched anywhere, which has only worsened since communism ended. Russia's life expectancy is about the same as Pakistan's, which is lower than most of Africa's.

At the same time, Russia's economy, fueled by its vast oil and gas reserves, has grown vigorously in the new millennium, resulting in the curious anomaly of Moscow, capital of the country with, until recently, the world's fastest-falling population, having the world's highest population of billionaires.[2]

Such numbers confound the conventional wisdom that having fewer people spells doom for robust economies. Nevertheless, Akihiko Matsutani's book about how shrinking Japan can remain prosperous has attracted scant attention from his country's financial circles and other economists.

"They'd rather translate American and European books about how to generate growth. They talk about rebuilding the fishing ports destroyed in the typhoon—except it will take up to twenty years to do that, and in twenty years only a quarter of the fishermen will still be alive, so three-fourths of the port facilities won't be necessary. Such simple discussion isn't taking place. People don't want to accept that things they know have changed. Some will say, okay, we can let more immigrant labor in. But at this point, we would need 24 million immigrants by 2030 to maintain our workforce at today's size. That won't happen."

What will happen, he says, is what's already happening. Not just to Japan, but to the world. "World population is still growing, but agricultural output isn't. Output from the seas is shrinking. Add those two together, and we get famines."

He looks at his glass-fronted bookshelves, filled with copies of his book. "In the animal world, when population exceeds its limits, species start reducing. Probably that is what will happen to us humans. Maybe we're lucky here in Japan, because we're not waiting until disaster reduces our population."

In the island city-state of Singapore, one of the world's most developed nations with one of the world's lowest birthrates—1.1 children per fertile woman—August 9 is celebrated as National Day, marking independence. In 2012, Mentos Singapore, a division of the multinational mint manufacturer, launched a promotion declaring the evening of August 9 to be "National Night"—during which, televised commercials urged, men should "raise the flag" and married couples should "go all the way for Singapore." Singapore had already sweetened this call to patriotic pillow duty with the world's most lavish baby bonuses: $4,000 apiece for a couple's first two children, and $6,000 each for the third and fourth. The government also matches, dollar for dollar, parental contributions to a child's savings account, up to $6,000 apiece for the first and second child, $12,000 for the third and fourth child, and $18,000[3] for each child thereafter.

During the 1970s, Singapore's government, fearing that the city-state would become overcrowded, had tried to convince everyone to "Stop at Two." That succeeded so well that by the mid-1980s they were trying to reverse it, and have been ever since. But to no avail: not even the extravagant baby bribes have tempted Singaporeans to have more children.

The Mentos campaign, set to a rap song —"it's National Night, so let's make fireworks ignite, let's make Singapore's birthrate right"—would have had even less chance in Japan. Each year, not only the number of babies but the number of Japanese marriages drops, further depressing childbirth in a culture where having a child out of wedlock is almost unknown. The falling marriage rates are often attributed to the disappearance of assured lifetime employment, once a staple with Japanese corporations. Without that security, fewer are willing to risk starting a family.

Government projections now assume that 36 percent of the current generation of young Japanese women will never have children.

On the eighth floor of an apartment tower in Takanawa, a posh central Tokyo neighborhood, Keiko, a thirty-five-year-old mother of a two-year-old daughter, greets her visitors. Two are friends who have brought their own daughters for a playdate; the third, who is unmarried, is a Spanish-language court interpreter (the accused are mainly Latin American drug mules). Keiko, round-faced with short dark hair, wears a gray T-shirt, capri pants, and a platinum wedding ring; Nanako, her daughter, is a miniature of her mother.

It is a Monday afternoon; Keiko's husband, an investment counselor at a finance company, left at 7:00 a.m. and won't return until 10:00 p.m. Keiko also used to work there. They had been married ten years when Nanako was born. "We didn't think we needed a child. We were having fun. Raising a kid is so much work, and none of my friends wanted the responsibility. But we decided to give our aging parents a grandchild."

They have no regrets—nor any intention of having more, she says, hugging Nanako, who's joined her on the charcoal gray couch. The apartment they own has maple floors and white shag rugs, but just two rooms, plus a compact kitchen. "It's hard enough with three of us. The size of a house pretty much limits the number of children." Most of her friends have just one. "A few have two. But more have none."

She hands Nanako a rice ball from a bowl on the granite coffee table, sends her back to her playmates, and confesses the extreme form of birth control she and her husband use to assure that they don't have another:

"Not having sex."

It's not as radical as it sounds, she says. "Frankly, Japanese people don't have sex much anymore."

That would definitely guarantee population decline. But surely there are other ways in Japan to prevent conception? "Of course," says Junko, the court interpreter. "But not having sex is the most common. Women here don't like Western medicine—I would never take pills, because of the side effects. And many women believe that an operation changes their hormones. Some use condoms, but young people don't like to. So either they abort, or do without sex."

"It's more than that," says Keiko. "Sex isn't how to prove affection in a marriage. When we were dating, we needed to do it to confirm our love.

But when people are married and become a family, they affirm their love just by living in the same house, eating the same food."

All these women—young, healthy, and quite lovely—nod in agreement. "Westerners can't believe it," says Keiko. "My German girlfriend keeps asking how is it conceivable that we don't have sex? But I don't miss it. I don't feel dried up, but I also don't feel that desire when I see my husband or any other attractive man. I'm very satisfied with my life. It's enough just for us to sleep together."

Again, no one argues. "My male friends say sex is just a form of recreation," says Junko. "Like going to a baseball game or the movies—in this case, to a bordello. Once a guy has a family, he doesn't see his wife as a woman anymore. She's family, like his mother or sister. Guys don't have sex with them, either."

A 2011 Japanese government survey showed that 36 percent of Japanese males aged sixteen to nineteen were either not interested in, or actually "despised," sex. A term for young men more enamored of animated video games than live female humans is "herbivores"—the implication being that, by comparison, dynamic Japanese career women are "carnivores."

"Japanese men are getting weak," says Junko. She glances out the picture window, where Japan's most blatant phallic symbol, the Eiffel-shaped Tokyo Tower, is spewing potent radio and TV signals. "And women don't have as many needs as men." More nods.

She laughs. "Our German girlfriend wouldn't agree."

Growth-Free Prosperity

Environmentally attuned Western economists have been mulling an economy of prosperity without growth for decades, especially since publication of The Limits to Growth and Paul and Anne Ehrlich's work. To the University of Maryland's Herman Daly, the dean of steady-state economists, it's simply the law of diminishing returns: produce too many goods, and they're not so good anymore.

"We then have uneconomic growth, producing 'bads' faster than goods— making us poorer, not richer," Daly, a former senior economist at the World Bank, has written. "Once we pass the optimal scale, growth becomes stupid in the short run and impossible to maintain in the long run."

Long before him, Thomas Robert Malthus, John Stuart Mill, and Adam Smith warned that economic growth, like everything else on Earth, was subject to resource limits. But identifying what doesn't work is one thing; figuring out what will, and how to transition to it, is another.

There's already an excellent model for the steady-state economy that Daly and his ecological economist colleagues have long espoused: the Earth itself. "Neither the surface nor the mass of the Earth is growing," Daly continually reminds people. On Earth, inputs and outputs have always cycled and recycled ad infinitum, transforming one into the other. Things only got out of whack when one species—ours—started demanding more stuff than ever before, requiring more concentrated energy for that stuff's manufacture than nature had ever accommodated all at once.

We're not the first instance of that happening in the planet's history. From time to time, there have been other exaggerated inputs—like the asteroid strike that knocked off the dinosaurs and nearly two-thirds of everything else alive. It took several million years for Earth to absorb its dust and spawn a new cast of characters to be fruitful and multiply. To avoid bringing something comparably drastic upon ourselves, the ecological economists propose we rethink the way we provision civilization—starting now.

It's a big job. Today's globalized economy literally means an economy the size of our planet—but as Daly points out, that also means there's no more room to expand. The addition of more fuel reserves than we once thought we had—in the form of gas we free by shattering bedrock, oil we wring from sand and shale, and newly ice-free Arctic deposits—seems impressive from a short-term perspective, such as an election cycle. But the math reveals that they'll buy us relatively little extra time, and may cost much more than they give. The techniques to harvest them make alarming messes, and burning them turns the skies even more uncontrollable and the oceans increasingly corrosive.

"The closer the economy approaches the scale of the Earth," Daly told the UK's Sustainable Development Commission in 2008, "the more it will have to conform to the physical behavior of the Earth." In a steady-state economy, we wouldn't be seeking more and dirtier ways to fuel the engine of growth, because we'd live within our planet's means. But if an economy permanently stopped expanding, wouldn't that mean it has failed?

No more, said Daly, than it means that the Earth is static—"a great deal of qualitative change can happen inside a steady state, and certainly has happened on Earth." In a steady-state economy, the population would stay more or less constant at a livable, optimal level, and so would the consumer base. Same with the labor pool, which would make just enough stuff for the consumers to consume. Manufacturing wastes, and products that had passed their useful life, would be continually recycled. Like a terrarium, everything would be in balance...

...which is easier said than done. The transition alone will be daunting, because throughout human history, we've been doing exactly the opposite, and nearly everyone alive knows no other way. What worked fine for our ancestors—run out of game, pick up and move to new hunting grounds—doesn't work when there's nowhere else to go that we haven't already picked over. But it's hard for most of us to see that, because, like Alberta tar sands, we keep squeezing more out of soil and water. The fact that they give steadily less is mainly apparent to a growing fringe at the bottom of the human tapestry: more hungry people than the population of the entire human race before industrialization began blowing the lid off our numbers.

So how do we get those of us at the top of the food chain to comprehend, lest we join their ranks?

The 2008 global financial crisis created a whole new batch of recruits to the world's chronic have-nots: growing numbers of underemployed and jobless, as the traditional economy fails them. University of Vermont economist Joshua Farley, coauthor of the 2010 book Ecological Economics with Herman Daly, has spent much time since that avalanche began thinking about something that few of us understand: monetary policy.

"That's the problem: Most people don't know where money comes from, nor how it's created."

Which, he believes, is the reason why our economy today resembles a chain letter based on the fiction of an infinite number of recipients, instead of a terrarium—such as Terra, the Earth itself. Farley, whose boyish looks are belied only by his shock of gray hair, has become adept at explaining it to policy makers who should already know it but don't, and to college undergraduates.

"Take the United States. There are about 800 billion dollars in actual bills, but that's a tiny fraction of the actual money we use." The rest is money that banks magically create whenever checks are written, because a bank only has to keep a fraction—usually around one-fifth—of actual deposits at any time, based on the usually reliable assumption that its customers aren't all going to simultaneously withdraw their savings.

This is the easy part: If a bank need only keep 20 percent of deposits on hand, it can lend out five times the amount of actual money it has. Which it does. Each time this happens, Farley explains, the economy has just grown again. "Banks virtually loan money into existence—and at interest." Of the interest it earns, four-fifths gets loaned out again.

Now comes the hard part: "So when I went to the bank and took out a mortgage for $100,000," says Farley, "the bank wrote me a check that essentially created that amount. As long as I haven't paid it back, that money circulates through our economy and lubricates the whole economic process. Except it isn't really money based on anything of value, except my promise to pay it back. It's debt that they've created. All the money in our country right now is debt: about $50 trillion in total interest-bearing debt in the United States alone."

In the days when money was backed by its face value in silver or gold, there were limits to how much wealth could flow around the world. Today, it's virtual money that the bank lends into existence on a computer screen. "And unless the economy continually expands, there is no new flow of money to pay back that money, plus interest." Hence the chain letter.

"As it stands now, if banks start loaning money more slowly than they collect debts, the quantity of money in the economy goes down, and it's impossible to pay back debts. So we get defaults on houses, defaults on mortgages, defaults on loans. We get collapsing businesses. Our economy plunges into misery and unemployment. Under our current monetary system, the only alternative to that is endless growth. So one absolute thing we have to change is the whole nature of the monetary system."

So how might we do that?

"It's fairly simple. It's a change that's been proposed by economists for centuries. We deny banks the right to create money."

Instead, Farley says, money creation would go back to where it used to be. "We restore that right to the government. It can spend money into existence on public goods, like rebuilding our infrastructure, our education systems, our sewage systems, and restoring our watersheds and forests. Or it can loan money into existence to state governments and local governments or to central industries, like renewable energy systems—but at zero interest. At zero percent interest, when it's paid back, the money's destroyed. So there's no continual increase in the money supply."

There's a challenge with that solution, he admits. "You're trying to take the right to create wealth away from some of the wealthiest people on the planet."

That does present an obstacle. And it's not simply confiscating Goldman Sachs's or HSBC's legal magic wands that allow them to conjure substance out of thin air by only maintaining fractional deposits: It also deprives them of vast interest income. The government would no longer have to borrow money, because it would literally create it by spending it on public goods and works. That also means no more needing to raise taxes in order to pay borrowed money back, plus interest.

The wealthiest 10 percent would appreciate the reduced tax part, but they wouldn't much like the loss of interest. "Since the top 10 percent of the economy is who receives interest payments, and the bottom 90 percent pays them, interest payments today essentially redistribute wealth from the bottom 90 percent to the top 10 percent."

In a steady-state economy, Farley says, the opposite would happen: Government would spend for things that benefit 100 percent of the people, creating jobs to build and maintain them, and redistributing money more equally throughout society. Taken globally, a fairer redistribution of wealth plus population reduction—either because we gracefully nudge our numbers toward some ecological balance, or because some unpleasant act of nature abruptly jerks us in that direction—are the inseparable sides of the new coin the human race must spend to afford the future.

It all makes sense, and sounds highly unlikely. Picture a world where economic decisions are made not to benefit the cleverest financial whizzes, nor the brawniest companies, nor the most powerful nations, but according to what's best for the most people and for the planet that sustains us all. Lovely, right?

Now, picture all the interested parties letting it happen. Not so pretty. The switch to a sustainable economy, wrote Herman Daly in Scientific American in 2005, "would entail an enormous change of mind and heart by economists, politicians, and voters. One might well be tempted to declare that such a project would be impossible. But the alternative to a sustainable economy—an ever-growing economy—is biophysically impossible. In choosing between tackling a political impossibility and a biophysical impossibility, I would judge the latter to be the more impossible, and take my chances with the former."

To have a world where the majority enjoyed a life that most of us would accept—something like a European lifestyle: less consumptive and energy-intensive than in the United States or China; more secure than in Africa—would require fewer people dividing up the world's goods, and leaving enough for nature to thrive. "Usually," says Jon Erickson, Farley's University of Vermont ecological economist colleague, "people presume that when economists talk about raising everyone's material standard of living—be it to a European, Japanese, or American standard—they mean for all seven or nine billion people. But mathematically, that clearly won't work. If we want a more affluent world, we have to drop population size. They go hand in hand."

The world's current, chronic economic crisis springs from everyone—from homeowners to entire nations—getting into more debt than we can possibly pay back. The idea of the whole world incurring even more debt just to pay off debts that can't be met is Ponzi financing in the extreme. That's where national economies—and even international, such as the European Union's—approach the brink of collapse. Yet thus far, says Erickson, it's the only kind of financing we've tried.

"We take on more debt, over and over again, assuming we'll simply grow more in the future and pay it off later. The only way we can possibly pay down that debt without growing is by consuming less."

There are only two ways to do that. "Either everybody on the average consumes less, or we have fewer people consuming."

Or both. Getting people to want less sounds tough, though from Farley's and Erickson's vantage point, perhaps not impossible. The Gund Institute for Ecological Economics, where they teach, which began at Herman Daly's school, the University of Maryland, moved to Vermont because, says Erickson, "at Maryland, it was like an outcast institute. Here, it's more central to what this university, Burlington, and Vermont are about: a transition to a reasonable economy."

Burlington, Vermont: whose last three mayors described themselves as either socialist or progressive, rather than Democrat or Republican. A city with a community land trust featuring a "ladder of affordability" for housing, offering everything from single rooms to co-op rentals, home ownership, and cohousing. A Lake Champlain waterfront converted mostly to public space. A supermarket-sized, city co-op grocery. Citywide composting. An electric utility that produces fifty megawatts from waste wood products.

Hard to get much more livable, boast patriotic residents. And yet, Erickson says, neither Burlington nor steady-state economics are radical. "It's good old Vermont conservatism"—and quite similar, he adds, to Akihiko Matsutani's prescription for Japan, which turns out to be very appealing for fiscal conservatives: If deficit spending is necessary to a growing society, in a shrinking society what's needed is exactly the opposite. As populations start shrinking —"as they must," Jon Erickson tells his students, "either by design or by default"—we will have to learn to live with balanced budgets.

Which, whether it likes it or not, Japan is en route to doing.

* * *

Yoshimi Kashitani, his khaki cargo pants tucked into black rubber boots, sloshes through the cold water cascading down his terraced wasabi patch. Bending, he inspects some one-year-old plants. "They are doing very well," he tells Yoshio Takeya, his new helper, who's watching closely from the next tier up.

Kashitani is a healthy, wiry man of eighty-three. He has been doing this right here all his life, as did his father before him. His wasabi grows high up a steep canyon above the village of Nosegawa in mountainous Nara Prefecture on south Honshu Island. Takeya, fifty years younger, is from Osaka, part of Japan's Keihanshin metropolitan area that includes Kyoto and Kobe, together home to 18 million people.

Nosegawa has five hundred people and counting—down. In 1975, twenty-three hundred lived here, working in forestry, growing wasabi and shiitake mushrooms, making chopsticks, and hatching amago trout. But mechanization and reusable plastic killed their hand-carved chopstick industry, which employed dozens who scraped and planed standard chopsticks from sugi cedar and fancy chopsticks from hinoki cypress. Mostly, though, the numbers withered away as older generations died off and fewer young people took their place. Nearly half of Nosegawa's residents are now over sixty-five.

It's the same throughout the Japanese countryside: fields and farmhouses vacant, elementary and middle schools down to handfuls of students, and elderly farmers still working the land because there's nobody else to do it.

"Once we were fourteen wasabi farmers here," says Yoshimi Kashitani, rain dripping from the bill of his cap. "Now just five of us are left." He has three daughters, born right after World War II before the short-lived baby boom abruptly ended. They now live in Yokahama and Osaka, and aren't coming back to grow wasabi. Only one of the five growers had a son, and he, too, left for the city. "So this young man is our only hope."

In a town where young means fifty years old, Takeya, who's dressed like his mentor except his rubber boots are white, is truly youthful at only thirty-three. After graduating from Osaka University in agriculture, he found few jobs awaiting in the dying countryside. But wasabi interested him. Despite all its soba and sushi eaters, Japan now mainly imports it from China, where, he says, the mass-produced, pesticided field wasabi barely resembles the native wasabi horseradish grown chemical-free in rivers like Mr. Kashitani's. Takeya found this place on the Internet: the prefecture's website described how the Nosegawans were using indigenous heirloom stock, hand gathering and nurturing their own seed. No one else he knew of still did that.

Figure 2 Wasabi growers, Nosegawa, Nara Prefecture, Japan

All around them, springs and waterfalls gush from the canyon walls. The mountain stream where Kashitani built sixteen stone terraces is lined with maple, beech, and Japanese oak, which retain water far better than the cypress and cedar that have replaced much of the native hardwoods in the mountains surrounding Nosegawa. Hinoki cypress and sugi cedar are also native, but in the postwar years the balance of Japan's deciduous conifer forests began to tip, as much of its hardwoods were clear-cut by the government to make way for faster-growing cypress and cedar for the construction and furniture industries.

The result is a national ecological snafu. As each of those species matures, it emits increasing amounts of pollen. By 2000, more than a quarter of the Japanese people were itching and sneezing from a hay fever pandemic, due to all the cypress and cedars their government had planted. Each year, with the trees' advancing age, more eyes redden and more sinuses burn. During the peak month of April, half the country is wearing face masks—and complaining.

But in this cool canyon, too steep for timbering, the air is bracing and fragrant. Leaf detritus and droppings of bears, boar, deer, fox, and monkeys that drink here provide the nutrients for the shiny, heart-shaped wasabi leaves poking up from the terraced streambed. As the rain eases, morning clears the mountaintop fog. The trills of Japanese bush warblers echo off the bedrock, as overhead, a Japanese mountain hawk-eagle, whose own population fell along with the hardwoods that once supported its massive nests, circles on barred wings.

Nevertheless, as the number of people here declines, the numbers of animals have increased. Villagers must fence off potato and cucumber gardens from bears, and hang netting over the stacks of oak logs injected with shiitake mushroom spores to protect them from herons and macaques. To young Yoshio Takeya, his bowl-cut hair rain-plastered to his forehead, it only makes his future more beautiful. He and his girlfriend from agriculture school will soon take over one of Nosegawa's abandoned wasabi patches for themselves.

As he sloshes his way to the next tier, a cloud of white butterflies circles his head. Their larvae eat wasabi leaves, but he doesn't mind: the presence of insects is proof that the ton of wasabi this mountain produces each year is unadulterated and organic. His girlfriend is a bit concerned that this isolated village has no supermarket, but here they can have something of their own, and be able to marry and have a child.

Kashitani approves of his protégé's plans: he and his colleagues, now in their eighties, are still strong enough to keep working for a while. "The air and water are so pure and good, we live longer here." Yet his own wife's recent death marked the first of their generation to go, and talk in the village has turned to wondering who will maintain their ancestors' tombs for them when they're all gone. For a while, their children will come back during the summer Obon festival to venerate them, but—"Unless more young people arrive, this village will disappear." He nods at young Takeya. "Maybe now they will come."

"They should," says Takeya. "Most of our classmates couldn't get jobs, because they wanted to stay near the cities, in agribusiness. They should spread out. This," he says, indicating the river plunging through the green terraces, "is real."

Which is exactly what economist Akihiko Matsutani, who sees prosperity in population reduction, expects more young people to realize. Right now, metro areas like Greater Tokyo and Osaka-Kyoto-Kobe are magnets for young people. But as today's workforce ages and becomes less productive, the megalopoli themselves will age. A smaller workforce will be employed in fewer heavy Japanese industries requiring coastal harbors for imported raw materials. By 2030, Matsutani calculates, shrinking Tokyo would need more than 6 million immigrants from elsewhere in Japan to maintain today's labor levels—an impossibility because, if for no other reason, they couldn't afford the real estate.

Instead of laborers seeking heavy industries, more nimble industries making lighter consumer goods will go where laborers are, spreading opportunity more equitably across the land. Smaller, more localized markets will take on new appeal, and as prosperity is redefined around shorter working weeks and quality of life rather than relentless accumulation, the hinterlands will be ever more attractive places to live.

The transition to a smaller population with, at least for a while, a higher proportion of older people—a completely new experience in human history—won't be painless.

"I wish we were wise enough to downsize gracefully and intelligently," says Matsutani. "The longer people fail to face what is happening, the harsher the adjustment will be." The part that makes most economists shiver is pensions, which have always been a way to share the fruits of economic growth across generations—"only fair," Matsutani writes, "since the previous generation laid the economic foundation for the affluence of the following generation." But in a shrinking, aging economy, when affluence is no longer growing, and with fewer workers paying into pension plans for all those long-lived seniors, people will have to save more for their own retirements, and make do on reduced income.

Like China's Jiang Zhenghua, now charged with planning how his country will deal with its own aging populace, Akihiko Matsutani sees those savings helping to finance communal public housing, parks, and cultural facilities that seniors will need. He's heard the scary rhetoric in Europe about how high payroll taxes must soar to meet the pension shortfall if populations fall, and how everyone should pump out more babies, lest their economies crumple beneath a mass of unproductive, gray-haired retirees. In reply, Matsutani reminds people that children, too, can be considered a burden on society, since they don't work and require their own infrastructure. Smaller populations won't need as many schools or subsidies for public and private universities. The size of government, too, will shrink along with the body politic: all representing savings that can be reallocated where they're needed.

"It's a more peaceful society when a large part of the population is aged," observes Japanese senator Kuniko Inoguchi, who is also a demographer. "The aged won't sacrifice health care for guns. Because of the graying populations in most democracies," she says, "in the twenty-first century there's hope for us to find a geriatric peace."

And with less dependence on foreign imports to sustain frenetic levels of production, a country might be less inclined to spend billions defending access to resources overseas, as the United States has done at such great financial and human cost. Without resource wars, there would be that much more available for caring for the elderly, until ages come back into balance, leveling out with each passing generation to a smaller, leaner population, with more breathing room to savor life.

Satoyama

As a boy in the city of Matsumoto in central Japan, Keibo Oiwa would accompany his mother to Genchi no Ido, an artesian well in the middle of town that's been used for thousands of years. He now teaches anthropology at Meiji Gakuin University in Yokohama, but following a Zen purification retreat in Matsumoto, he's returned to the old wooden portico that shelters the well. Thirst quenched and ablutions completed, he bows before a statue of a standing Buddha holding an infant, with two other babies tugging at his robes. "Buddha as compassionate mother," notes Oiwa.

Few Japanese mothers have three children anymore, but Oiwa's actually headed to see one: his former student Mari Tokuhisa. Oiwa, lean and denim-clad, is the founder of The Sloth Club, a group that promotes the sustainable life he envisioned in his popular book Slow Is Beautiful. His friends Mari and her husband, Kin, recently found an old house in Shiga, a nearby farming village, where, like most of rural Japan, the median age is in the seventies and empty houses rent cheaply—in this case, for ¥10,000 a month, about US$130.

The half-hour drive there climbs through a cypress forest still ribboned with oak, beech, and camellia. Descending, the road crosses a narrow valley of terraced rice paddies, bisected by a small river. On the opposite side, Shiga's wooden houses fill a mountain pass lined with red pines.

It is very quiet, because few live here now. Mari, in a peasant blouse and long skirt, and her three small boys, Kyusen, Gennosuke, and Yosei, await in front of their new home, the former village chief's house. The town is now so small that legally it no longer exists.

"It's beautiful here," Oiwa says, greeting Mari with a hug.

"Hai." With the same haircut as her sons, they resemble a family of pixies. The house, about a hundred years old, has curved Japanese eaves. Its interior, carpeted in woven straw mats, has a reed ceiling and window shades. Shoji screens that divide the large space into rooms are open so that afternoon light fills the house. A brick chimney is retrofitted with an iron woodstove made by Mari's husband, who's off building stage sets for a theater company. They met as students; disillusioned with the shaky Japanese job market after their first son was born, they escaped to Amami Oshima, a tiny island near Okinawa at the Japanese archipelago's southern tip, to practice permaculture. So far from the big crowded islands, life there turns around families, which tend to be larger than the rest of Japan, and they soon had two more. "I still want more. My friend just had her fifth."

Before becoming a mother, she worked in one of the slow food cafés that Keibo Oiwa has sponsored around Japan, which feature local ingredients prepared from scratch. When they decided to return to Honshu, they were committed to becoming as self-sufficient as possible, a decision underscored by the Fukushima earthquake-tsunami-nuclear disaster of March 11, 2011— known evermore in Japan as 3/11.

"Our life here is simple. We grow our food and make our furniture. Our sons' nursery school meets outdoors. But if we're not free from nuclear power, it's not enough. So since 3/11, we're heating our bathwater with firewood."

Yes, it takes more time, she says. "But it's also more fun. When we had a modern life in Yokohama, we would waste time. Now, by putting effort into making things, it's like we're regaining time."

"Hai," says Oiwa. "Exactly. That is the slow life. People think environmental living means being ascetic. But every culture has a huge storage of fun. Sure, there's fun technology. But today we see so many sick, unhappy, empty people. Before 3/11, people gave thanks to nuclear power for allowing us to have our lives. But now, post-3/11, we realize that we all die. We who survived aren't immortal; we're in the palm of Buddha. Knowing that we die is the first wisdom of human beings, the beginning of philosophy. Every day I wake up still alive, that is happiness."

They're having tea around a table hewn by Mari's husband from cypress slabs. "We humans have a proper speed, and when society speeds beyond our limit, we get social problems," Oiwa says. "Psychological problems. Things break down. We've now contaminated much of this island, but they still say we need economic growth. They act like we'll live forever. But if we can face the wisdom that everyone dies, we'll see that we live not because of nuclear power, but because of the sun and the air. Once we realize that, maybe we can turn this around."

They go next door to see Mari's seventy-year-old neighbor, Michiko Takizawa. A widow early in life, she raised her two children by growing vegetables and rice and keeping cows, angora rabbits, and silkworms. With pleasure, Oiwa inspects her two-hundred-year-old house: traditional post-and-beam, strong enough to sustain a second story of thick, earthen walls. The main beam, fully a half-meter wide, is from a single Japanese red pine.

They kneel at a low round table, where Michiko-san sets bowls of sliced eggplant, zucchini, green beans, and plums she pickles in sugar and vinegar. "Take," she says, handing a plum to Mari's oldest, whose second-grade classroom has just four other students. "And that's after they combined two schools. After we die"—other than Mari's family, Michiko's youngest neighbor is fifty-five—"all these houses will be empty." Her unmarried son, who works construction, still lives nearby. "But women don't want to marry men here. Women today would rather have a job than get married." One man brought a Filipina bride, she says, "But she left.

The culture was too different. She said she didn't like wasabi."

"Aren't more city people moving here?" Keibo asks.

"More are still leaving than coming." She looks sadly at Mari, who just smiles at her until she has to smile back.

"You will see," Mari tells her. She and her husband have rented one of Michiko-san's rice paddies, which they will cultivate organically. A discussion ensues about how to keep water in the paddy all winter, despite the snow, to control weeds.

Afterward, they end up in Michiko's cornucopial vegetable patch. On her hands and knees, she harvests sweet peppers, eggplants, okra, and soybeans for her guests. Oiwa gazes raptly at her bountiful garden, bordered by lilies and filled with dusky blue butterflies. Beyond it are rice paddies latticed with channels of water borrowed from the river, the brilliant green stalks heavy with grains about to turn golden. Past them is a perfect triangular wedge of mountain covered with mixed forest—and farther, more cool mountains dissolving into fog.

This, Oiwa knows, is a blessed remnant of satoyama, the harmonious marriage of human and natural landscapes that for thousands of years defined the Japanese countryside. In these tranquil mosaics of cultivated lands, wildflower meadows, ponds, streams, orchards, and forests, Japanese culture was born. On islands where, since ancient times, humans have shaped and manicured all but the craggiest terrain, satoyama has been the salvation of Japanese biodiversity. For millennia, people dwelling in satoyama landscapes harvested firewood and charcoal, pastured animals, and grew crops with an aesthetic that invited and nurtured fish, frogs, dragonflies, butterflies, fireflies, grasshoppers, songbirds, ducks, storks, and falcons.

But in the 1960s, farmhouse chimneys gave way to oil burners. As synthetic fertilizer took over the fields, coppiced woodlands that once provided warmth, fodder, and leaf mulch for rice paddies were no longer visited daily. Pesticides banished the grasshoppers and caterpillars, and the herons, egrets, and majestic Oriental white storks that fed on them failed to return. Concrete lining for ditches to drain fields wiped out tadpoles, snails, and sludge worms. As cows and beef cattle switched from pasture to imported corn and soy feed, grasslands and meadows that once surrounded Japanese cities disappeared beneath housing developments and golf courses.

Within a half-century, Japan no longer resembled a timeless ink-on-silk painting. But as numbers recede, and as a smaller younger generation seeks alternatives to the corporate soldiering that came to define Japanese work, there is a chance for a slower life to return, along with landscapes to sustain it.

The last wild Oriental white stork in Japan was seen in 1971. In 1989, a stork hatchery at Toyooka, an hour from Kyoto in Hyogo Prefecture, successfully produced offspring using breeding pairs from Russia. But the local rice fields, soaked annually with organo-mercury pesticides, proved too toxic for the fledgling birds to be released. In 2004, a ten-year-old schoolgirl named Yuka Okada learned that storks like the caged birds in Toyooka's now crowded hatchery had once filled the skies and nested on every chimney. After learning why they no longer did, she went to the mayor and demanded that Toyooka serve organic rice for school lunches.

To do that meant eliminating mercury, inviting back grasshoppers but also making the rice paddies safe for storks. The mayor, hearing the simple truth from a ten-year-old, could only agree. His city's slogan became "An environment good for storks must be good for humans, too." The next plantings were pesticide-free. A year later, the first stork was released, and today, wherever they nest, the rice is twice as valuable because the presence of storks guarantees its purity. An economy that had bottomed was rejuvenated, and today tourists flock to Toyooka to watch hundreds of storks do the same.

The value to be reaped from tourists and fancy organic rice is easy to quantify. Harder, but most critical, is calculating the value of nature—what conservation ecologists call natural capital. How much is a grasshopper worth, anyway, if nature always provided them for free? Trees in forests were free. Rivers and the atmosphere were free places to toss wastes.

Free, but ultimately costly, when they vanish or can hold no more.

The accounting of nature's capital has never been included in corporate balance sheets, but every prechemical farmer knew it well. In a Japan with far fewer Japanese, as Japan will inevitably become this century, there is a chance for natural capital to replenish, and for people to enjoy healthier, even happier lives.

The rice fields may yield less, if humans must share the grains with grasshoppers—but with fewer humans, that won't be such a problem.

NOTES

1. Source of English translation: Connolly, Kate. "Angela Merkel Declares Death of German Multiculturalism." *Guardian* (UK), October 17, 2010.
2. In 2009, the population of Russia rose for the first time in fifteen years, and has increased by a few thousand per year since then. The growth is due not to rising birth rates, but to immigrants from other former Soviet republics.
3. 1 Singapore dollar is approximately $0.80.

Acknowledgments

The editors would like to acknowledge the Board of Directors and the staff of Population Connection, as well as our 40,000+ members. Thanks go to Lauren Boucher, Estelle Raboni, Mina Silberberg, Pam Wasserman, and the folks at Print Matters. Special thanks to Marian Starkey and Shauna Scherer for their help, patience, and unflagging enthusiasm.

Contributors

Katherine Baicker
Professor of Health Economics
School of Public Health, Harvard University

Noah Berger
President of the Massachusetts Budget and Policy Center

David E. Bloom
Clarence James Gamble Professor of Economics and Demography
Department of Global Health and Population
Harvard T.H. Chan School of Public Health

David Cutler
Professor of Economics
Harvard University

Brian Czech
President, Center for the Advancement of the Steady State Economy

Herman Daly
Emeritus Professor, School of Public Policy
University of Maryland

Peter Fisher
Research Director, Iowa Policy Project

Matt L. Huffman
Professor, Department of Sociology and the Paul Merage School of Business
University of California-Irvine

Lori M. Hunter
Professor, Department of Sociology
Faculty Research Associate, Institute of Behavioral Science
University of Colorado at Boulder

Ronald Lee
Professor of the Graduate School, Demography and Economics
University of California, Berkeley

Jay W. Lorsch
Louis Kirstein Professor of Human Relations
Harvard Business School

Hal Marcovitz
Writer; former newspaper reporter and columnist

Robert D. Plotnick
Professor of Public Policy and Governance
Daniel J. Evans School of Public Policy and Governance
University of Washington

Lee S. Polansky
Director of Planning and Strategic Support
Population Connection

John Seager
President and CEO
Population Connection

Zirui Song
Doctoral candidate at Harvard Medical School

Alan Weisman
Author, *Countdown: Our Last, Best Hope for a Future on Earth?*